Technical Resource Management
Quantitative Methods

Technical Resource Management
Quantitative Methods

Marvin J. Cetron
Raymond Isenson
Jacob N. Johnson
Ambrose B. Nutt
Howard A. Wells

The M.I.T. Press
Cambridge, Massachusetts, and London, England

Set in Monophoto Times Roman
Printed and bound in the United States of America by
The Maple Press Company, York, Pennsylvania

ISBN 0 262 03034 9 (hardcover)

Library of Congress catalog card number: 77-86608

Foreword

Despite the growth in importance of science and technology, research and development (R&D) activities remain among the most "undermanaged" of corporate and governmental functions. A number of factors contribute to but do not excuse this state of affairs. The relative youth of organized R&D and its rapid growth until recently have left it without firmly established managerial traditions and practices. Some mistaken ideas borrowed from the history of academic research even suggested that the least-managed R&D activity is the best-managed. Furthermore, R&D's uncertainty, intangibility, uniqueness of accomplishments, and long time delays in the feedback of results have discouraged and hindered attempts to develop a factual basis for the field. These same phenomena, combined with the concentration of operations research analysts and management scientists on the more straightforward problems encountered in the production and distribution functions, have limited the quantitative developments applicable to R&D.

Until the past few years methods for planning, budgeting, and control of technical programs were simple in concept and implementation, seldom demanding more than arithmetic for computational operations. Bar charts or Gantt charts were used for project scheduling, off-the-cuff allocations or percentage-of-sales calculations were used for budgeting, standard accounting methods were used for control. Among the professionals interested in the problems of technology management, Burton Dean of Case Western Reserve Institute and a few others were concentrating their attention on sophisticated methodological approaches to a variety of R&D problems.

A turning point in attention to quantitative methodology for R&D management, observable only after the fact, was the publication in 1963 of Dean's collection of a number of papers treating divers areas.[1]

---

[1] Dean, Burton V. (ed.), *Operations Research in Research and Development,* New York: John Wiley and Sons, Inc., 1963.

This was accompanied concurrently by many books on the Program Evaluation and Review Technique (PERT), which under governmental pressure and mistakenly attributed acclaim rapidly became a widely used method for quantitative scheduling and control of R&D projects.

In 1964 my book, *The Dynamics of Research and Development*, became the first published text that presented quantitative analyses of a large number of project management factors, based upon a complex mathematical model and extensive computer simulations.[2] This has been followed by several recent books on technological forecasting, the most recent area of interest of those trying to apply quantitative techniques to R&D management.[3]

The present book by Marv Cetron and his colleagues is clearly a product of the technological forecasting school of thought. It addresses in several ways the problems of resource allocation for technologically based programs and organizations. The authors are leading contributors to the development of the methods now being tentatively deployed by a number of government agencies and industrial firms, and are themselves users of these methods for the U.S. military R&D programs. Their joint effort has resulted in the assembly in one volume of several of the most strongly advocated methods for technological resource allocation, as well as of several strong defenses of the use of these methods. As such the book is an important and up-to-date contribution to the advancement of quantitative developments for R&D management.

When I was asked to prepare this Foreword I felt both complimented and cautious. Over the past several years I have enjoyed close professional and social relationships with all the co-authors of the book. But during this same interval I have also been among their most vocal critics.[4] Lest I be co-opted by friendship into refraining from a warning to the readers of this book, I shall finish the Foreword on a note of concern.

[2] Roberts, Edward B., *The Dynamics of Research and Development*, New York: Harper & Row, Publishers, 1964.

[3] Bright, James R. (ed.), *Technological Forecasting for Industry and Government*, Englewood Cliffs, N.J.: Prentice-Hall, Inc., 1968; Cetron, Marvin J., *Technological Forecasting: A Practical Approach*, New York: Gordon and Breach, Science Publishers, Inc. 1969; Jantsch, Erich, *Technological Forecasting in Perspective*, Paris: Organization for Economic Cooperation and Development, 1967.

[4] Roberts, Edward B., "Facts and Folklore in Research and Development Management," *Industrial Management Review*, vol. 8, no. 3, Spring 1967, pp. 5–18; Roberts, Edward B., "Exploratory and Normative Technological Forecasting: A Critical Appraisal," *Technological Forecasting*, Vol. 1, No. 2, Fall 1969.

In many places throughout the book, Cetron and the other authors state that the manager had better not accept as gospel the outputs of the techniques they are presenting. They warn that the methods are aids for decision-makers, not replacements for them. This theme is consistent with one of my major sources of hesitation about the quantitative approaches described here. Regardless of these warnings, many managers are bound to accept uncritically the results generated by seemingly objective quantitative techniques. And yet the methods sometimes are guilty of being merely objective and complex manipulations of subjective and simple inputs. "Garbage in" still produces "garbage out"; similarly, questionable subjective inputs can never result in unquestionable conclusions. In fact, R&D management can take a step backward in its meager progress to date if effective intuitive R&D managers are overwhelmed by staff men armed with impressive but misleading computer printouts.

The methods presented in this book are potentially important tools for planning and controlling research and development. Their balanced use, in combination with improving factual bases for R&D management, should help heretofore intuitive managers to improve their operational effectiveness significantly.

Edward B. Roberts

Contents

Preface

At a time of rapid technological and scientific changes, managers are becoming increasingly aware that the key to effective work is a smoothly functioning planning and resource-allocating system. In spite of this, not every organization avails itself of even the very simple systems. Too often the approaches used are neither complete enough nor rigorous enough to do the desired job effectively. In the worst cases, the planning and allocating systems do little more than formalize the subjective judgments of managers, based primarily on past experience.

We will not dwell here on the question of whether it is really possible to rationalize the planning and allocation of resources for R&D. These arguments (for quantitative management methods) are dealt with throughout the book. But we should state our thesis briefly. Technological resource management is too important to be handled with the traditional methods still in use today in a majority of companies and government agencies. More importantly, over the past decade a wide range of planning tools have been developed and tested. We think that they work and, if applied to an R&D organization, will result in a significant improvement of the effectiveness of that organization.

This book gives a broad view of the most significant resource-allocation techniques now increasingly used in government and industry. However, it is important to remember that the systems cannot usually be adopted in toto. They generally require modification to fit special situations in a particular laboratory or shop. But the methods and cases discussed will provide a basis for improving R&D planning in any technical organization we can think of.

This book is aimed at the wide cross section of those with a need to know about technical resource allocation. These include, with no order or priority intended, students in engineering and management schools who are taking courses in planning, management theory, or operations research; managers and other R&D specialists who are intensively studying planning and allocation; managers in technological areas who are responsible for the planning job and must consider upgrading or revamping their system; and finally those managers —whatever their current assignment—who are interested in the new methods of analysis and problem solving that are utilized in the techniques and case studies presented.

At this point, a few words of thanks and appreciation are in order. The thoughts and work that went into the creation of the methods discussed here are the result of the efforts of hundreds of gifted and dedicated men who have worked for many years in a wide range of organizations. While they are too numerous to be listed here, we can say that, if this book helps provide the same kind of foundation for work to be done in the future they have provided for us in the past, we will be proud indeed. We would also like to thank the IEEE for permission to use material in Chapter 2 and Appendix A that was originally published in *Transactions of Engineering Management,* March 1967.

A special note of thanks is due to Herbert E. Klein, who served as editor, inquisitor, and chief representative of the potential reader. He combined the drafts of the several authors, organized them, and turned what began as material for planning specialists into a book for a wide range of interested readers. We can't count the times when he asked us, "What does that mean?" But forcing us to give the answer to that question kept the bit in our teeth.

Naturally, the author listed for each chapter accepts full responsibility for any errors of fact or logic that might appear.

Our wives, Gloria, Maggie, Donna, Elaine, and Polly are to be thanked for their patience and understanding. Our gratitude is extended as well to our business associates for their cooperation and help in testing these models.

Spring 1970

Marvin J. Cetron
Raymond Isenson
Jacob N. Johnson
Ambrose B. Nutt
Howard A. Wells

Introduction:
The New Dimension
of Resource Management

"The Golden Rule: He who hath the gold, maketh the rules."

It would be highly unrealistic to suppose that the day will ever come when researchers will not be subjected to the decisions of the men who control the funds—and a strong case can be made for the idea that this control, properly applied, is necessary for effective work. There is a real question, however, whether the managers of R&D, whatever their level in an organization, are carrying out their control functions as effectively as possible. This question has received growing and urgent attention in the past decade, as research and development work, especially in military and space areas, has expanded rapidly. It has become clear to most professionals in the R&D field that more precise means are needed to make sure that the man who hath the gold has a more precise way of deciding how he should make the rules.

The main job in providing useful guidelines for the manager with responsibility and authority in planning and allocating R&D work has been to develop new sources of data and to build a systematic method of using these data to aid the decision-making process. This book attempts to show how sophisticated and effective these new techniques have become.

This is not to say that a great deal of work still does not have to be done to improve resource-management techniques. But even a casual scanning of the chapters in this book should make it plain that there are already in existence systematic, highly rational ways to bring a wide range of information to bear on the complex problems of planning and allocating limited resources in research, exploratory, and advanced development.

Need for a System

At the risk of belaboring the point, it is worth discussing one of the key factors that is impelling R&D managers to explore new planning and allocating techniques. We have already mentioned that R&D has been a rapidly growing area. Therefore, size alone would require a greater attention to the management function. But the size of budgets is not the only factor in greater control. In most cases rapidly rising research budgets were the result of some outside force or an unexpected research breakthrough. The federal government's 300-percent increase in funding R&D in the last decade was the result of the cold war and the space race more than that of a well-reasoned analysis of the most effective use of resources.

The same picture can be painted for much of the increase in industrial R&D expenditures over the last 10 or 15 years—that portion of R&D that did not grow out of federal contracts or the hope for a bigger share of the federal spending programs. The most obvious case is the computer field, where the key to success was a no-holds-barred technology battle. The same can be said for the commercial electronics industry, the office copier market or the jockeying for position in the oceanography race.

But there are strong signs that R&D, while not becoming a stepchild, will have a more severe fight with its competitors for both government and corporate funds. Managers who have had more money to spend than they could effectively use—though they would never admit it—are having their budgets put under a microscope. Not only do they have to make better decisions, but they have to have a stronger case than ever to back them up. A more mature R&D industry now needs more sophisticated control tools.

The Scope of the Manager's Task

Perhaps the best way to outline all the elements that go into designing and using an effective technical planning and resource-allocation system is to discuss briefly the scope and purpose of each chapter in this book. Readers will find a certain amount of overlap. This is intended to help those who will read only the chapters they feel apply to their needs. We hope that those using the book for a more comprehensive study will excuse the redundancies necessitated by this approach.

Chapter 1 introduces the methodology generally used throughout the book. Although the term "systems approach" is often misused, and overused to the point of becoming a cliché, it can justifiably be applied to the technical resource allocation job. In briefest terms, the system is a three-step progression: identification of goals; planning how to meet these goals; and allocation of resources of men, materials, and money to implement the plans.

Chapter 2 shows how technical effort serves as the vital bridge between basic knowledge and the specific goals of an organization, be they a new weapons system or an improved washing machine. The key point here is to develop a means of assigning a "value" to research. Admittedly there is subjective judgment involved in putting some kind of a numerical value on research projects, but properly used such numbers can help a manager make decisions without causing him to ignore his experience and judgment.

Chapter 3 introduces the economic concept of marginal utility to the planning and allocation problem. The main question is: how much will an additional investment of funds in an applied research or exploratory development project aid the organization's major goals?

Chapter 4 tries to zero in on how a single laboratory can select the most worthwhile projects from the whole spectrum of possible projects it could try to carry out. The methodology used here can be applied to organizations with a single R&D facility or adapted to situations where planning must be done for each of a number of related laboratories.

Chapter 5 presents another method for approaching the project-selection problem. But it goes a step further by including in the system framework a way of determining the specific level of support for each project after it has been selected.

Chapter 6 expands the discussion from the levels of basic research and exploratory development to the question of planning advanced development. It outlines a way of constructing an organization's optimal "product mix," based on quantitative assessments of utility, feasibility, and cost.

Chapter 7 takes the next logical step and deals with the actual production of the organization's final output or product. Here a manager is likely to be preoccupied with the problem of scarce resources. He needs an effective means of monitoring and controlling these resources, whether they be men, materials, or money.

Chapter 8 takes a wide-angle look at the whole planning and allocation problem. Up to this point it has been assumed that the total budget of the planning unit, whatever its size, had been set by some higher authority. This authority could be Congress, the head of a government agency, or top company management. But how do you determine what this total amount should be? The method outlined uses the results of the Defense Department's research project called Project Hindsight, a study that investigated the R&D efforts that went into a wide range of products. These results are combined with data from the National Science Foundation's surveys on how much each industry actually spends on R&D. This provides a rough guide for estimating how much an organization should allocate for its total R&D budget.

Chapter 9 illustrates the tight interaction of technological forecasting and the planning job. It is placed last, but some readers might find it worthwhile at least to scan it earlier in their work on the planning and allocation problem. While the advancement of technology is a basic aim of all the techniques discussed in this book, some form of technological forecasting is either implied or required in all the methods.

Pace of Innovation

To a large extent, the material in these chapters is tied to work done in various sections of the Department of Defense. This reflects not only the job experience of the authors but also the fact that much of the research and development on R&D is now being carried out at government installations or with government funds. After all, the federal budget is supporting about 80 percent of all research and development.

This reliance on examples from government, however, should not be taken to mean that industry is not interested in bringing the systems approach to its R&D efforts. Techniques like those in the book have been observed by the authors in a wide variety of firms, including those in such fields as electronics, oil, glass, computers, textiles, minerals, and contract research.

The fact is that many organizations, including government agencies at times, are reluctant to talk about their planning and allocation systems. For one thing, by letting out details of their methodology, they may encourage research people to try to beat the system and make sure that their favorite projects meet the requirements for maximum funding. Whether or not this is possible is arguable, but the fear still exists.

A stronger argument against release of information is the fact that even a relatively rough outline of a planning and allocating model may help a competitor to outguess you. And a detailed look at a company's reasons for supporting or withholding funds from a list of projects can give you all kinds of potentially useful data, from future new products to an expert scientist's opinion of the potential worth of a particular line of research. Arguments for restricting information about planning models, especially data about how key factors are weighed, often apply to people within a company. In an industrial climate that often encourages job mobility, today's trusted employee can quickly become tomorrow's dangerous competitor.

Another real problem, however, has more psychological impact than direct bearing on scientific or economic questions. One of the greatest potential dangers in any systems approach to jobs like planning and allocation is that it will be misunderstood by the managers who use it, their subordinates, and their top management supervisors. Again and again, throughout the discussion of the various methods explained in this book, the authors warn about the dangers of regarding a decision-making aid as a replacement for a human decision-maker.

A lack of understanding of this vital point can occur at any level of management. Just a few examples will make the point clear. Top managers can use a system, especially if it has a sophisticated-looking computer printout, to take decision-making out of the hands of R&D managers who have the experience to evaluate the results properly. The R&D managers, for their part, can use the system as a crutch and abdicate much of their creative leadership role. And the working scientist and engineer can begin to feel that he is a pawn in some numbers game where the dedication to his work carries little weight against the manipulation of the "computer boys."

Problems like these, real or imagined, are a fact of life for everyone working in the planning and allocation field today. They must be faced squarely and handled successfully; otherwise no system is likely to be installed or used effectively.

Ending this introduction on a pessimistic note, with a warning of potential problems for the R&D planning practitioner, would certainly be an overreaction to the situation. The fact is, few subjects in management deserve a more optimistic approach. Not only is the need for better systems for planning and allocating R&D resources being recognized throughout the nation—and the world, for that matter—but the systems that have been developed have proved their worth.

More exciting to anyone studying this subject is the fact that the greatest period of discovery, innovation, and growth lies in the immediate future. The technical man who specializes in this area of research on research can hope to play a significant role. The technical manager who studies it carefully can expect to bring a new dimension of understanding and effectiveness to his profession.

Although the processes called research are far from being fully understood, enough is known about them, about the nature and growth of technology, and about the psychology of the market place to permit the development of procedures to satisfy most organizational requirements. Undoubtedly new and more powerful techniques will be developed in the future. Even today, however, there is no longer any need to rely solely on the wisdom or experience of the research manager to estimate a research budget that will meet the vital R&D needs of any organization.

Technical Resource Allocation: An Overview

Marvin J. Cetron

"Then I looked on all the works that my hands had wrought, and on all the labour that I had laboured to do: and behold, all was vanity and vexation of spirit, and there was no profit under the sun." Ecclesiastes 2:11

The idea of applying a precise rating system to research and development was until fairly recently highly suspect—somehow anti-intellectual. The old stereotype of the independent researcher following his private star dies hard. But the history of the past twenty-five years has sounded the death knell of this romantic approach. World War II, Sputnik, the Apollo moon program—not to mention the new worlds of electrons, medicine, and transportation—have all made science and technology into a big business of tremendous complexity. When the Department of Defense alone has an R&D budget of over $8 billion, there *must* be a logical, rational way of selecting the tasks to be worked on and the resources to be expended on the effort.

The fact is that research today is an input to an organization—whether government or private. Like production and sales, it must be subjected to examination, and its usefulness to the organization's mission must be evaluated. This means that much of the halo and aura of mysticism and infallibility usually attached to R&D must be discarded. Although most scientists and engineers aren't romantics, they tend to resent the use of "relevance numbers," "figures of merit," and other techniques for evaluating their work. Procedures that they themselves have developed, such as operations research, seem like Frankensteins when put to use in judging R&D itself.

But the job of allocating technical resources must be done. And as the scope of the effort becomes larger and the complexity increases, more and more factors must be considered to arrive at an effective decision. The point is soon reached where even one small decision may affect the operation of all efforts—at least to some degree. When that happens, the human brain alone cannot do the job as well as is needed.

The situation is particularly hard to handle when many R&D projects must be considered for inclusion in a fixed government or corporation resource ceiling. Priorities must be set, or decisions made concerning which projects to back and which to drop or delay. Numerous efforts are interrelated with regard to time, resources required, purpose, and possible technical transfer. Choices must therefore be made with regard to the total effect. Whether a manufacturer, a service industry, a government agency, or a university laboratory, every organization must seek the greatest payoff from its resource investments.

What alternate methods are available for helping to make allocations? How do you evaluate them? The basic point is that the resource-allocation problem is usually too big to keep in one man's head. Data inputs come from areas completely outside of his control. The inputs involved multiply rapidly to the hundreds or thousands when an allocation problem is really subjected to careful analysis.

It might be useful, at this point, to back off and take a look at how these problems were usually handled in the past. A familiar approach was to take care of the "squeaking wheel." Some requested resources were cut from all estimates. Then the manager could sit back and see who complained the most. On the basis of the loudest and most insistent cries of anguish, he would then restore some of the resources withheld. When he reached his budget ceiling, he simply shrugged.

Another common approach developed the minimum noise level and resulted in fewer squeaks. It allocated this year's resources in just about the same manner as last year's. But if the level funding or status quo approach is continued very long in a rapidly changing technology, the organization involved will end up in serious trouble.

One easy approach, which often made R&D managers feel most secure, was to be guided by the glorious past. Last year, or the year before, or perhaps several years ago, a division or organization had a very successful project; therefore, why not fund the unit for the next five years on any projects advocated by them? This method eliminated the need for analysis of the proposed projects. If an individual or laboratory had a past record of success, it got whatever it asked for.

I am sure all readers are familiar with the "white charger" technique. Here the various department heads came dashing in to top management with multicolor graphs, handouts, and well-rehearsed presentations. If they impressed the decision-maker, they were rewarded with increased resources. Often the best speaker or the last man to brief the boss won the treasure hunt.

Finally, there was the committee approach, which freed any individual manager from resource allocation decisions. The committees called the shots—increasing, decreasing, or leaving all allocations as they were. Too often, the committee did not have enough actual experience in the organization nor sufficient information upon which to base its recommendations. Its members, especially if it was an ad hoc group or from outside the organization, could avoid responsibility nicely since they did not have to implement their recommendations. This is not to say that committees are never useful.

Obviously, these allocation methods are neither scientific nor objective. Anyone who has lived with them knows that they must be supplanted. An increase in the number of reports and recommendations that can be demanded of every level in the R&D organization does not help the situation. More data without a system for using them only compound the manager's problem.

The Basics of Resource Allocation

A more realistic alternative is being built by specialists in operations research. Information assembled by them can be used to assist managerial judgment significantly. This is the point where quantitative evaluation techniques enter the picture. Each major aspect of a program can be examined, first separately and then as it becomes interrelated to competing programs. Items such as timeliness, cost utility or payoff, confidence level or risk, personnel, and facilities can be evaluated by specialists in each field and the total picture made available as a basis for decision. Payoff areas can be identified and problems highlighted. Inputs can be accurately recorded, made clearly visible, and analyzed to help make the final decision.

The use of quantitative techniques permits input factors and outcomes to be reexamined readily, and different possible managerial decisions can be tried out with simulation techniques. The manager can still hedge his allocation selections, deciding to buck the system or play a hunch. He can increase resources to previously successful groups, back a high-risk effort—that is, a low-cost project with seem-

ingly slim chances of success which ultimately might yield gigantic results. The decision-maker can incorporate any desired intangible
criteria, such as the politics of selection, competitive factors, or technological barriers. But he does this with the full knowledge that he is
bucking the odds.

In general, the allocation question is one of manipulating men,
money, and materials. Figure 1.1, in a broad allocation diagram, shows
the interactions of numerous managers, from the technical specialist
to the department manager, the head of research, and the corporate
planners. The data flow between these must be fitted into an over-all
planning approach if it is to be really useful. Corporate goals are the
main question and therefore occupy the central position in the chart.
In order to establish these corporate goals, the major preliminary steps
are systems analysis, needs analysis, and deficiency analysis.

Systems Analysis

The over-all job of the systems-analysis work is to assess corporate
policy, including philosophy and strategy questions. These are just a
few: Shall we be the industry leader? Shall we keep abreast of the industry technically and see if a major market develops? Of course,
competitors' actions must be followed closely, but there are other
factors, such as interest rates, business expectations, and economic
forecasts that must be identified.

The technology-forecasting element of Figure 1.1 acts as a catalyst
in setting and implementing over-all corporate goals. The truth is that
at present only a handful of the largest corporations are really utilizing
their technical potential. Most do not really have a clear idea of the
future possibilities in their laboratories. But even with good forecasts,
how do you relate them to the total picture?

A discussion of the numerous resource-allocation methods would
be a long story in itself. For example, all systems employed by the Department of Defense utilize three major factors in the approval process:
military utility, technical feasibility, and financial acceptability. Each
of these factors is amenable to quantification and can be fitted into a
model that compares the value of each component project or system.
Owing to the complexity of the analysis, it is necessary to program the
job on a computer in order to get valid information and to get it quickly
enough to be useful.

In addition to future technology, the future environment (competition, climate) also must be considered. Who are the competitors likely

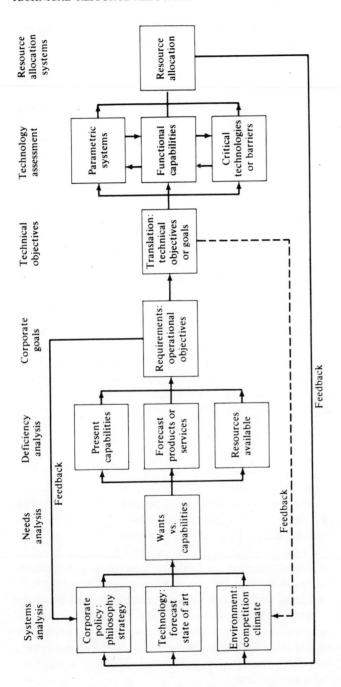

Figure 1.1 Technical Resource-Allocation System

to be? What unique skills, products, or finances will they possess? What will the industry-wide climate be? Will the industry demand continue to expand rapidly, will there be a sudden drop in demand, or is a leveling of demand to be expected? These factors and others considered under the systems analysis allow the future requirements as well as the unique or strong capabilities of the firm to be identified.

Needs Analysis

The first point here is that the national or international economy provides the broadest scope for analysis of the needs for the firm's products or services. The stage of development in the country, the requirements from related industries, the availability and cost of capital and governmental controls may all require attention for the process of determining what the firm "wants" to do.

The industry share-of-the-market for the firm relates directly to its volume. That is, in an industry of rapid growth the individual firm may grow and yet remain constant relative to its competitors. Conversely, the share-of-the-market may need to be greatly increased to remain at a level stage in a declining industry.

Finally, the desire of the firm and of the individual groups within the firm must be assessed. However, these desires may not be attainable within the capability of the firm. Thus, a careful analysis must be made to balance needs against capabilities.

Deficiency Analysis

After the wants of the organization have been established, the capabilities available to meet them must be measured, and areas of deficiency must be identified. Ordinarily, the present capabilities of an organization will be known in general, but often effort is required by management to obtain a comprehensive statement of the organization's technological capabilities in terms of men, money, and equipment. Because we are dealing with futures, the products and services, such as new manufacturing methods, new materials, and advanced skills that are forecast to be available must also be carefully identified. Other resources available to the organization will also constitute important information. Skills or manufacturing processes or equipment, and so on, may exist that can be made available from outside the organization when and if required.

Corporate Goals

Identifying and analyzing present capabilities, forecast products and services along with other resources available will make the deficiencies and excesses evident. The analysis now permits management to concentrate upon realistic technical goals for the organization.

The most important phase of the resource-allocation system, objectives, may now be brought into focus. These may be viewed by top management from the wants (desires or needs) of the organization that have been carefully considered for feasibility against the present or potential capabilities of the organization. Several passes through the analysis are usually required before acceptable goals are achieved by top management. These corporate goals will be translated into requirements for performance of the organization or into operational objectives.

The idea of applying quantitative approaches to resource allocation has too long been suspect by management. Currently, both industry and government are seeking tangible improvements in the results from use of available resources. Economy drives and cost-versus-benefit analyses have resulted in pared budgets. This makes it more critical than ever that hard choices be made among alternative programs. The application of objective measurements to resource assignments has too long been classified as visionary and impractical.

Let us look at a relatively simple question: How does a corporation decide whether its allocation this year for research and technology is adequate? You might begin by querying the scientist or engineer and requesting a justification of his selection of a program or a task. In the past, asking for projected benefits has often been construed as an assault against the scientific professional's prestige and prerogatives. Today, however, scientists and engineers are more confident that they are appreciated at the highest organization levels. One of the signs of this ascendancy is their high visibility and responsibility in the making of management decisions. Technical managers, particularly, are aware that their intuition can no longer be accepted as infallible and beyond top management review.

Several project-evaluation and selection techniques have as their basis a belief in the efficacy and acceptance of Bayesian statistics and theories of probability. The basic idea in the Bayesian approach is that it is correct to quantify feelings about uncertainty in terms of subjectively assessed numerical probabilities. Assessments are made of probabilities for events that determine the profitability or utility of all alternative actions open to the decision-maker.

Using this approach, one can assess whether a research project is feasible. It is also possible for an expert in the field being assessed to assign a figure of merit or "subjective probability" number that the event will actually occur—often by choosing a scale between 0 and 10. Men with wide experience in a field usually have no difficulty in using this kind of probability once they realize that what may seem like guesswork can lead to an objective analysis. Other criteria, such as the utility of the research to the objectives of the organization or its relevance to desired priority systems, can be rated in a like manner.

The use of Bayesian subjective probabilities makes feasible the incorporation into the decision process, in a formal and visible way, of both the nonobjective and objective criteria and variables that were previously taken into account by the decision-maker when he applied his judgment to the data available to him.

Once the experience, knowledge, and judgment of the various experts are summarized by collecting and analyzing the subjective probabilities they assign against the respective criterion, the ultimate decision-maker has a clear view of his alternatives. Usually, a computer is used to summarize the probabilities and make the various calculations and listings required by the allocation system. It can also be used to determine consequences if the probability assignments are changed or if the final decision-maker adds new information or weighting factors, etc.

There is a key point here that I have skipped over briefly, but that often turns up in the arguments of those who have doubts about the Bayesian approach. How, they ask, can a collection of admittedly subjective ideas be turned into a reliable "objective" tool? They feel that people are fooled into thinking they have "data" when they assign a number to an opinion or guess. Perhaps the best first answer should be that this approach isn't really new but has been used successfully in other fields.

Mr. Robert Freshman, one of the key Air Force laboratory planners, who was previously a professional educator, likes to answer this attack by citing the experience of the academic community. High-school students are admitted to universities, he explains, on the basis of quantitative judgments made by teachers. These teachers grade about five subjects a year, for four years of high school. The different teachers, different subjects, different tests, and different subject matter taken in high schools throughout the nation are all expressed in numbers or letter grades. Teacher opinions on how to grade, biases and prejudgments, oral recitations, grades on nonstandardized, unstructured subject matter and tests are all injected into the conglomeration to form the individual teacher's final grade in one subject. High-school grades for the four years are then averaged to produce one number: the high-school average. Miraculously, there is a good, positive correlation between this magic average and success in college. It is recognized in most cases that this "quantitative estimate" of many judgments is the best indicator of success in college.

Since opinions and judgments are gathered and weighed by every decision-maker in one way or another, why not formalize the process?

This book describes some of the most advanced and sophisticated attempts to do this that have been made so far. They do not pretend to give all the answers; but they do show that technical resource allocation can and does work. They are offered to interested students, managers, and allocation specialists in a spirit that is expressed in these two points:

1. The quantitative management techniques outlined do not result in good decisions. Rather, they provide a basis of information upon which decisions can be made.

2. The most important thing at this stage is that an objective attitude be maintained concerning all new resource-allocation techniques. Calling them impractical before they have been fairly tested in a scientific manner does little but protect the status quo—and this simply isn't good enough.

How Is Technology Assessed?

Assessment of technology or subsystem analysis is employed to answer the question: Which, when, and how many resources should be allocated where among the alternative projects? Since the topic is multifaceted, it is necessary to draw information from a variety of sources, including operations research, project selection techniques, and technological forecasting.

Assessment is commonly considered to mean "setting a value to." Assessment of technology thus means setting a value to technology. By technologies we mean areas of special knowledge such as gas turbines, diesels, thermionics, thermoelectrics, fuel cells, or energy conversion—not sciences such as surface physics, cryogenics, or magnetics. The kinds or measures of value given to technologies will be discussed later in this chapter. Also, it should be remembered that the nature of the assessment of technology depends on the person who assesses it, the reason for performing assessments, and the nature of the technology itself.

You can get to the heart of one technique of assessing technology by using a simple analogy. To assess the value of two baskets of fruit with contents as listed in Table 1.1, first determine the value of the baskets in one of many respects such as weight (which would be a critical criterion in submarines, for example), volume (a critical criterion for spacecraft), calories (a critical criterion for weight-watchers), and cost (budgeting or economic analysis).

Table 1.1

Basket No. 1	Fruit Cost (¢/unit)	Basket No. 2
5 apples	10	10 apples
8 oranges	20	2 oranges
6 bananas	30	9 bananas

In this example, assessment can be readily done in terms of financial cost with monetary values assigned to the individual items as follows: 10 cents per apple; 20 cents per orange; 30 cents per banana. Therefore Basket 1 is worth $3.90, and Basket 2 is worth $4.10.

You can think of the baskets of fruit as technologies: the different types of fruit represent the characteristics (parameters) of the technologies; and the cost values of the fruit represent their "relative importance factors."

The assumption here is that the parameters of technologies (the fruit), while differing from each other, provide measures that can be taken collectively (each basket) to determine a single numerical value. This can be compared to a similarly derived value of another technology. Note that the assessment could have been made for the purpose of comparing other importance factors—values of weight, volume, calories, etc. It is easy to see that the selection of the relative importance factors is dependent upon the parameters (kinds of fruit, in the example), and upon the purpose of the assessment. Of course our example does not do the impossible job of adding apples and oranges. Instead, a system is constructed that allows them to be stacked against each other in some meaningful way.

Another hypothetical example of technological assessment is employed by Keith Ellingsworth of the Annapolis Division of the Naval Ship Research and Development Center, Division Planning Office. This one is neither an analogy nor trivial. It concerns the design of a boat for river warfare use. The design has proceeded to the point where

Table 1.2

Boat No. 1	Importance Factor	Boat No. 2
25 K		20 K
80 db		50 db

a choice must be made between two parameters, speed and noise level, of two boats, as illustrated in Table 1.2.

Here it appears difficult to assign relative importance of factors, but there are methods: a mission analysis can allow us to make the determination. Imagine the boat patrolling a river and scanning up and down the river with its radar. Its mission is to prevent enemy junks from crossing the river. The more noise the boat makes, the farther up the river the enemy can hear it. The farther away the boat can be heard, the more time the enemy has to escape by crossing the river or by ducking back into a shallow creek where the boat can't follow, and the faster our boat must be to catch the enemy.

It is simply a matter of physics and geometry to determine, say for a given boat noise, the speed required to achieve a stated level of mission effectiveness. The results of a mission analysis might be that for every 16 decibels of noise, 4 knots of speed are required in order to make it possible to intercept those junks up to a mile away and in the middle two-thirds (width) of the river. In other words, 4 decibels of noise correspond to 1 knot of speed; these are the relative importance factors needed. The boat is then selected as illustrated in Table 1.3. The calculations of value derived from the data are:

$$V(\#1) = 25 \times 4 - 80 \times 1 = 20;$$
$$V(\#2) = 20 \times 4 - 50 \times 1 = 30.$$

This assessment indicates the choice of Boat #2. It's a slower boat, but its reduced noise makes it more effective by the criteria established.

Table 1.3

Boat No. 1	Importance Factor	Boat No. 2
25 K	4	20 K
80 db	1	50 db

This sort of assessment might be done to determine operational capabilities, to determine design criteria, or, in resource allocation, to determine the appropriate levels of effort in the two technological areas of boat power and noise reduction.

Intuitively, nearly everyone assesses technology at some time, for some purpose, and to some degree of sophistication. The shopper for example, may assess the aggregates of the technologies of color versus black-and-white television. He may consider the collective value of parameters such as cost, picture quality, repair frequency, and pressure from his wife in order to choose which, if either, to buy.

That nearly everyone has different values is obvious. But there are some points about this statement that bear review. For one thing, personal values vary widely; they might be called theoretical, economic, esthetic, social, political, or religious. And, the values that are most important to an individual have a profound influence on his strategic decisions. The point here is that, too often, managers are unaware of their own values and tend to misjudge those of others. Therefore, the man who will take steps to understand his and others' values better can gain an important advantage in developing workable decision-making methods.

Taking this discussion back to technology, it was stated earlier that the assessment of technology depends on who does the assessing, why the assessment is undertaken, and on the nature of technology itself. Consider the case of assessors examining the technology of storage batteries and three of its parameters: volume, cost, and time between rechargings. A broad range of assessors might be as in Table 1.4. The four people listed might assess battery technology by using the tech-

Table 1.4

Technology Involvement	Situation
User	Lt. USN; Commanding Officer of a boat, which contains batteries, drifting on a Vietnamese river on night patrol
R&D Manager	Chief of Naval Development; responsible for Navy's total Exploratory Development. Program (Applied Research): considering each year's fiscal budget
Boat Designer	Naval Architect, Naval Ships Systems Command, designing a boat for use in Vietnam
R&D Engineer	Project engineer; working in a Navy R&D laboratory to improve the general performance of batteries

Table 1.5 Technology: Batteries

Parameter	User	Manager	Designer	Engineer
Volume	3	2	10	8
Cost	0	10	2	2
Time between Rechargings	10	2	1	1

niques illustrated earlier and come up with results like those shown in Table 1.5, assigning values to the parameters based on intuition. The tendencies shown by the variations of relative importance might be exaggerated, but they have a basis in fact.

The boat operator's life depends to a large extent on his boat. He is probably very concerned when, in the situation described, he must start up his loud engines to charge the batteries. He therefore considers the necessity and the time to recharge very important. He is probably not too concerned with the volume of the batteries so long as they do not infringe significantly on ammunition storage space. Nor does he care what the batteries cost.

The R&D manager is likely to place more importance on cost and less on individual performance characteristics. This is probably due to his responsibility for a large number of current and projected R&D programs which involve many different parameters of many different technologies; the one common element among these is cost.

The boat designer is concerned with the over-all performance of the boat. He must be sure that all components required fit onto the boat, and he therefore considers volume relatively more important than either cost or recharging time.

The project engineer, on the other hand, is concerned with many characteristics of batteries; he is concerned with the improvement of batteries in general. It is not specially required of him that he produce a profit. He therefore may not be particularly cost conscious. Unless he was specifically told to produce the smallest possible boat battery, he would place less importance on volume than the boat designer does.

These considerations show that the selection of relative importance factors for parameters describing a technology is strongly influenced by the assessor's environment. This points up how hard it can be to obtain and maintain an alignment of relative importance factors between the users of technologies and those responsible for improving the capabilities of technologies.

Focusing on Facts

We are well aware of many of the omissions and weaknesses of quantitative selection or resource-allocation techniques based on the type of analysis illustrated here. It should be stressed again that the parameters generated do not yield decisions, but rather information that will facilitate decision-making. Indeed, these techniques are merely thinking structures to force methodical, meticulous consideration of all the factors involved in resource allocation. In other words, data plus analysis yield information; information plus judgment yield decisions.

Those of us who are working to build these allocation systems are firmly convinced that if we had to choose between any system with miles of computer printout and the human brain, we would select the brain. The brain has a marvelous way of learning from experience and an uncanny way of pulling out salient factors and rejecting useless information. It is wrong to say, however, that one must select intuitive experience over analysis, or minds over machines. They are not alternatives but should complement each other. Used together properly, they can be counted on to reduce the most complex problem to an answerable question.

A close look at a few quantitative resource-allocation methods will show that most of these approaches are still experimental management techniques. The fact that a computer or an adding machine may be used to facilitate data handling should in no way distract from the basic fact that human subjective inputs are the foundation of these systems. Accurate human calculation, as opposed to use of a computer for the calculations of all the interrelationships considered, would not alter the basic principles of these management tools in any respect.

These approaches represent the latest thinking on how to use the collective judgments of technical staffs and decision-makers in such a manner that the most logical and sound decisions evolve. The goal is the greatest payoff achieved for the resources committed, whether in men, money, or facilities. To make an incorrect decision is understandable, but to make a decision without really trying to get as much usable information as possible is unforgivable. The managers who design and work with information systems, however, must realize that the technological forecasts, quantitative estimates of project value, and other aids to resource allocation are simply planning tools.

Even this caveat, however, does not defuse critics of the whole idea —and there are some very vocal ones around both in government and business. Some of the criticism is a reaction to the fear of "mechanization" of a task felt to be rightfully in the province of human evaluation. Other critics claim that building up a logical system, computerizing the output, and quantifying what are essentially intuitive and judgment decisions may insulate some managers with a false sense of security. In some way, they fear management responsibility will be hard to pin down.

Systematic analysis, however, tends to force managers to consider their resource-allocation tasks more comprehensively and highlights problem areas that might easily be overlooked by more traditional approaches. At the same time, quantitative methods are considered threatening by some managers because they may tend to expose their value judgments to critical analysis by others. As the high degree of sophistication of these planning devices improves, however, managers will be won over, especially when they find that they will be able to spend more, not less, time doing real decision-making. It is hoped that the following chapters will make this point clear.

Quantifying Military Utility

Marvin J. Cetron

"I wish to have no connection with any ship that does not sail fast, for I intend to go in harm's way." **John Paul Jones**

Over recent years the Department of Defense, often under the prodding of Congress, has been working hard to develop a logical method of allocating its resources to the sciences and technologies. QUEST (Quantitative Utility Estimates for Science and Technology) is one of the earliest methods developed to relate research and exploratory development directly to military missions and make possible a more efficient allocation of dollars and manpower.

In outline, the approach is to assign a "figure of utility" to each military mission and then determine the value to each mission of the work being done in each technological area. Similarly, the relevant impact of each of the scientific disciplines is related to each technological area. Since we have already related the technical areas to missions, we now have a method of relating the impact of each scientific discipline on military missions.

To complete the analysis, technological forecasts for each scientific and technological area (under given resource levels) must be generated; these help determine the probability of success (risk) of each project. Combining the military utility and the probability of success, an "expected value" is produced which the Department of Defense top planners can use to aid them in allocating resources to both research and exploratory development.

The underpinnings of this approach are ideas such as "relevance numbers," "figures of merit," and other numerical techniques for evaluating alternatives that are already standard procedures in operations research and other management science methods. There are still differences of opinion, however, on how and where these techniques can be applied. Some doubt that the operations research approaches have been applied successfully to R&D. Robert Anthony, for example, suggests that these techniques are in essence game theory, and that the difference between the complexity of real life and the relative simplicity essential in applying game theory probably accounts for the fact that there are few published reports of the application of the theory of games to actual business problems. Even if it is assumed that illustrations in texts and articles on the subject are taken from real life, although this is not usually the case, most of the reported applications turn out to deal with operating problems.[1]

But the potential benefits of developing a quantitative system are well worth struggling with the obstacles. Note this comment from a potential user of this appraisal information, Capt. Edmund Mahinske, USN, as stated in a Management Memo: "A Planning Appraisal System which operates on task area proposals . . . is a crucial necessity to our attempts to derive our program on a basis of relatively unimpeachable logic . . . . An appraisal system is the crux of our problem and *must* be solved. . . . Remember our goal is to *improve* our management of the program, *not* to perpetuate the 'control' we now exercise."[2]

But realizing the need for a system and putting experimental systems into use represent a big step for managers. Nevertheless, from all indications (conferences, articles, and implementing instructions), I now think the step is being taken. We are well into a transition period, where new allocation techniques based on sophisticated quantitative analyses are being applied to R&D management.

Some Basic Definitions

Since QUEST is concerned with both military R&D concepts and similar ideas in the nonmilitary world, it may be useful to relate the

---

[1] Anthony, Robert N., *Planning and Control Systems—A Framework for the Analysis*, Boston, Mass., Harvard Business School, Division of Research, pp. 5–57.
[2] Mahinske, Edmund B., *Memorandum on Exploratory Development Planning Appraisal System*, HQ Naval Material Command, Nov. 22, 1966.

certainty, the decision process considers the maximization of known objectives (such as military utility or profits) that are subject to known constraints (such as costs). Under conditions of uncertainty, the functions and/or constraints are not known precisely, and the decision maker or his advisers must make subjective estimates of the most important criteria.

Wherever possible, new techniques try to attach significant numerical values to these estimates. For example, in the Bayesian probability approach, the decision-maker lists the set of values of outcomes that a particular parameter may take and the corresponding subjective probability of each outcome. These subjectively "weighted" outcomes are then summed to result in what is known as the "expected value of the parameter."

Also of concern is the measurability of utility. Utility may be defined as something that serves a purpose or is helpful in accomplishing an end. Some economists have adopted the same idea that experimental psychology did when it began measuring aspects of sensation. If a subject reacts to changes in a physical stimulus and the pattern of his reactions is known, then a functional relationship can be set between the stimulus and the response. Since the physical stimulus can be measured, measures of the response from the functional relationship can be derived.

C. West Churchman puts it this way: "To see how this might work out for utility measurements, suppose we want to compare a person's preference for various commodities (apples, beer, pigs, TV sets, and so on). Suppose we could find a physically measurable commodity of this nature: When we present a subject with x units of this "standard" commodity and y units of apples, he feels that he is indifferent as to which he received. That is, he feels he prefers equally x units of the standard commodity and y units of apples. Then why not say that his degree of 'pleasure' associated with y apples is measured by the x standard units? If this could be done for all quantities of every commodity, then we would apparently have a general 'pleasure' scale (sometimes called a preference scale and sometimes a utility scale)."[3] Value, as defined by Webster's dictionary, is that which renders anything desirable or useful; worth usually refers to price. However,

[3] Churchman, C. West, *Prediction and Optimal Decision,* Englewood Cliffs, N.J., Prentice-Hall, 1961, pp. 42–43.

Churchman says, "values are a basis of predicting choice when the probabilities are known."

A distinction must be made here between risk and uncertainty. Risk refers to relatively objective probabilities that can be computed on the basis of past experience or some a priori principle. Examples of the use of past experience are the actuarial probabilities in the insurance business that certain proportions of fires of various magnitudes will take place or that certain numbers of people of various ages will die. Examples of the a priori type are the odds that a coin will turn up heads or that an ace will be drawn from a deck of cards. In any of these cases the probability of the outcomes can be computed with considerable precision. In risk situations experience is repetitive and provides a frequency distribution about which inferences can be drawn by objective statistical procedures.

Uncertainty, on the other hand, is relatively subjective, since there is insufficient past information or insufficient stability in the structure of the variables to permit exact prediction. Most business decisions take place under conditions of uncertainty, for each decision is made in a somewhat different environment. Sometimes the term *objective probability* is used in connection with risk and *subjective probability* in connection with uncertainty. Expected value, in our usage, is future value under conditions of uncertainty.

Finally, there is balance. In our context, balance is a situation in which due consideration has been given to program requirements, including what the customer has specified as his needs: utility; timeliness; success expectancy; credibility and performance of participating organizations; exploitation of technological opportunities; technological forecasts; adequacy of funding; availability of funds, and so on. Only by making trade-offs among all these areas can you achieve a "balanced" program.

In some sense or other, the funds allocated to various technological areas must not only be properly balanced with respect to each other but also with respect to the goals of the entire program. Naturally, if unlimited resources were available, all the desired programs could be pursued fully. In practice, however, choices must be made. In general, each avenue of technological advance will be pursued at somewhat less than the maximum possible rate. The problem of balance, then, is one of deciding at what rate each area of technology should be advanced, recognizing that advances in one area are only obtained at the cost of slowing down advances in some other area.

The Concept of R&D Planning

The funds available to the formal Department of Defense (DOD) program should be considered principally as an indicator of the interest in important areas—a vector toward desirable goals. The level of funds applied represents a firm indication of interest and serves as a guide to the work of universities, industry, and the national research complex as a whole. It is vital, therefore, that these funds be applied wisely. It is also vital to have a thorough knowledge of the ongoing national efforts in the major technical areas so that planning efforts can be oriented to emphasize those areas where there is a requirement for greater efforts in order to be sure that the technical knowledge will be available when needed.

In this major problem of deciding which directions R&D should go, selectivity is the key. The question of selectivity, however, is very complex since research and exploratory development must be responsive to specific recognized needs and also opportunistic with respect to the unknown possibilities of new technology and science. In addition, the technical program must provide for the transition of new ideas from research into promising new or improved techniques, materials, and processes for future applications. At the same time, the total national needs must be considered.

Focusing on the military aspects of the matter, the program must generate the technology for the next generation of systems and subsystem components, and help minimize the time between concept and operational capability. The major portion of the technological effort must therefore ensure that work in the many independent areas of technology will ultimately lend themselves to integration.

The value of such efforts depends largely on our ability to predict the capabilities desired in the future. For the short term we can do this quite well; often the user is actually knocking at the door. For the long term, unfortunately, no one has 20-20 vision, and only generalized concepts or broad mission area descriptions can be derived.

While efforts are being made to meet current as well as projected needs, another segment of the R&D effort must cover the unpredictable but intuitively promising areas—the search for unexpected new techniques and "breakthroughs." This segment embraces a category of high risk effort and relies for its success on the technical competence and judgment of those managing the R&D program. On their analysis of the possibilities—and sometimes guesses—rests the technological base for the next family of desired operational capabilities.

In planning any technical program, management must decide upon an appropriate balance between research and development. This balance will vary from time to time, from one science or technical area to another, and will be influenced by the environment of the time. It is a function of corporate management to set the guidelines for establishing this balance and to make sure the balance is in fact maintained.

In the selection of opportunistic or fringe-area types of effort, however, the man who knows best is usually the scientist or engineer who has a day-to-day intimacy with a particular science or technology. One must rely heavily upon the judgment of the individual engineer or scientist, provided he has a good general understanding of problem areas facing him and is knowledgeable with respect to the scientific potential and technical risk of his work.

In the selection of efforts that are responsive to operational needs or deficiencies, on the other hand, we move into an area that can be evaluated in a more precise quantitative manner. Here time phasing becomes more important and technical risk becomes more critical— especially with respect to the contribution expected for known operational needs. In addition, the costs involved are usually higher and may involve expensive facilities and large manpower resources. Here, the major source of guidance in determining areas for emphasis are the generalized statements of desired operational capability. These capabilities represent the over-all objectives identifying the technology desired, the time phasing required, and the relative importance of various R&D tasks.

Purpose of QUEST

The rest of this chapter describes an experimental evaluation procedure that is designed to provide greater "visibility" for the information managers when selecting support levels for programs in the research and exploratory development categories. The procedure is primarily oriented to show the relevance and criticality of an area of technology and the supporting sciences that contribute to its military capabilities. The procedure is neither absolute nor optimal, and may not even be the decisive factor in planning and programming. It is, however, an extremely useful aid for the decision-maker, regardless of whether he is in an individual laboratory or at higher echelons of management.

It is admittedly a subjective approach. But it combines many subjective judgments into one over-all picture. The key point is that the procedure involves the assignment of quantitative values to the judgments made by experienced people. It then brings together these values in an orderly, visible manner as an aid in making gross allocation decisions among technical programs—in different areas of both technology and science.

The obvious question arises: Why is there a need for a quantitative approach? For one thing—and this would be answer enough—Congressional appropriation committees have requested quantitative justification from DOD regarding the dispensing of its R&D funds. But even without this spur, I do not think that in the past the DOD has appraised, evaluated, and allocated its research and development resources in the most objective and productive manner.

The traditional approach to the problem of resource allocation has been to give the researcher what he had last year, and the engineer fragmented funding on a "piecemeal justification" basis. Technological funding would be given to those areas whose champions could convince top management that their areas have greater requirements for resources than other areas. (While I am talking about the DOD, the same could be said about many large industrial organizations.)

The traditional approach has several serious deficiencies, however. The two most important are that it is too sensitive to the salesmanship qualities of the lower management echelons and that it has the tendency to base justifications on a single factor, i.e., short-term military utility. The fact is that funds should be allocated only after a complete evaluation of all of the three factors pertinent to project selection: probability of success, costs, and military utility.

Too many technical managers, both in and out of government, regard all research as "pure" and "valuable" for the future. These executives and the scientists and engineers supervised by them often tend to refuse even to consider the problem logically for fear that a logical system will lead to interference from higher levels and butcher some of their sacred cows. Many times, government or industrial research managers fight new allocation systems with the statement: "We fund the man, not the work." This may be good procedure for achieving results, but the results may not bear any resemblance to the needs or goals of the total organization involved.

I believe firmly that research not only can, but should, be planned carefully. In the Department of Defense, the great bulk of it must be guided along the lines of relevancy to DOD missions. Yet, it should not be so constrained that it produces applied research exclusively. A given percentage of the R&D budget, say 20 percent, should be un-fettered for "knowledge for the sake of knowledge" in research and for "technological opportunities" in the case of exploratory development. A well-structured planning tool does not have to ignore the fact that a scientific curiosity today may be a military necessity tomorrow.

QUEST is designed to do this planning job. It has five key elements or functions:

1. To define the purposes of the research and exploratory development programs and relate these to DOD missions or companies' goals or needs by assigning a quantitative "relevance" number to each scientific discipline and a quantitative "contribution" number to each techno-logical or functional area.
2. To develop a structure that will aid in the understanding of the relationships between the sciences, technologies, and the missions to which they contribute.
3. To see that the scientific or technological areas are objectively evaluated to insure balanced support and continuity for long-term objectives.
4. To develop a mechanism to insure that *all* scientific and technological areas are considered, so that no opportunities are overlooked.
5. To make available a statement of the R&D program that can be used to explain to higher authority how, where, and why resources were used and how they should be used in the future.

Methodology

In the most basic terms, current research and exploratory programs are supported by DOD to make sure that scientific and technological knowledge will be available in the future when it is needed. With tech-nology, too, links can be fairly clear between R&D and future missions or systems. With science, however, the path from workbench to battle-field is often less obvious. To solve this problem, QUEST uses tech-nology as the coupling between science and military missions.

This system assumes that two elements of information are required prior to the allocation of funds to a science or technology: the potential military value of each R&D area in the future and a technical forecast of the probability of achieving technological objectives or useful scientific results.

Military Value

When dealing with military value or relevance, the first step is to determine the future value of each technology to specific missions, and then the future value of each scientific discipline to technology. These steps are carried out by building two interdependent matrices:

Matrix 1, Value of Technology to Mission. The mission-oriented parameter of this matrix is the initial input and must be quantified by the major military organizations (Combat Development Command; Commandant, Marine Corps; Chief of Naval Operations; Strategic Air Command; Tactical Air Command, and so on). These numbers, or "figures of utility," are assigned to each warfare category and should be updated annually prior to budget time. They are based on a combination of evaluations of the world situation and forecasts of the future environment, including the probable situations that will bring that future environment about (scenarios). The number assigned to the most important category ("figure of merit") should be 100; the rest will fall in appropriately. The "producer" commands of all three services (Army Materiel Command, Naval Material Command, Air Force Systems Command) should then assign numbers from 0 to 10 ("contribution number") to indicate the contribution of each technological area to each mission (Table 2.1). If the contribution number is multiplied by the figure of merit for each mission, an "impact number" can be determined for each mission. Adding up the impact numbers for each individual mission results in a quantitative contribution of each technology to every mission.

Three of these "technology-to-mission charts" may well be required: one for now, one for five years from now, and one for ten years from now. These should aid in determining future adequacy. If a sensitivity investigation shows there is very little difference, this triple approach may be discontinued.

Matrix 2, Relevance of Science to Technology. By using the contribution numbers evolved from Matrix 1, the technology parameters should be filled into a grid similar to that of Matrix 1, evaluating the contribution of *Science* against that of *Technology*. The research branch of the services (Office of Naval Research, Army Research Office, Office of Aerospace Research) should determine the relevance number (between 0 and 10) to each of the scientific disciplines listed as it applies to each technological area (Table 2.2). The product of the quantified technological area contribution and the relevance number will then represent the significance of that scientific discipline to that particular

Matrix 1. Value of
Technology to Missions

TECHNOLOGY

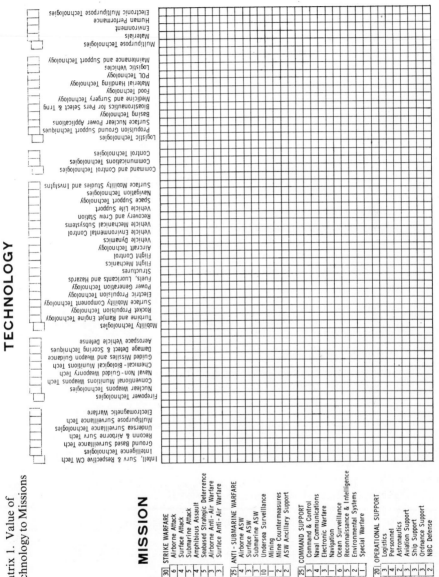

MISSION

30	STRIKE WARFARE
6	Airborne Attack
4	Surface Attack
5	Submarine Attack
4	Amphibious Assault
5	Seabased Strategic Deterrence
3	Airborne Anti-Air Warfare
3	Surface Anti-Air Warfare

25	ANTI-SUBMARINE WARFARE
4	Airborne ASW
3	Surface ASW
3	Submarine ASW
10	Undersea Surveillance
1	Mining
2	Mine Countermeasures
2	ASW Ancillary Support

25	COMMAND SUPPORT
3	Command & Control
4	Naval Communications
3	Electronic Warfare
1	Navigation
6	Ocean Surveillance
5	Reconnaissance & Intelligence
2	Environmental Systems
1	Special Warfare

20	OPERATIONAL SUPPORT
3	Logistics
4	Personnel
2	Astronautics
2	Aviation Support
3	Ship Support
3	Ordnance Support
2	NBC Defense

Table 2.1   Contribution of a Technical Effort to a Desired Operational Capability (Mission)
(The assumption is that the objective of the technical effort will be accomplished)

Absolutely essential	
Failure to have this technology will absolutely prevent the attainment of the capability desired	10
Major contribution	
Failure to acquire this technology will result in a significant decrease in one or more of the major performance parameters needed to attain the capability desired. Such degradation would probably prevent a favorable decision for developing of equipment for the inventor	7
Cost reduction Success in achieving this technology will provide a major reduction in the cost of achieving the capability desired	5
Substantial contribution	
Failure to achieve this technology will result in the loss of a highly desirable but not essential capability. Such lack of success, while important, probably would not prevent a favorable decision on the development of equipment to attain the capability desired	4
Refinement of capability	
Achievement of this technology will result in some refinement of the present capability. The desired capability, however, could be achieved without this effort	3
Indirect contributions	
Achievement of this technology will only be an indirect contribution to the capability desired	2
Remote association	
This effort has only a remote association with the capability desired	1
No contribution	0

Table 2.2   Research Evaluation

No progress is possible in this technology without vigorous pursuit of this science	10
Major improvements in this technology will require major advances in this science to achieve success	8
Current knowledge will permit only crude or cumbersome solutions to advanced technology requirements. New and significant knowledge is required to make satisfactory solutions possible	5

Only minor and straightforward extension of existing knowledge is needed to permit this technology to meet advanced technology requirements 3

Current knowledge in this science is adequate for advancing this technology 1

The technology does not draw on this science at all 0

---

technological area. The resultant summation of that discipline to all quantified area would then represent the "mission relevance" for each scientific discipline.

In this matrix, the scientific disciplines are listed as follows:

Physical Sciences
General physics
    Solid-state physics
    Atomic and molecular physics
    Quantum and classical wave physics (new)
    Acoustics
    Plasma and ionic physics
    Theoretical physics
    Relativity and gravitational physics
    Quantum fluid physics
    Instrumentation

Nuclear Physics
    Cosmic radiation
    Elementary particles
    Nuclear structures

Chemistry
    Physical chemistry
    Organic chemistry
    Inorganic chemistry
    Analytical chemistry
    Solid state chemistry
    Biochemistry
    Chemistry techniques

Mathematical sciences
    Theoretical mathematics
    Applied analysis, theoretical, mechanical, and mathematical physics
    Biological mathematics
    Numerical analyses
    Mathematical statistics and probability
    Theories and technologies of logic, analysis, and decision making
    Theories and technologies of information processing

Information processing systems and devices
Methodological topics relevant to specific military problems
Basic methodology in systems research
Interdisciplinary research
Communication and control systems

Engineering Sciences
Electronics
Electromagnetic wave propagation and radiation
Electromagnetic wave detection
Phys. properties of solids, liquids, and gases
Electromagnetic materials and components
Electronic theory
Communications theory
Information processing
Electro-acoustics
Plasma electrodynamics
Quantum electronics

Materials
Organic materials
Lubricants
Inorganic materials
Metals and alloys
Composite and fibrous materials
High-temperature and specific materials
Surface phenomena, corrosion and prevention
Radiation-resistant materials
Ceramics
Characterization
Macromolecular research

Mechanics
Flight mechanics
Simulation research
Hydroelasticity
Aeroelasticity
Biomechanics
Aeromechanics
Hydromechanics
Mechanics of materials
Stress analyses and structural stability
Continuum mechanics

Energy conversion
Fuels and propellant
Single-step energy transformation
Multistep energy transformation
Energy utilization
Combustion dynamics

Environmental Sciences
Oceanography
   Physical oceanography
   Chemical oceanography
   Marine biology
   Marine geophysics and chemistry

Terrestrial sciences
   Seismology
   Geology
   Geodesy
   Gravity
   Selenodesy
   Geography
   Geomagnetism
   Geoelectricity
   Glaciology
   Arctic Research
   Environmental factors

Atmospheric sciences
   Meteorology
   Atmospheric optics
   Aeronomy
   Ionospheric physics
   Planetary atmosphere

Astronomy and astrophysics
   Solar physics
   Radio and radar astronomy
   Lunar and planetary research
   Observational astronomy
   Galactic phenomena
   Magnetic fields, cosmic rays
   Meteor physics
   Astrophysics
   Laboratory astrophysics

Life Sciences
Biological and medical sciences
   Genetics
   Molecular biology
   Botany
   Entomology
   Regulatory mechanisms
   Immunology and hematology
   Biological response to environment
   Microbiology
   Biochemistry
   Hydrobiology

Biophysics
Epidemology
Biological orientation
Ecology
Neurology and neuropsychiatry
Surgical sciences
Medical sciences
Radiology, pathology
Pharmacology
Physiology
Mathematical biology

Behaviorial and social sciences
Sensory mechanisms
Neural and perceptual processes
Motor mechanisms
Psychological traits
Selection methods and performance criteria
Learning and training
Individual effectiveness
Group effectiveness
Engineering psychology
Psychology of individual performance
Social psychology and sociology
Social sciences—interaction
Policy-planning studies
Intercultural effectiveness

These are evaluated against the following list of technological areas:

Intelligence, Surveillance, and Respective CM Technologies
Intelligence technologies
Ground-based surveillance technologies
Reconnaissance and airborne survey technologies
Undersea surveillance technologies
Multipurpose surveillance technologies
Electromagnetic warfare

Firepower Technologies
Nuclear-weapons technologies
Conventional munitions and weapons technologies
Naval nonguided weaponry technologies
Chemical-biological munitions technologies
Guided Missiles and weapon guidance
Damage detection and storing techniques
Aerospace vehicle defense

Mobility Technologies
  Turbine and ramjet engine technology
  Rocket-propulsion technology
  Surface mobility component technology
  Electric propulsion technology
  Power-generation technology
  Fuels, lubricants, and hazards
  Structures
  Flight mechanics
  Flight control
  Aircraft technology
  Vehicle dynamics
  Vehicle environmental control
  Vehicle mechanical subsystems
  Recovery and crew station
  Vehicle life support
  Space support technology
  Navigation technologies
  Surface mobility studies and investigations

Command and Control Technologies
  Communication technologies
  Control technologies

Logistic Technologies
  Propulsion ground-support techniques
  Surface nuclear power applications
  Basing technology
  Bioastronautics for personnel selection and training
  Medicine and surgery technology
  Food technology
  Material-handling technology
  POL technology
  Logistic vehicles
  Maintenance and support technology

Multipurpose Technologies
  Materials
  Environment
  Human performance
  Electronic multipurpose technologies

This procedure may also have to be repeated for three time frames (now, five years from now, and ten years from now) in order to show how long-term research makes its impact on future military systems.

Because this method includes technological transfer in the matrix, this criterion need not be broken out separately. Timeliness and responsiveness are also implicit in the "figures of utility" for each mission that are given by the operational inputs from each service.

Forecasts

Before allocating funds, the planner must know the probability of
success (risk) of the scientist or engineer in achieving his goals. This
input can be based on a technological forecast in a given area. A technological forecast may be defined as the prediction, with a given level
of confidence, of the occurrence of a technical achievement within a
given time, when a specified amount of resources are applied.

Generally speaking, a scientific forecast in applied research should
be based on background, present status, projections, military implications, and references. A technological forecast in exploratory development should consider the current state of the art, status, projections,
operational significance, and references. Figure 2.1 shows how the
results may be charted.

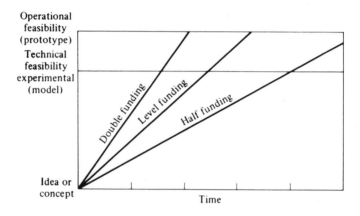

Figure 2.1   Trend Extrapolations for Technological Forecasts

Detailed Description of QUEST

For simplicity, military terminology and government budgetary
words—and dollar amounts—will be used, but the QUEST system
may well be applied to other allocation situations.

To begin with, a set of desired military capabilities or missions to be
performed must be given; they must satisfy the assumptions that each
mission can be assigned a critical weight (W) based upon its opera-

tional importance, and that the weights of the missions are additive (i.e., the importance of two missions, taken together, is the sum of their individual weights.)

It is important to gain some insight into this weighing process. First, a list of missions is generated for each Service that covers the complete spectrum of possible wartime and peacetime missions. For each mission m_1, the Service staff will be asked to assign a relative weight W_1 according to a well-defined procedure.

For example, a committee of, say, five persons will be given the list of missions and asked to select the most important mission and assign to it a weight of 100. They will next select the least important mission, and give it a weight that indicates its importance relative to the most important mission (i.e., if it is half as important, it gets a weight of 50; if one tenth as important, a weight of 10.) Next, each mission on the list is compared with the most important mission and assigned the appropriate weight, in the same manner as for the least important mission. When this process is completed, each mission is compared in turn with the least important mission, and the correctness of the previously assigned weight checked. Adjustments may be made if indicated. If necessary, the process is repeated with the most important mission.

Eventually, the group will produce a set of weights for the missions that has two important properties. First, it is internally consistent, and second, the weights are additive. The weights will be given for a specified time frame (e.g., 1971–1976), but in actual fact will probably reflect current service program emphases. The instructions to the group doing the weighting should specify that the weights be based on operational importance, that they reflect neither technological cost nor difficulty, and that they be oriented to the specified time period rather than to the present.

The weighted list of military capabilities is then formed into a matrix with a set of technologies. These are defined so that the subtechnologies within each are relatively homogeneous. That is, they must be more like one another than they are like subtechnologies listed under other technologies. Further, each technology must be costed to arrive at the annual funding—preferably based on a five-year projection. Of course, shorter periods of projection would apply to technologies that are likely to terminate prior to five years. The matrix looks something like this:

At each intersection on the matrix, between a technology (T_j) and a mission statement (m_1), the evaluation team considers the potential contribution of the technology to the mission. The contribution might, for example, be improvements in a system, subsystem, component, or material or perhaps a procedure needed to achieve the desired capability.

Then for each intersection the evaluation team must assign two separate quantitative judgments (Table 2.1 provides the numerical values to be used). The first judgment will be the criticality (C_{ij}) of the technology efforts progressing within the special annual budget ceiling to the respective desired capability. Next, the team will estimate additional funding which could be used within current manpower ceilings and with existing facilities. With this in mind, they will judge the criticality C_{ij}^* of the technology that could be provided by the overceiling funding. In practice, the value assigned to the overceiling effort should never exceed, and rarely equal, the value assigned the inceiling case. As an aid to planners at a step further along in the system, those items that receive a value of 7 to 10 should be listed, with a brief verbal description.

At the completion of this work, the matrix would appear approximately as follows:

Military Capabilities (Missions)	W Mission Weighting		$T_{\text{Ia}(1)}$	$T_{\text{Ia}(2)}$	$T_{\text{Ia}(3)}$	$\cdots$	T_r
	100	m_1	7 / 4	5 / 2	2 / 1		
	20	m_2	10 / 1	2 / 0	0 / 0		
	10	m_3	7 / 5	1 / 1	0 / 0		
	70	m_4	0 / 0	10 / 4	10 / 0		
	⋮	⋮					
	2	m_n	0 / 0	0 / 0	4 / 4		
	N_{total}		970 / 470	1250 / 490	908 / 108		

For each intersection on the matrix the mission weighting (W_{mi}) is multiplied by the criticality values C_{ij} and C_{ij}^*. The vertical column is then totaled to find N_{Tj} for each technology area specified at the top of the matrix for both inceiling and overceiling resource levels.

Each technology area is then ranked in decreasing order of N for the entire matrix. This ranking can be by inceiling only, overceiling only, or combinations of both. For purposes of this example, we will consider the inceiling ordering only (Table 2.3). After the ranking, the proposed annual rate of the exploratory development funding for the fiscal years involved is lined up with each technology area in a simple table. The dollar entry includes both work to be contracted and in-house support required for the effort.

The next step requires the preparation of a visual display of the data arranged in the table. First, the dollar column is added to some arbitrary accumulated total, say 50-million dollars. A graph is then made of dollars versus technological area at the T_{Ia}, T_{Ib} level for this

Table 2.3   Inceiling Ordering of Technology

	Decreasing N	Annual Rate (Millions of Dollars)
$T_{Ia(2)}$	1110	.050
$T_{IIIe(4)}$	1100	.100
$T_{Ia(1)}$	1070	1.000
$T_{IVc(2)}$	900	.500
$T_{Vb(3)}$	820	.300
$\vdots$	$\vdots$	$\vdots$
T_r	50	etc.

50-million dollar increment (Fig. 2.2). Next, the dollar amount in the table is added to the 100-million cumulative total and this increment is plotted on the same graph as the previous 50-million. This process is continued until the entire budget is included on the graph.

Obviously, the first 50-million increment shows the profile of those areas that have highest direct relevance to the military problem areas used in the matrix. The last increment has the least direct relevance.

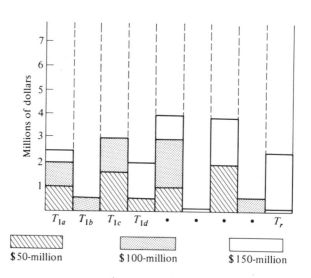

Figure 2.2   Resource Allocations by Technology

The overceiling program can be displayed in a similar manner. Further, a combination inceiling and overceiling graphic presentation can be prepared from the same data. If a proposed budget is applied as a transparent overlay to the given series of profiles, it will show either the similarity or the dissimilarity between the funding proposed and the funding profile developed from the relevancy relationships. Any dissimilarities found are areas that management should examine in detail. They show, for example, where more funds are being allocated than is justified by the value of the technology.

Adding Research to the Picture

By using the set of technologies developed, and a similarly developed set of sciences, a technology-to-science matrix can be built as shown here:

	S_1	S_2	$\cdots$	S_m
T_1				
T_2				
$\vdots$			C_{ij} / C_{ij}^*	
T_r				

At the intersection T_i and S_j, the evaluation team will consider the contribution of S_j to T_i. The team will then assign two quantitative judgments to these contributions (using the numerical values of Table 2.2). As in the technology-to-mission matrix, the first judgment will be the criticality C_{ij} of the research efforts within the special fiscal year budget ceiling to the technology T_j. Once again, the team will estimate the additional resources that could be used within current manpower ceilings and with existing facilities. It will then judge the criticality C_{ij}^* of the research made possible by the additional resources. As before, the criticality of the overceiling research resources should never exceed, and rarely equal, the criticality of the inceiling research. If the criticality of any research is judged to be eight or greater, a supporting statement backing up this judgment should be prepared by the evaluation team.

The rest of this analysis proceeds as before. Each technology will have received a score N_{Ti} during the evaluation of exploratory development. The products $(N_{Ti})(C_{ij})$ are summed for S_j, giving a value V_j for each science. The sciences are then ordered according to V_j, and science profiles prepared in the same manner as was explained for exploratory development.

Evaluation of QUEST

For all its complexity, as compared to more traditional evaluation methods, the QUEST system does not go as far as it might in bringing all critical factors into the analysis. For one thing, it does not consider changes in value per change in dollars since it is based upon the total value of a package measured against total dollar budget. Therefore, it is not a system that permits managers to assume that each additional dollar expended produces the same improvement in value, regardless of the discipline concerned.

Also, the procedure does not consider technical transfer in a direct and visible manner. For example, the achievement of success in some materials work may contribute to propulsion efficiency, but this multiplier effect is not given a direct value in the matrix.

Nor does QUEST provide separate consideration of high-potential "opportunistic" efforts. These are not easily fitted into mission type objectives, no matter how broad they may be. This feature can, however, be added as a separate table.

The amount of effort contributed from other agencies is not shown directly, although this factor is inherent in the cost-estimating steps. And QUEST does not consider day-to-day management decisions concerning over-runs, impracticability of termination contract phasing, and so on. Finally, this system does reflect programs outside of research or exploratory development which may affect funding levels.

The truth is, QUEST is just a part of a general effort to improve allocation procedures. Many systems are being developed and used in government and industry. Ultimately, the widespread installation of such systems appears inevitable; it is part of a strong trend toward organizing and mechanizing information for long-range planning—a task that is gaining the attention of more and more specialists and managers every day. It is obvious that efficient planning and programming of R&D programs depend on an ability to manipulate data on large numbers of individual R&D projects in an efficient manner. Only quantitative appraisal and selection techniques like QUEST, along with powerful computers, can give the decision-makers the information they need in order to do their jobs with great efficiency.

3
Balancing Research and Exploratory Development
Marvin J. Cetron

"Having lost sight of our objectives, we redoubled our efforts."
C. E. K. Mees

A series of developments during the past two decades has greatly changed the character of research and development management. The most obvious change is in the magnitude of the management problem. In 1949, resources devoted to R&D in the United States amounted to less than two billion dollars. Currently, annual expenditures on R&D are about 25 billion dollars. Concomitantly, the entire character of general management has changed. Long-range corporate planning, an almost unknown phenomenon in 1950, is now commanding a recognized position among corporate activities.

With the advent of computer systems, operations research has transformed many "vest-pocket decisions" into rational choices made between systematically evaluated alternatives. Management in the scientific and technical community, meshed as it is with the government—particularly the Department of Defense—has been profoundly influenced by the "McNamara era." These developments have generated a large number of analytical techniques for dealing with problems of R&D management.

The need for an objective approach to the problem of resource allocation, particularly funds, has been one plaguing the R&D community for many years. This need has become critical as the funds that have been poured into R&D have soared. Numerous industrial and government specialists have recognized this need and under the prodding of their leaders have been working to develop usable alloca-tion systems.[1,2]

This chapter will describe one of these systems, called MACRO (Methodology for Allocating Corporate Resources to Objectives). It is a method for developing the necessary decision processes to balance funds between research and exploratory development.

It might be noted here that much of the work on project selection appraisal has been done in the United States. A survey of this subject has appeared in the IEEE Transactions on Engineering Management[3] and lists thirty different techniques for quantitative resource allocation. Most of those described are American developments.

Interest in the problem, however, is not limited to the United States. As this chapter is being written, numerous western European nations are exploring resource allocation rationales with a view to experimental evaluation. Most of these efforts are still on a small scale and have not been implemented in major laboratories. The British Ministry of Technology, in particular, is actively pursuing resource allocation studies.[4] And De l'Estoile in France has developed a system that involves four factors: military utility, probability of technical success, possibility of realization in France, and direct and indirect economic impact.[5]

The orientation of most quantitative methods for R&D decisions is toward the public sector, particularly toward defense efforts. MACRO, however, was developed specifically to aid the decision processes of corporate management. The technique provides an analytical frame-work which corporate executives can use to deal systematically with the problem of achieving a balance in the allocation of funds between various projects in applied research and development. It is not intended for use with basic research, nor for development beyond the prototype stage.

The basic idea behind MACRO and similar efforts is that an organi-zation invests resources in scientific and technical investigations because of a real need for the results of these efforts. Generally, the amount of money spent in advancing an area of science or technology is a direct

[1] Andrews, W., "Air Force To Try Systems Analysis (TORQUE) on Exploratory De-velopment," *Defense Management* (April 1968).

[2] Beller, W. S., "Decision-Making in Washington," *Space-Aeronautics Magazine* (December 1967), p. 98.

[3] Cetron, M. J., Martino, Joseph, and Roepcke, Lewis, "The Selection of R&D Program Content-Survey of Quantitative Methods," *IEEE Transactions on Engineering Manage-ment,* Vol. EM-14, 1 (March 1967), pp. 4–13.

[4] *New Technology* No. 7, Published by British Ministry of Technology (July 1967), p. 7.

[5] De l'Estoile, "Resource Allocation Model." Ministère des Armées, Paris, France.

reflection of the interest of the organization in that area. The relative amounts spent in several areas therefore point up the varying degrees of corporate interest among those areas.

The problem of allocation—or of achieving balance—becomes a matter of determining how much an additional advance in one field is worth compared to an advance in some other field that might be bought with the same money. Planners have always made these decisions in one way or another, but most would agree that there is a need for a logically sound system to help them manipulate the great amounts of data that can and should be involved.

The MACRO technique, to sum up, proposes to clarify the matter of balance by requiring that the following questions be answered for each area of science or technology: What achievements are desired? What is the relative worth of each? When are the achievements needed? What will be the cost?

The bases for this analysis involve human judgments and estimates. Basically, these are the judgments and decisions by top management and the systems and technological analyses gathered from throughout the customer and R&D communities. If feasible, MACRO will facilitate the simultaneous consideration of most of the management judgments and decisions that impinge on the development and possibly on the applied research program.

To help the reader in working through this methodology, he is referred to the glossary of terms at the end of this chapter.

Setting of Goals

Two general goals can be assigned to the development efforts of an organization: First, the larger portion of the effort and funds must be directed specifically toward generating technology needed for corporate capability objectives. Where R&D effort is motivated by this kind of end-product application, a systematic method of relating magnitude of effort to urgency of need is of obvious value. Second, some of the effort is, and always should be, expended to seek and capitalize on unexpected developments in science or technology.

The design of MACRO makes it possible to balance the efforts designed to fulfill the first goal while placing no arbitrary restrictions on expenditures related to the second goal. Given a limit on total funds, however, it will indicate the cost of the more speculative efforts in relation to the other investigations that might not be funded even though they are directly tied to a current or known end base.

This methodology is based on the premise that not only do the relative amounts of money spent in various areas of science and technology reflect the varying degrees of interest in those areas, but that this is as it should be. This system is based on three factors: relative worth, date needed, and cost of each achievement. These three factors, when combined into a quantified measure of the usefulness of money spent in each research area, can make possible a precise judgment comparing a budget change in one area with an equivalent one in another area.

The first plan of goal-setting is done by the corporate planning and policy staff, which specifies the long-range corporate objectives. It is on this level that corporate strategies for exploitation of markets should be generated. The technology or corporate technical capability necessary to meet these corporate goals is specified, for utilization in MACRO, in the form of corporate capability objectives (CCO's). Examples of CCO's are shown in Table 3.1.

Table 3.1 Corporate Capability Objectives

Weights	Objectives
12	Achieve a low-volume, high-margin business
15	Gain at least a 10% share of the market
18	Reach an annual growth rate of 12 to 15%
14	Maintain a product of high versatility
10	Obtain maximum profits within 5 years
12	Keep government business below 25%
19	Attain a minimum discounted cash flow of 6% of investment
—	
100	

Once these broad objectives have been outlined, each is broken down into the products and technologies needed to meet them (Fig. 3.1). An interdisciplinary team of marketing and engineering personnel then analyzes each of the objectives to determine ways in which they can be accomplished.

The next step is to assign a number representing the criticality of the technological capability to the objective. This may range from a low number, representing a capability that contributes only minimally, to a high number implying that the objective cannot be attained without this technological achievement. Table 2.1 (p. 26) contains one possible criticality index. Finally, the team must assign to each level of technological capability the earliest date needed and the latest date by

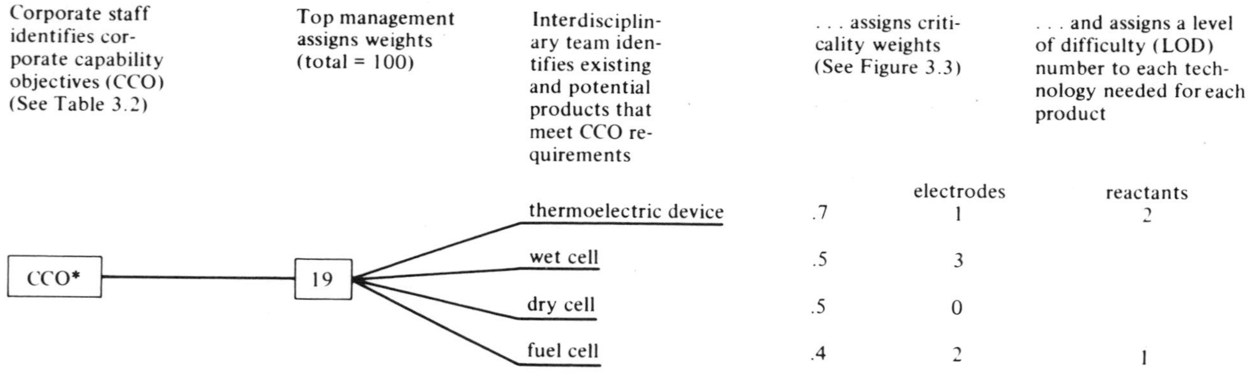

Figure 3.1   Schematic Relating Corporate Objectives to Technological Levels of Difficulty

*One objective, for example, might be to gain a 10% share of market

which the achievement can still be used with full effectiveness in realization of the CCO's.

The technological capabilities desired are collected into "packages" representing single areas of technology. In many cases these will cut across objective lines. A team of specialists in a given technology then arranges in order of increasing levels of difficulty (LOD) the technologies that have also been assigned to them and estimates the cost of achieving each capability by the required date. The cost for a given LOD reflects, but does not include, LOD's that have to be achieved first (Figure 3.2).

Fiscal year	68	69	70	71	72	73	74
LOD_1	150	100	—	—	—	—	—
LOD_2	—	50	100	100	—	—	—
LOD_3	—	—	—	50	100	50	—
Total	150	150	100	150	100	50	—

Figure 3.2   Technology Costing (000's omitted)

In practice, the current year's budget may represent only a fraction of the total cost of achieving the highest LOD. Provided that all the technology leading to the accomplishment of the LOD is funded at the level specified by the technology team, each LOD is expected to be achieved when needed.

Of course, the worth of the LOD will be decreased if the achievement date is postponed by budget reductions. For example, a 30-percent budget reduction would result in a slip in the completion dates of the LOD's (Figure 3.3). There is a tardiness penalty T which assumes an arbitrary form and will be presented later in this chapter.

Under the MACRO system, a computer will determine the worth of having each LOD achieved by multiplying its objective weight by its criticality number and then modifying the result by a timeliness factor and the LOD cost fraction. The utility of a budget level allocated to a particular technology is the sum of the worths of each of the LOD's in that technology.

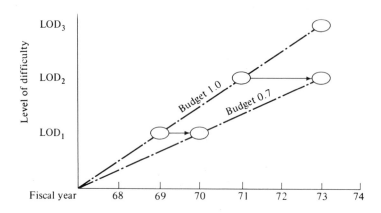

Figure 3.3   Slip in Completion Dates

Utility can also be computed separately for several possible budget levels for the current year. The computer can select the combination of allocation levels in each of the various categories that, with a given budget, will buy the maximum utility. Hopefully, the budget will be allocated so that each technology will be advancing at the maximum rate consistent with the worth of its products and the funds available.

Generating a Sample Budget

When properly gathered, the data obtained from the various teams are sufficient to permit allocating the available budget to the various technologies—under certain assumptions. Each of the technology teams has given an estimate of the budget required to achieve its objectives, including an estimate of the budget for the forthcoming year (in our example it is fiscal year 1969). However, it is most probable that the total of all the estimates for fiscal year 1969 will exceed the budget available.

What happens to the total cost of achieving an LOD and the date at which it is achieved if the rate of annual expenditure is changed from that given by the technology teams? Some assumption must be made to permit estimating the effects of various budgets. It can, for example, be assumed that the total cost remains fixed and that the time required is inversely proportional to expenditure rate. That is, cutting the budget in half doubles the time to the final result and the total cost remains constant. But this assumption is not the only one possible.

Any other rational assumption or set of assumptions can be made and used in the allocation method.

Another factor that must be considered is the effect of achieving a level of difficulty earlier or later than the "latest" date specified by the interdisciplinary team. For simplicity, if an achievement is late, its worth will be assumed to decrease with time, using a time function to be described below. If the LOD is achieved too early, this means that the rate of progress of some other technology was reduced unnecessarily. Thus, early achievement of the LOD is also penalized, as will be shown. Finally, it is accepted that the latest date is only an estimate, and the LOD should not be penalized if it misses that date by a relatively short time, either early or late.

The penalty for missing the latest date is calculated according to a "timeliness function" (Figure 3.4). No penalty is assessed for being

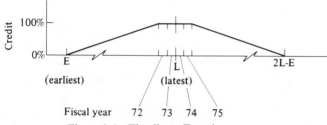

Figure 3.4   Timeliness Function

within two years of the latest year. For being early, the slope of the timeliness function is linear from the earliest year. For simplicity, the slope for the late side of the timeliness function is made the same as for the early side on our figure. Again, this particular timeliness function is not essential to the method; any other timeliness function could be used.[6] As experience with the method is gathered, a planner will be able to design a more realistic timeliness function for his organization.

[6] The algorithm used in the computer program is the following:

$$\text{Technology utility} = \sum_{j}^{N_s} S_j C_i \frac{F_i + S_1}{T_j + S_2} t_j$$

Systems supported

Time

Tech. criticality to system
System relative value

F_i = Current year funds
S_1 = Sum of current year funds — previous LOD's
T_j = Total LOD funds
S_2 = Sum of funds — previous LOD's

Table 3.2   Sequence of LOD's

LOD	Earliest date (Fiscal year)	Latest date (Fiscal year)	CCO
A	1968	1972	O_3
B	1969	1973	O_5
C	1970	1974	O_1
D	1970	1975	O_4
E	1971	1976	O_3
F	1972	1977	O_6

Let us now consider the sequence of LOD's given in Table 3.2, the CCO's having been weighted earlier. The dates refer to years when the links between CCO and the technology associated with it require the technology in question. Here the LOD's are assumed to have been ordered in increasing difficulty. In practice, the first action may be to perform this ordering. The timeliness function is added in Table 3.3.

Look at LOD B, for example. It is stated to be required by the end of fiscal year 1973. It receives full credit for achievement in any of the years 1972, 1973, 1974, or 1975. It receives zero credit for achievement before its earliest year of 1969. Its credit for achievement between the beginning of 1969 and the end of 1971 increases linearly, as shown.

Let us consider the year in which the LOD's will be achieved for various budget levels. The levels considered will be 1.0, 0.8, 0.7, and 0.6 of those requested (see Table 3.4). It must be remembered that a budget level of 0.6 means that the budget is reduced to 60% of that requested and that the program time is stretched to $1/0.6$ times the original duration.

Since the 1968 budget represents a certain proportion of the total costs of achieving each of the LOD's, the various proportions can be

Table 3.3   Timeliness Function

	68	69	70	71	72	73	74	75	76	77	78	79	80	81	82	83	84	85
A	1/4	1/2	3/4	1	1	1	1	3/4	1/2	1/4	0 ———→							
B	0	1/4	1/2	3/4	1	1	1	1	3/4	1/2	1/4	0 ———→						
C	←		0	1/4	1/2	3/4	1	1	1	1	3/4	1/2	1/4	0 ———→				
D	←		0	1/5	2/5	3/5	4/5	1	1	1	1	4/5	3/5	2/5	1/5	0 ———→		
E	←			0	1/5	2/5	3/5	4/5	1	1	1	1	1	4/5	3/5	2/5	1/5	0 ———→
F	← 0	1/7	2/7	3/7	4/7	5/7	6/7	1	1	1	1	1	6/7	5/7	4/7	3/7	2/7	1/7

(Year of Achievement (Fiscal Year))

Table 3.4   LOD Achievements

	Year of Achievement (Fiscal Year)			
	Budget Level			
LOD	1.0	0.8	0.7	0.6
A	72	73	74	75
B	73	75	76	77
C	74	76	77	79
D	75	77	78	80
E	76	78	80	82
F	77	79	81	84

added to the analysis. One set of possible proportions is given in Table 3.5. For instance, if the estimate were $50,000 and it were $\frac{1}{2}$ of the total cost of achieving LOD A, or 0.0833 of the total cost, Table 3.5 could have been developed utilizing the same procedure.

All of the data described so far must now be combined into a single measure of utility to be associated with each of the possible budget levels for fiscal year 1968. That is, we want to answer this question: What is the utility of a given budget level in terms of achievement of the various LOD's at some time in the future and in terms of their worth?

Each LOD is associated with a CCO which has a certain weight associated with it. The criticality of the LOD to the CCO is a number between 0 and 1 and gives the proportion of the weight which is "earned" by achieving the LOD. The worth of achievement is further modified by the timeliness function according to the date at which the

Table 3.5   Proportion of Budget

	Budget Level			
LOD	1.0	0.8	0.7	0.6
A	.0833	.0666	.0584	.0500
B	.0555	.0445	.0388	.0353
C	.0435	.0349	.0305	.0261
D	.0345	.0276	.0242	.0207
E	.0270	.0216	.0189	.0162
F	.0217	.0182	.0152	.0130

LOD will be achieved at a given budget level. Finally, the 1968 budget represents a certain proportion of the ultimate cost of achieving each LOD. The worth of achievement is further modified by this "cost fraction," to get the measure of utility of a LOD which is "earned" by a budget level. That is, for each LOD we take the product:

CCO Weight × Criticality × Timeliness × Cost Fraction.

The sum of these products, for each LOD toward which a budget leads, is the measure of utility of the total technology package for that budget level.

How Valid Is MACRO?

It should be pointed out that the MACRO technique offers no panacea to one of the R&D manager's ever-changing problems: that of achieving the most effective balance in the allocation of exploratory development funds. One complicating factor is that it does not take into account the effects of competitors' research and development on the corporate posture. For a new product on the market may call for a drastic shift in R&D that could not have been predicted.

Also, the MACRO system does not take into account the relative cost of doing R&D in different science and technology areas. Other factors not accounted for are an organization's inability to work effectively in some area of science or technology due to lack of qualified personnel, ceiling limitations on budget, and the problem of one firm doing work that might benefit another.

Finally, MACRO does not consider a potentially vital area. It offers no formula for assuring the organization's future by allowing some logical proportion of the total funds to be used in high-risk, high-payoff efforts. These may be in areas of low apparent relevance, but a significant breakthrough may lead a company into a new and highly profitable business. A manager can, however, add this factor when he transforms MACRO data to an actual budget.

However, these shortcomings have not prevented the successful testing and use of the method in the many areas where it has applied.

To date, MACRO-like techniques have been applied in three industrial firms, two in the chemical industry and one in electronics. In two of these cases, management went through the "drill" and compared the results with those obtained by the traditional methods. Where there were major differences, management knew it had a situation that required special study. In the other company, the manager has used the information right out of the computer. In the author's opinion this was wrong, but the company planner said: "How else am I going to allocate money over 100 pieces of R&D work? This system is better than just plain 'guesstimates,' or what we gave them last year."

Acknowledgment

The author is indebted to the other members of an interservice team for their valuable assistance in preparing the methodology for the military version of MACRO (TORQUE). In alphabetical order, they are: Mr. Patrick Caulfield, Mr. Harold Davidson, Dr. Harold Liebowitz, Dr. Joseph Martino, and Mr. Louis Roepcke.

Glossary for Chapter 3

Alternate approaches to meeting corporation objectives

These approaches are conceptual descriptions of systems, subsystems, etc. which are the means to achieve the ability to carry out an objective.

Balanced resources allocation

An allocation which, based upon contribution to desired corporate capabilities, determines the relative utility of a technology, its criticality, cost, and appropriate time phasing, thus providing an input toward rational funds allocations.

Criticality (of a technology to an objective)

This is a method for indicating the importance of a Level of Difficulty (LOD) of a technology to a Corporate Capability Objective (CCO). The criticality is expressed as a numerical value from zero to 1.0 and is obtained from a predefined scale.

Interdisciplinary (I.D.) team

This is a team comprised of users, long-range planners, systems analysts, preliminary design groups, and consulting technologists who propose methods (i.e., systems or subsystems, etc.) for carrying out the Corporate Capability Objectives (CCO's). It also estimates the technologies required to support the alternatives and the criticality of the technologies to the achievement of the alternative proposed.

Level of Difficulty (LOD)

A quantitative statement of a technological capability required to achieve a CCO. One or more similar LOD's at different levels comprise a technology package.

Corporate Capability Objective (CCO)

A description of a portion of the role or mission of a corporation. It is a rather broad statement of a desired operational function rather than a precise statement of how or with what equipment the function is to be carried out.

Technology Package

A set of one or more related levels of technical capability stated in quantitative terms. When more than one level of capability is sought, the levels represent homogeneous technological capabilities and the lowest capability is required before any higher level can be attained.

Technology team

This is a group of scientific and engineering personnel who are knowledgeable in a given area of technology. They are responsible for arranging LOD's within a technology rationally and for stipulating the annual expenditure of resources required to achieve the LOD's (and consequently technologies) in the given number of years stipulated by the I.D. team.

MACRO (Methodology for Allocation of Corporate Resources to Objectives for R&D)

A resources allocation system which applies analytical techniques to the determination of balanced corporate research and exploratory development budgets for the corporation.

Utility of a funding level

A quantitative determination of the importance of each of several levels of funding in a technology package.

Weight of an objective

This is a numerical value assigned to each member of the set of objectives of the corporation. This value represents the relative importance of an objective compared with all other objectives of that set and has the characteristic of being additive.

4
Task Selection in
Exploratory Development
Marvin J. Cetron

"The cost of development is far greater than the cost of research, and if a big development gets off on the wrong foot, the price is terribly high."
F. R. Kappel

Over the past decade, managers throughout the R&D community have been aware of the need for improving the methods of evaluating and comparing proposed projects. The need applies not only to project selection itself but also to the planning and controlling of resource allocations once the selections have been made. One of the early systems that was developed is called PROFILE (PROgrammed Functional Indices for Laboratory Evaluation). Its aim is to provide a quantitative model for the selection of jobs that are to be backed in an exploratory development program. After several years of development and use at the Navy's Marine Engineering Laboratory (MEL), the system demonstrated that it had internal consistency and was of real value to laboratory management.

This chapter gives a brief outline of the management thinking that lead to the PROFILE effort and of the management needs that went into the design of the method. Following this, there is a step-by-step look at how data are generated and where they fit into the model structure. Finally, there is a description of an experiment that was run to test the way PROFILE operated and the usefulness of the data it generated for management use.

I do not suggest that this model has universal value in exploratory development project selection. But the techniques used and the thinking behind them are useful for anyone who wants to grasp the fundamentals of quantitative approaches to the selection of R&D projects to back. And, although many of the terms used are tied to military applications, the method is easily adaptable for an industrial situation. "Marketing," for example, could be substituted for "military utility."

Purpose of PROFILE

Over a period of years, top management at the Marine Engineering Laboratory realized that a quantitative approach to the problems of resource allocation would help them do their primary job better: to meet the Navy's future mission objectives. In addition, it would aid management in strengthening the over-all effectiveness of their organization, in improving the rate of useful short- and long-term growth, and in keeping the Laboratory ahead in those areas where it was supposed to provide leadership to the over-all Navy R&D program.

It was found that the usual methods of task selection and appraisal were fragmented and rarely based on objective analysis. Rather, it was based either on rough guidelines handed down from higher head-quarters or on intuitive judgments—sometimes made by just one man. Even when some "facts" were available, they were too mixed with subjective judgments to be of much use. Generally speaking, in the past the Laboratory had reacted rather than acted and, management was therefore ready to accept most tasks if funds were provided for them and if they seemed to meet some need. With a logical allocation approach, however, the Laboratory was able to take on more responsibility for determining many of its own goals. It had facts to back it up in negotiations with its parent bureau, so that its program could be mutually agreed on.

PROFILE was the system developed to provide the needed allocation data. In addition to helping top management select tasks and appraise the total Laboratory R&D program, it placed a numerical value on each task, which made it possible to be more precise in deciding which tasks should be increased, curtailed, or eliminated. PROFILE also compared and appraised each task's funding in relation to its importance; in these terms it pointed out tasks that are adequately funded, overfunded, or underfunded.

Because of PROFILE'S flexibility, it could be adapted to help answer many management questions. For example, the use of resources could be analyzed in three possible environments: cold war, limited war, and general war. It could also isolate factors within each task and show where each is strong and where each is weak. This can alert management to potential headaches before they occur.

Finally, PROFILE gives top management a logical and constant means of explaining to various inspecting groups how its program is arrived at and how likely the resources available will make it possible to achieve the goals of the program.

Profile of PROFILE

PROFILE can be characterized as a combination of a vertical relevance tree for the higher levels and a mixed horizontal–vertical evaluation at the task level based on a decision-theory approach. The relevance tree developed for MEL, shown in Figure 4.1, may serve to illustrate the PROFILE approach. For each task an evaluation is undertaken in ten task contribution sectors, representing different criteria acting horizontally and vertically (they will be enumerated and defined later). A set of weight numbers is assigned to the ten task contributing sectors for each of the three types of conflict on level B, as seen in Table 4.1.

Three factors are the basis of the Department of Defense's evaluation of programs. These are military utility, technical feasibility, and financial acceptability. When exploratory development in a laboratory is military oriented, these factors become the basis for setting the overall goals of the laboratory.

Table 4.1   Weighting Factors

Task Contribution Sectors	General War	Limited War	Cold War
Value to naval warfare	* 40	30	30
Task responsiveness	25	20	15
Timeliness	5	5	5
Applicability to MEL long-range plan and mission	–	10	15
Probability of achieving task objective	15	10	10
Technological transfer	5	10	10
Manpower	4	3	3
Facilities	3	3	3
Funding	3	4	4
Intrinsic value to MEL	–	5	5

* Dummy Figures.

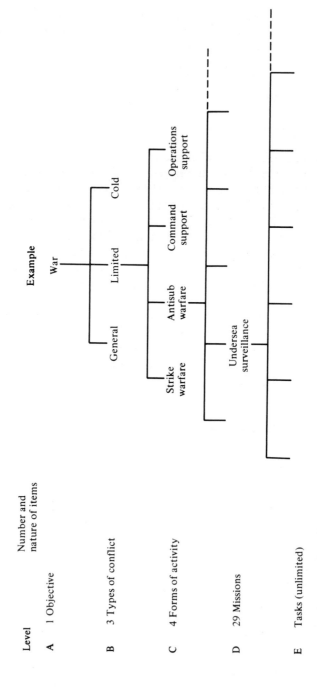

Level	Number and nature of items
A	1 Objective
B	3 Types of conflict
C	4 Forms of activity
D	29 Missions
E	Tasks (unlimited)

Figure 4.1 PROFILE Relevance Tree

Military Utility in MEL is a measure of work in terms of its usefulness to the Navy. To be useful, hardware or information must provide a new or improved capability in the shortest possible time after its need is recognized. This military utility is measured by three interdependent criteria.

First there is "value to naval warfare" (Table 4.2), which considers the extent of the contribution of a task objective in terms of its inherent value as well as its military operational value. The importance of a task is measured by its relative impact on any individual naval-warfare category, as well as the number of categories to which it contributes. The calculation is simple: multiply the assigned value of the warfare category by the impact value of the contribution and you have a value for each individual category. The sum of these values will determine the value of the task objective to naval warfare at the time of the rating. Note that the Chief of Naval Operations (CNO) provides the figures of merit based on the world situation and the most probable future conditions. The total number of points assigned to all 29 naval warfare categories will equal 100.

The second criterion is "task responsiveness" (Table 4.3), which measures how important the given task is when viewed from the prime consideration of the operational readiness of the fleet at any given point in time. Beyond this, there is a priority list of needs that must be taken into account. However, each category of work should be compared within its own area—research with research, exploratory development with exploratory development, and so on. In this regard, the statements for different categories may be assigned different values.

Finally, there is "timeliness" for research or exploratory development (Table 4.4). This criterion evaluates the task in terms of its completion time. Engineering or systems tasks are considered separately from developmental or applied research, since the problems involved in scheduling are different. The point values that may be assigned reflect this difference.

Technical feasibility represents the confidence in the successful completion of a task that is shown by the specialists doing it. It also recognizes the "forcing of technology" by the benefits of the task to a range of possible applications. These factors are evaluated by the following three criteria: the first, "applicability to long-range plans" (Table 4.5) assumes that the greater the familiarity or experience of a laboratory with a certain type of work, the higher the probability that it will produce expeditious results. The matrix used to express this is subject to change at irregular intervals, but its purpose remains un-

Table 4.2   Value to Naval Warfare

Column 1—Categories	Column 2—Impact of Task Contributions										Column 3—Value to Individual Category
	1.0	.9	.8	.7	.6	.5	.4	.3	.2	.1	
* 30—Strike Warfare											
6—Airborne attack											
4—Surface attack											
5—Submarine attack											
4—Amphibious assault											
5—Seabased strategic deter.											
3—Airborne anti-air warfare											
3—Surface anti-air warfare											
25—Antisubmarine Warfare											
4—Airborne ASW											
3—Surface ASW											
3—Submarine ASW											
10—Undersea surveillance											
1—Mining											
2—Mine countermeasures											
2—ASW ancillary support											
25—Command Support											
3—Command and control											
4—Naval communications											
3—Electronic warfare											
1—Navigation											
6—Ocean surveillance											
5—Reconnaissance and intelligence											
2—Environmental systems											
1—Special warfare											
20—Operational support											
3—Logistics											
4—Personnel											
2—Astronautics											
3—Aviation support											
3—Ship support											
3—Ordnance support											
2—NBC defense											

4. Total Value to Naval Warfare =

* Dummy Figures.
Scale of Definitions for "Impact of Task Contribution" (Column 2):

Points
1.0	Creation of radically new mission concepts (meets overriding critical need)
.7	Revolutionary extension of capabilities
.4	Incremental or marginal improvement of capabilities
.2	Increase in economy

changed: to insure a fully integrated R&D program within the laboratory and minimize the miscellaneous and less relevant tasks that could better be handled by others. Thus this criterion awards greater value to those tasks which fall into the laboratory's area of expertise and competence, since this will enhance the laboratory's long-range technical growth and value.

The second criterion to be considered by technical feasibility is the "probability of achieving task objectives" (Table 4.6), which tries to

Table 4.3 Task Responsiveness

Research	Exploratory development	Advanced development	Systems and above	
		10	10	Immediate fleet problem—ship inoperative or subject to construction delays
		9	9	Immediate fleet problem—limited operation, e.g., inability to perform complete mission
	10	10	7	Technical development plan approved or item scheduled under current shipbuilding program [concurrence by DOD (Department of Defense), CNO (Chief of Naval Operations), CNM (Chief of Naval Material), NAVSHIPS]
		8	8	Fleet problem—minor system inoperative
	7	6	6	Specific Operational Requirement or Advanced Development Objective issued (concurrence by CNO, CNM, NAVSHIPS)
	6	5	5	General Operational Requirement issued (concurrence by CNO, CNM, NAVSHIPS)
10	5	3	4	Exploratory Development Requirement or Navy Research Requirement [CNM and NAVSHIPS or CNR (Chief of Naval Research)]
7	4		3	Fundamental research or independent exploratory development (FR/IED)(Laboratory discretionary funds)
	2		2	Routine testing for Government agencies (if not covered by higher category)
	1		1	Routine testing for non-Government organizations

Table 4.4   Timeliness

Points	Engineering
10	Fits current shipbuilding program and is expected to meet operational needs for at least five years
8	Fits current shipbuilding program
6	Can be substituted for present equipment to solve Fleet Problem
4	Retrofit
2	Expensive retrofit
	Exploratory Development
10	Will have application to present systems and advances the state of the art
8	Will be available when needed for many advanced development (prototype) tasks (many technical areas)
6	Will be available when needed for one advanced development prototype
4	Deadlines cannot be established but the objective is still valid
2	No other solution will satisfy need but the information will be late

measure the stage of development of the work. The degree of confidence in achieving success is based on the predictability of accomplishing the desired results. This might be called a measure of technical risk. (A technological forecast would be a much better criterion of the probability of achieving the task objective, but when PROFILE was developed, MEL did not have a formal technological forecasting (TF) program. It does have a very fine TF program now, which may well have replaced the stage of development indicator as the criterion.) Also important here is "technological transfer" (Table 4.7). In this, greater value is given to those tasks which will provide assistance to other tasks. This cross support can be considered a fringe benefit of meeting a task objective in addition to building up the "need pressure" brought by the other potential users.

Financial acceptability is the third major category in the PROFILE analysis. In the Navy this is defined as applying competent manpower and facilities and suitable funding to effectively carry the work toward completion. Financial acceptability is not a measure of the willingness but of the capability to perform the work. Resources needed are rated as follows: "manpower" (Table 4.8), a measure of the ability to apply adequate manpower to the task, becomes critical in times of manpower shortages and/or ceiling restrictions; "facilities" (Table 4.9) is a measure of the extent of the facilities which are available or can be made available; "funding" (Table 4.10) assumes that the urgency of a task is shown in the availability of funds—dollars per se is not a measure, whereas sufficiency of funds to achieve the task at the right time is.

It must also be remembered that the laboratory must give consideration to both the immediate and long-range results of any undertaking.

Table 4.5 Applicability to MEL Long-Range Plan and Mission

MEL's Functional Areas \ MEL's Long-Range Program Plan	Deep Submergence	Antisubmarine Warfare	Reliability and Maintainability	Automated Ship Concepts	General Purpose Vessels	Active Buoys–Countermeasures	Advanced Vehicle Concepts	Fixed Underwater Installations	Submarine Safety	Nuclear Propulsion	
Fuel cells											
Fuels and lubricating oils											
Hydraulic systems											
Piping systems											
Seals and bearings											
Ship-control equipment											
Shipboard electrical systems											
Ship silencing											
Atmosphere control											
Thermoelectrics											
Water treatment											
Naval alloys											
Magnetics											
Systems engineering											
Other ship or Submarine Machinery and Components											

Total

If the task objective falls into one of MEL's above assigned functional areas, check as many as possible of the program plan areas in which this function could be used.

Table 4.6   Probability of Achieving Task Objective

Points

10	The current technology is adequate in all respects and prototype testing is complete; only Fleet evaluation required
8	The current technology is adequate but prototype testing is required
6	Feasibility has been demonstrated by experimental models but improvements in such areas as service life, reliability and efficiency are needed
4	Basic concepts have been proven but extensive testing is required to demonstrate actual feasibility
2	Preliminary concepts are available but rigorous analysis is necessary to prove validity.
1	Problem only vaguely defined.

Today's decisions affect tomorrow's growth. Thus, "value to MEL" (Table 4.11) has been added to the schematic (Figure 4.2) to increase the quantitative subjective ratings given a task, to show whether it provides greater over-all benefits to MEL, and to make the whole system more palatable to top management. If this "management environment" is not taken into account, the system probably will not even be considered for implementation.

All these individual task rating numbers are finally brought together in an over-all profile of the individual task (Figure 4.3), which is used by management in the "management by exceptions" manner. The PROFILE of each task tends to flag or highlight graphically any criterion of a task that is outside of normal limits (3 to 8); these exceptions are then singled out for special managerial attention.

Specifically the sample PROFILE of Figure 4.3 shows that the value to naval warfare is exceptionally high (9) whereas the applica-

Table 4.7   Technological Transfer

Points

10	Supports two or more major systems
9	Supports one system
8	Supports two or more Applied Research areas
7	
6	Supports a single Applied Research area
5	Supports two or more basic research areas
4	
3	Supports a single basic research area
2	
1	No cross support

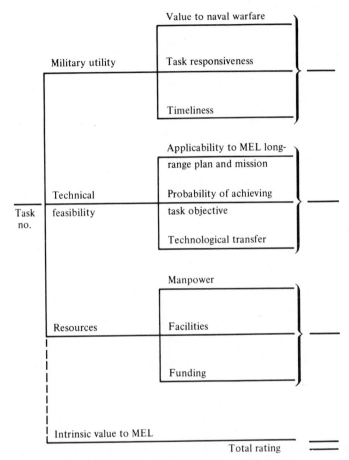

Figure 4.2 Factors Used in Appraising an R&D Program

bility to MEL long-range planning and mission is exceptionally low (2). Normally this would be a cause for concern, since it would mean that here is an important task that really should not have been given to this laboratory to begin with. However, further examination indicates that the probability of achieving the task objective is high (8) and that the rest of the criteria ratings are in the normal spread area. It also shows that the two key criteria, value to naval warfare (9) and technical risk (8) can be multiplied to give management an expected value rating (in this case 72) for the task at hand. Laboratory management could at this point divide the expected value by the dollar amount assigned to each task in order to determine the "desirability index" of each task—it could then rank them accordingly.

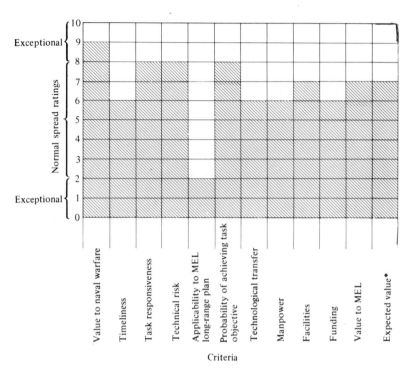

* Expected value = value to naval warfare × probability of achieving task objective (9 × 8 = 72)

Figure 4.3   Individual Task Profile

Table 4.8   Manpower

Points	
10	Competent personnel on board and free for task—awaiting assignment or currently assigned to the task with no other commitments
8	Competent personnel on board but not free. However, they are assigned lower priority work
7	
6	Competent personnel can be obtained—ceiling available
5	
4	Competent personnel available, but not within present ceiling or grade limitations
2	Competent personnel on board but on high priority work
1	Inexperienced personnel may be obtained and trained

Table 4.9 Facilities

Points	
10	All facilities available and free for use
9	Contract let—will be available to meet needs
7	Military Construction (MILCON) funds appropriated by Congress
6	Funds have been approved by parent organization
3	Funds have been budgeted in five-year financial plan
2	Scheduled by CNO under MILCON—not available when needed to start work
1	Non-MILCON funds suitable for use when available
0.5	Not available—must be scheduled under MILCON
0.1	Rejected under latest MILCON schedule—must be resubmitted

Evaluating PROFILE

In many ways this may seem like a quick and dirty way to rank tasks, and it is. The fact that scientists and engineers must structure their thinking and assign numbers to questions that appear nonquantifiable tends to rub many technical men the wrong way.

One measure of evaluating PROFILE might be to see if its approach tends to provide some consistency to the rating games. This was the aim of one evaluation experiment in which two groups of engineers and scientists were involved. The first group used PROFILE in the morning and their own criteria in the afternoon. The second group reversed the procedure. They were assigned a representative list of sixteen tasks to rate. In the morning sessions, the group using PROFILE first had a high correlation in their rankings (77% at a 1% confidence level),

Table 4.10 Funding

Points	
10	Great urgency—sufficient funds available for several approaches to be worked on concurrently
8	High priority assigned and adequate funds available until conclusion
5	Adequate funds available for this fiscal year
3	Limited funding—not enough to achieve task objective in realistic time frame
1	Limited funds available to start the work—no assurance of future funding

Table 4.11   Intrinsic Value to MEL

2	Attracts and holds superior people
2	Enhances MEL's image to the public and Navy (prestige)
1	Fully utilizes our resources
1	Increases lead lab list (new areas)
1	Long-term benefits
1	Stabilizes funding
1	Increases technical potential
1	Improves morale and esprit de corps
	Total points of applicable statements

whereas the group using their own criteria had a low correlation (18%). The first group seemed to carry over much of the PROFILE structure in their minds when they used their own criteria in the afternoon (89% correlation). The second group, not surprisingly, had a higher correlation using PROFILE in the afternoon (47%) than they had with their own systems.

Does this prove that PROFILE is the total answer to the whole allocation problem? Of course not. But it would seem that a manager who can get a group of diverse people to think about a set of problems and come up with relatively consistent solutions is in a better position to make a final decision than he would be if evaluations are scattered all over the lot. This does not mean that the manager may not sometimes be in the position of President Lincoln when he told his cabinet: "One aye, seven nays; the ayes have it."

Acknowledgment

The author is indebted to Mr. Robert Freshman and Mr. Al King for their valuable assistance in preparing the methodology, and to Mr. John Sivy for his help in testing it.

5
Building a Laboratory-Wide Allocation System

Ambrose B. Nutt

"Only by having some reasonably well defined goals can researchers make those choices which they face at every turn as to which of several possible lines to follow. This statement does no violence to the classical concept that true research is without restraint and follows the intellectual curiosity of the researcher." Ralph Brown

This chapter will describe the development and use of a computerized planning program called Research and Development Effectiveness (RDE).[1] It was built to introduce new analytical techniques to the management of R&D resources in the Air Force Flight Dynamics Laboratory, which is part of the Flight and Technology Division of the Air Force Systems Command (AFSC).

It might be worth noting at the beginning that this program's capability for giving management detailed insights into the R&D efforts on short notice has spurred the development of an over-all management information system for the Laboratory. This was intended to complement the RDE program by providing past resource consumption trend data that can be keyed into the planning data obtained from the RDE program. The result is probably one of the most comprehensive R&D planning tools in existence.

[1] Rea, R. H., and Synnott, T. W., "Project RDE, a framework for the comprehension and analysis of Research and Development Effectiveness," *TM 64-22, Air Force Flight Dynamics Laboratory, Wright-Patterson AFB, Ohio* (October 1963).

A brief description of the mission and research program of the Flight Dynamics Laboratory (FDL) will show the environment in which the program is used. FDL is one of eight Laboratories of the Directorate of Laboratories of the AFSC. Its primary mission is conducting exploratory and advanced development leading to the solution of technical problems and creation of design criteria for future AF flight vehicles. The primary areas of responsibility are flight control, aerodynamics, structures, equipment, and dynamics. It also provides technical support, as required, to Air Force systems offices, other product divisions of AFSC, and, where certain of its unique development facilities are needed, other government agencies and industry.

During the development of RDE, from 1963 to 1965, it had a staff of 762; of this number, 418 were professional scientists or engineers. The annual budget was $34.6 million, of which $16.5 million was earmarked for exploratory development. The RDE program was built to help in the allocation of these exploratory development funds. In all, about 70 percent of the scientific and engineering manpower worked in the development area.

The technical program used was made up of 22 projects, covering over 200 individual research tasks. In setting down the objectives of the exploratory development budget, the following were found to be the key criteria for resource allocation:

1. Future systems needs and the relative importances and probability of their development.
2. The state of the art in various areas within the Laboratory's technical competence.
3. The degree of support afforded each future Air Force system and area of technology by each technical activity or task in the Laboratory.
4. The most effective research approach—in-house or contract.
5. The relationship of progress in each technical activity to the resources level applied.
6. The cost of technical alternatives relative to limited resources.

Defining an Allocation Matrix

The research budget allocation problem faced by the FDL is outlined in Figure 5.1. Its similarity to a capital budgeting problem in industry is apparent.[2] The number of variables affecting task resource

---

[2] Weingartner, H. H., *Mathematical Programming and the Analysis of Capital Budgeting Problems.* Englewood Cliffs, N.J.: Prentice-Hall, 1963.

Figure 5.1   Factors Impacting on the Total Allocation Problems

allocations, based on all possible mutual interrelationships, runs into the thousands. However, the basic considerations in resources allocation for the Laboratory are relatively few in number.

The solution to the problem is to structure management judgment in such a way as to take into account all basic considerations for budget allocation while still giving unbiased and equal consideration to resource allocations to each research activity or task. To organize the needed data and consider all important interactions rapidly, the data-handling capability of a digital computer is needed.

This process can be illustrated with a graphic representation of the RDE program (Figure 5.2). The AF mission matrix in the top block of the diagram, which represents the total set of Air Force operational responsibilities, is used as the basis for the entire program. Since the Laboratory's job consists of providing technology to meet Air Force needs, a way must be found to express these needs quantitatively. Such quantitative elements will then make it possible to build a model that relates the allocation of resources to each task in the support of over-all objectives.

A simple matrix (Figure 5.3) expresses the operational environment in which exist the technical needs of the Air Force in its role of supporting national objectives. It indicates in effect that the Air Force conducts its four basic types of operation in three kinds of potential war environments and that technical needs exist in each of the resulting twelve mission elements. Each element n_{ij} of the matrix is given a value representing the technological improvement required at some time future in support of the corresponding mission element; this value must be relative to that for each other element of the matrix.

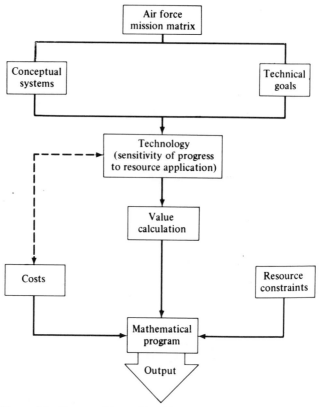

Figure 5.2   Program Data-Flow Diagram

This first weighting job was done initially by staff planners at Air Force headquarters, using the military, economic, geopolitical, and intelligence data available to them. They used a mathematical technique known as the Churchman, Arnoff, Ackoff (CAA) method for the determination of relative value.[3] The values were then normalized so that $\Sigma n_{ij} = 1$, so that the sum of all relative values of the elements of the matrix equaled unity. These then are the numerical values used in the simulation model to be described later. The matrix must be reevaluated by a higher headquarters plans office each time the program is run, to make sure it reflects the latest thinking in terms of the changing world environment. In industry, this would be a top management review.

[3] Ackoff, R. L., *Scientific Method: Optimizing Applied Research Decisions.* New York: John Wiley and Sons, 1962.

	General war	Limited war	Cold war
Combat operations	n_{11}	n_{12}	n_{13}
Reconnaissance	n_{21}	n_{22}	n_{23}
Logistics	n_{31}	n_{32}	n_{33}
Show of force	n_{41}	n_{42}	n_{43}

Figure 5.3   The Air Force Mission Matrix

The technology block of Figure 5.2 represents all the exploratory development research tasks of the Laboratory. To determine the extent to which each task assists the Air Force mission, the support of future Air Force flight vehicle systems (as defined in the higher headquarters guidance documents) and that of the technical goals of the Laboratory (as defined by Laboratory management and planning guidance) must be linked together. A relative value of importance for each of these systems and goals is determined by CAA method. For details of this and other aspects of the value calculation block in Figure 5.2, see Appendix A to this chapter.

In actual operation of the RDE program, each task engineer plots the progress of his task, based on the actual work and resources required to progress from one confidence level (CL) to another, on a graph of CL and P_s versus years (a typical plot is shown in Figure 5.4). This is done by first determining the quantitative objective to be attained upon completion of the work covered by the task. Next, each discrete effort leading to the completion of the task is determined and briefly described on a Work Package Description form. The cost in dollars and man-years of completing each effort is estimated and noted opposite the effort description, as is the advance in confidence level attained (in CL units) for each effort completion. Obviously, the annual funding level for the task determines the rate of progress for the work. For example, an effort requiring $50,000 would take two years if the annual funding were $25,000. (For purpose of plotting, man-years are converted into equivalent dollars and added to the dollars required.) Probability of Success is equated to Confidence Level for purposes of the plot and simulation model, i.e., a P_s of .4 equals a CL of .4 (see Appendix A).

Three curves are plotted, one using tentatively programmed resources (dollars as well as scientific and engineering manpower), the

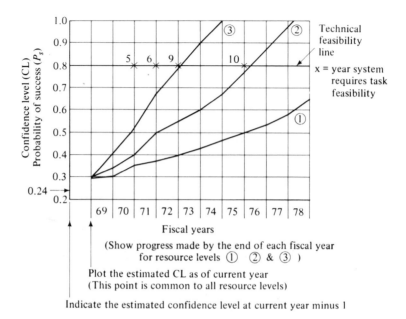

Figure 5.4 Task Progress Plots, Showing the Effect of Varying Resource Levels on Rate of Progress

second using one-half the programmed manpower, and the third using twice the manpower. For the latter two, the funds in dollars are estimates commensurate with the aggregate of manpower and facilities that would have to be made available in these situations. The contract-versus-in-house question is included in these estimates by considering the ability of the staff personnel and any special requirements of the research to be performed. Although Figure 5.4 shows three curve plots, a subroutine in the computer input program makes possible the computation of three intermediate resource levels. Laboratory management, therefore, can consider six possible resource levels for each task during the allocation process.

A task applicability factor in the model relates the relative importance of each task (from 0.1 to 1.0) to the system on which it would be used. This factor is applied by the Assistant Chief for Research and Technology of each division in the Laboratory for each of his division's tasks.

There is also a timeliness function applied to each task for each system and goal it supports (valued from zero to 1.0 in the model) to evaluate each task in terms of whether or not it will achieve technical feasibility in time to be of use to the system and goals it supports. Each system and technical goal has a desired initiation of acquisition and "completion date." These relationships can be shown graphically as having a trapezoidal form since the approach used provides a penalty for being too early or too late. Since task support for each system or goal is considered and computed individually in the simulation model, the length in years at the base and top of the trapezoid that constitutes the timeliness function will vary, depending on the year when the task technology will be required for a given system or goal.

Finally, the technical contribution or importance of a task to a system or technical goal (aside from the timeliness aspect) is determined in the model by reference to a predefined contribution scale calibrated from zero to 1.0. This represents a gamut from remote association to absolutely essential in the case of systems, and from minor contribution to potential breakthrough in the case of technical goals. The value of the systems and of the technical goals are determined by their relationship to the mission matrix (see Appendix A and Figure 5.3).

The block in Figure 5.2 labeled Mathematical Program represents the linear program put into the computer for solution of the budget allocation problem.[4] It utilizes: the effectiveness parameter of each resource level of each task as computed by the mathematical model; the dollar and manpower resource level of each task as stipulated by the task engineer, represented by the lower left-hand block of the diagram in Figure 5.2; and the total annual resources in dollars and manpower made available to the Laboratory by higher headquarters, the block labeled Resource Constraints (see Appendix B for details).

A flow chart is furnished each task engineer as a guide to preparation of input data and as a schedule for showing which preliminary inputs must be checked at each stage in the process (Fig. 5.5).

The basic solution to the problem consists of a recommended dollar and manpower allocation for each of the Laboratory's tasks. It is of interest to note that in a program run near the end of the three-year development process, 135 of 236 tasks in the program—either running or proposed—were recommended for support.

The output format is designed to print out the allocation by project, task, and division within the Laboratory. All input data are printed out

[4] Dantzig, G. G., *Linear Programming and Extensions.* Princeton, N.J.: Princeton University Press, 1958.

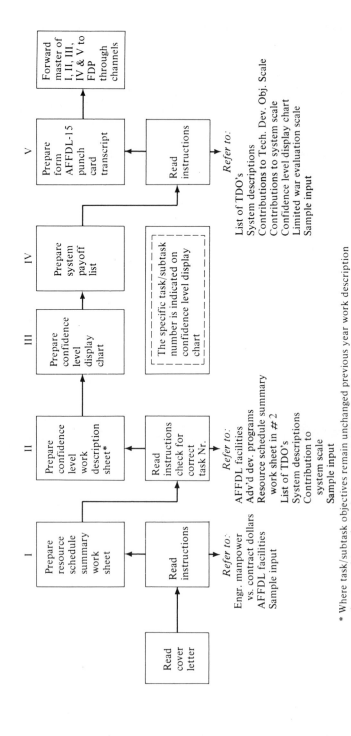

Figure 5.5   Flow Chart of RDE Input Preparation Process

for checking purposes, as are the measures of effectiveness, as computed with the simulation model, for each resource level of each task. Output formats are also designed to print out priority lists of selected and nonselected tasks. This is possible since the program solution includes a computation of the value, or "implicit price," of a unit of each kind of resource (dollars, contract direction, and in-house manpower) in terms of *effectiveness units*. By subtracting the resource "cost" from the measure of effectiveness of a given task resource level, a net "profit" or "loss" can be determined for each task. This computation is performed by the computer in preparing the task priority list.

In addition, since the model projects for five consecutive years ahead, technology and system profiles are printed out that graphically show the yearly increase in confidence level for each task supporting each system and technical goal. By noting the desired year of initiation of system acquisition, a manager can decide quickly from the profile whether or not the total Laboratory technical program is supporting a given technical goal or future system on a timely basis.

A sensitivity analysis was performed on the RDE program (as constituted per Appendices A and B at the end of this chapter) to check the effect of changes in recommended allocations arising out of changes in the value of each variable in the model over its possible value range, with all other variables held constant. This was done to check whether or not the results were too sensitive or too insensitive to changes in individual variable values. The RDE program was adjudged to have a satisfactory degree of stability.[5]

Gathering the Input Data

Naturally, no matter how good the model, the results can only be as good as the input data themselves. One of the major questions related to this is who should be responsible for what data. The following is the distribution of effort that evolved:

1. Calculation of relative values of systems and technical goals— senior staff personnel
2. Stipulation of task applicability factors (relative importance of tasks within a Laboratory division in terms of their importance to flight vehicle systems which they support, as determined by division management)—assistant division chiefs

[5] Chester, L. B., "Analysis of the effect of variance on linear programming problems," M.A. thesis, Air Force Institute of Technology, Wright-Patterson AFB, Ohio (September 1964).

3. Task resource estimates—task engineers (see format, Fig. 5.6)
4. Task progress plots—task engineers (see Figure 5.4)
5. Punch-card transcript forms—task engineers
6. Review of input data—branch and division management
7. Analysis of output data—all levels of laboratory management
8. Objective review of engineer's evaluation of task values—advanced systems analysis group and selected system project offices.

The first three years of the program were somewhat experimental in that changes in the measure of effectiveness model were made frequently. After that, changes were restricted or relatively minor, with the result that time for preparation of input data was markedly decreased. In many cases the updating of input plots already prepared were utilized instead of constructing entirely new ones. An added benefit was a feedback function, since task engineers' past progress was reflected on the marked-up progress plot sheet. This resembled Figure 5.4 with the curves removed and a point on the fiscal year 1968-1969 vertical line showing predicted progress for the current fiscal year. The starting points for the two previous fiscal years remain on the plot.

Measuring the Output

From a theoretical viewpoint, the modeling methods and the input responsibilities are important but for managers it is the usefulness of the results that counts. The most important impact of the program on the Laboratory allocation process is that total exploratory development-fund allocations to divisions have actually been made using the results of the RDE input. In one example, the Laboratory had to absorb an over-all exploratory development budget decrease. A special RDE program was run, using the decreased Laboratory budget as a new funds constraint in the linear program and the actual planned tasks' funds as coefficients. As a result, the Laboratory's top management was furnished with a list of the tasks that should get less funding.

This example also illustrates how a system like this is used to assist, rather than substitute for, management decision-making. The RDE model was set so that it came up with a total of proposed cuts exceeding those required by about 50 percent. Management then could select the final cuts. Some tasks could not be decreased in funding because of policy or other reasons, despite their relatively low value. Manage-

Date _____

Fiscal year	69	70	71	72	73	74	75	76	77	78
Resource level 1										
Contract dollars										
Support dollars										
Total dollars (1000's)										
Engineer manyears— contract monitoring										
Engineer manyears— in-house work										
Resource level 2										
Contract dollars										
Support dollars										
Total dollars (1000's)										
Funds—other agencies*										
ADP manpower†										
Engineer manyears— contract monitoring										
Engineer manyears— in-house work										
Resource level 3										
Contract dollars										
Support dollars										
Total dollars (1000's)										
Engineer manyears— contract monitoring										
Engineer manyears— in-house work										

* Insert appropriate code letter in parenthesis after final amount in blocks
  A. Army
  B. Navy
  C. NASA
  D. ADP (Write out title and number here)_____
  E. USAF other than exploratory and Advanced Development
  F. Other—(Write out source here)_____
† Show that part of total manpower (contract & in-house) expended on Advanced Development Program if applicable. If not, leave blank

Figure 5.6   Resource Schedule Summary Work Sheet

ment, however, was able to focus its attention on a much smaller area than would be the case if the entire Laboratory task list had to be reviewed. A similar procedure can be followed for budget increases.

Results like these should not imply that this allocation modeling project went off without problems. From time to time there were reviews in depth of the input data covering a randomly chosen set of selected and nonselected tasks. Previous reviews of this type had revealed a number of improperly prepared inputs sufficient to warrant only limited use of the program as an allocation aid. But by fiscal year 1966 most of the bugs seemed to be eliminated.

It should be pointed out that the RDE program does not explicitly cover the allocation of resources for all aspects of the Laboratory mission. Such items as selection of new facilities, resources in support of current operational Air Force systems and certain Laboratory advanced development programs (except for manpower), and certain projects specifically directed by higher headquarters are generally outside the direct scope of RDE. These items, however, are either few enough—in the case of facilities—to be handled by the direct exercise of management judgment, or else are of such a nature that, since they are unpredictable in occurrence, they cannot be preplanned in detail. Obviously, in many situations the cost of adapting the system would not be worth the results.

One basic rationale for operation of the program is that it does not require any planning that ought not be done in any event. For instance, in the normal intuitive planning cycle, project engineers in exploratory development should consider the needs of future high-priority advanced Air Force systems, the availability of facilities that will be required for the research, the current state of the art of the technology under consideration, and all the other variables included in the RDE model. Supervisory levels above them should consider similar factors, but in a less detailed fashion.

The bias usually shown by a project engineer in recommending his program for adoption in an intuitive planning environment is also considered in the operation of RDE. Here this is handled by having the task engineers' evaluations of the importance of their tasks also evaluated by specialists from outside organizations. In the case of RDE, these are "objective" engineers from the Advanced System Analysis Group which is not part of the Flight Dynamics Laboratory, and engineers from selected advanced systems project offices. Where deviations of more than 0.2 from the selected value are found, these differences are brought to the attention of the Laboratory division office concerned for settlement.

Lessons of the RDE System

After going through the birthpangs of the Research and Development Effectiveness system, the conclusion is reached that its benefits have been well worth the investment of time and money. For those who might get involved in similar projects, it may be a good idea to summarize the benefits in the order in which they occur.

The first order of business and the first payoff are a much more detailed review and analysis of research objectives than are required in a laboratory's normal planning process. To quantify objectives requires not only precise definition of these objectives but also detailed comparisons of all objectives in order to obtain relative values. In the case of the Flight Dynamics Laboratory, this meant the structuring of broad technical needs of the Air Force in varying mission situations against a set of future weapons systems—postulated in guidance documents—and against the Laboratory technical objectives. The system also requires that over-all technological objectives be time-oriented so that their achievement can be related in time to each research task objective.

Second, there is the didactic effect on all professional personnel down to task engineer level. They must be exposed in a very concentrated fashion to a common set of planning data, which includes detailed descriptions of all research objectives, descriptions of all advanced development programs, and brief descriptions of planned new facilities. The fact that they come to understand the criteria used to determine how research dollars are used should be important to every manager who feels his technical men are often oblivious to financial considerations. The key to the benefit here is not only the fact that each task engineer must relate his task to each objective to maximize the benefit factors within his RDE input, but that he must take into account the future task support that is required.

Further, the system forces each task engineer to describe the specific character, timing, and size of the work efforts needed to achieve his task objective. This permits ferreting out those efforts that will require major cost increases in the future. By reviewing the ten-year task resource summary sheet, management can forecast high-cost items well in advance, so that programs can be rescheduled to balance out spending or other adjustments made so that the required funds will be available when needed.

One of the outputs plots of task time against progress permits instantaneous evaluation of the timeliness of each task effort to over-all research objectives. This is because desired dates for achievement of task-objective technical feasibility relative to each laboratory task objective is shown directly on the plotting sheet (See Figure 5.4.). Since a large percentage of tasks (about 80% in the Flight Dynamics Laboratory) have unchanged objectives year after year, comparisons of progress achieved to be fed back to the task engineers—showing the year-to-year feasibility status or distance from task completion.

Particularly for higher levels of management, the fact that the program produces a task priority list in addition to a recommended set of funded tasks permits a greater degree of management by exception. Tasks that have the lowest priority can be singled out for detailed review. The input data are so inclusive that in many cases they permit such reviews to zero in on the probable cause of any ineffectiveness quickly and accurately. Recommendations by management resulting from such a review are based on all facets of the situation rather than on random data and intuition, as is often the case in normal practice. The fact that RDE brings together the low-priority tasks from various parts of a large laboratory organization may help management spot pockets of research "poverty" that would be missed if buried in the usual unit-by-unit report. Some general policy may well be suggested that would help in many separate situations.

Obviously, laboratory management gains valuable insights from the fact that all tasks have been evaluated with respect to major research objectives. This makes it possible to determine, by subroutines in the computer, the total support provided to each major objective by the over-all program and the cost of this support. The timeliness of this support can also be printed out in a format known as a system or technology profile (depending on the nature of the objective system or technology). This profile shows in graphic form which tasks are lagging, and how they stand with respect to any others or to all time-oriented objectives.

These are but a few high spots of possible RDE outputs. Because such large amounts of data are put into the computer to solve the basic allocation problem, possibilities exist for all sorts of "cuts" at this data bank for management information purposes. A long list of examples of direct and derived outputs is contained in Appendix C.

Spreading the Word

The major elements of the laboratory allocation program described in this chapter are by no means unique. What may be unique is that they have been put into a meaningfully structured plan. When properly set up, the plan permits many payoffs to management with a minimum expenditure of manpower compared to that used in the usual non-structured planning and allocating situation.

Although this system was developed in an Air Force laboratory, it has attracted the attention of other government organizations as well as large companies. Use of such a system was recommended for the NASA Electronic Center, Boston, Massachusetts, by Arthur D. Little, Inc.; NASA Headquarters is studying the use of a similar system for the NASA Office of Advanced Research and Technology. The Department of Defense is testing a quantitative resources allocation system for use in all DOD laboratories. North American Space and Information Division, Downey, California, has programmed a similar test in its organization.

The process by which a large, wide-range, relevant allocation system is established is complex. The number of information elements to consider is staggering; moreover, the interdependence of these information elements contributes another order of complexity. The only solution is the power of the computer, utilizing the analytical methods of operations research. All of this means that discussion of allocation systems may be left to the specialists, and they may wind up talking to themselves most of the time. A key job, therefore, is communication. Reducing everything to a "communications problem" may be a cliché but in this case it is also a reality.

To get an allocation system installed, top management must be convinced that the payoff will justify the resources required. Initially, it may still get the benefit of the doubt, but once it is on stream to any real extent, it must begin to prove its worth. Any lingering doubt at this point will more than likely lead to the system's speedy demise.

The emphasis on top management does not mean that all levels of management need not be convinced also and involved early in devising and implementing the system. This effort will have large subsequent benefits. Managers will have greater faith in the system, help insure better and more timely inputs, and feel that the system is something that can help them do a better job rather than be an additional burden on their backs.

At the individual engineer's or scientist's level, it is important to strive constantly for simplification of the input process. Despite all the talk about management tools, his natural inclination is to look on anything not directly concerned with his task as an additional "exercise." Proper briefing by staff specialists can help, but it is up to middle management to create and maintain a working interface between the man and the system.

Finally, the inclination to use the computer printouts of such a system as a "Bible" must be resisted on everyone's part. No model can begin to cover all eventualities. A healthy degree of pragmatism must be maintained by all users, whether they be staff or line management, if the most effective use is to be made of a resources allocation system.

Appendix A

To find a relative value of importance for each of the Laboratory's systems and goals, proceed as follows:

1. Determine the relative value (expressed as $R_{S_m}^{n_{ij}}$) for each System S_1 thru S_m in support of Mission Matrix element n_{11}.
2. Repeat this determination for each element of the matrix resulting in M sets of values of $R_{S_m}^{n_{ij}}$.
3. Multiply each $R_{S_m}^{n_{ij}}$ by the corresponding element of the matrix n_{ij} and sum to get M values of $n_{ij}R_{S_m}^{n_{ij}}$.
4. Normalize, so that $\sum n_{ij}R_{S_m}^{n_{ij}} = 1$, giving a relative value for each System in providing improved capabilities for the AF in carrying out all elements of the AF Mission Matrix.

Similarly, for P technical goals, obtain $\sum n_{ij}R_{TG_p}^{n_{ij}} = 1$, giving a similar relative value for each technical goal.

To determine the measurement of the effectiveness or value of each research task, the following factors must be considered: rate of technical progress; state of the art; relative importance of task applicability to systems; number and relative importance of technical goals supported; timeliness of effort; relative contributions to systems and technical goals; and relationship between progress achieved and resources required.

These factors are combined into the following model:

$$V_i = \frac{\Delta P_{si}}{\Delta t}\frac{1}{P_{si}}D_\tau \sum_{j=1}^{M} f(t)_j b_j' c_j + \frac{\Delta CL_i}{\Delta t}\frac{1}{CL_i}\sum_{k=1}^{L} f(t)_k g_k h_k,$$

where

V_i = RDE model objective function coefficient
P_{si} = current level of probability of success in task-level i
i = task resource level
$\Delta P_{si}/\Delta t$ = change in this probability of success during the reference time period
D_τ = task applicability factor
M = number of systems
j = system

$f(t)$ = timeliness function
b'_j = contribution of task to a system
c_j = value of system j
CL_i = confidence level for task resource level i
$\Delta CL_j / \Delta t$ = change in confidence level over the reference time period
L = number of technical goals
k = technical goal
g_k = contribution of task to a technical goal
h_k = technical goal effectivity

This model is the value calculation block referred to in Figure 5.2. In an over-all sense, the model says that the measure of effectiveness V_i of each task resource level is comprised of two parts: the effectiveness the task has in support of development of future AF flight vehicles, represented by the term to the left of the plus sign; and the effectiveness the task has in support of the achievement of the technical goals of the Laboratory, represented by the other term.

The Confidence Level CL referred to in the model indicates technical progress on a given task from the idea conception and problem definition to the acquisition of adequate technology. These values, from 0.1 to 1.0, are predefined for the task engineer in ten discrete steps. The probability of success (P_s) is defined as the probability that, in a normal system development cycle, the task technology at a given confidence level can be successfully incorporated into a system development without further state-of-the-art development. For all tasks, a P_s of 0.8 is equated to a CL of 0.8 and is defined as the point where technical feasibility of a technology is demonstrated (see Fig. 5.4).

Appendix B

The input matrix for the program in Figure 5.2 is as follows:

Maximize value of:

$$v_1 X_1 + v_2 X_2 + \cdots + v_n X_n = V_T$$

Subject to:

$$a_1 X_1 + a_2 X_2 + \cdots + a_n X_n \leq \text{Contract \$} + \text{Support \$}$$
$$b_1 X_1 + b_2 X_2 + \cdots + b_n X_n \leq \text{Engineers (Contract)}$$
$$c_1 X_1 + c_2 X_2 + \cdots + c_n X_n \leq \text{Engineers (In-House)}$$
$$X_1 + X_2 + \cdots + X_s = 1$$
$$X_{n-s} + X_{n-4} + \cdots + X_n = 1$$
$$X_n = 0 \text{ or } 1$$

There are approximately 200 unitary constraint equations.

In the matrix, X_n represents individual resource levels for each task and v_n is the measure of effectiveness for each resource level of each task, as computed using the mathematical model described. This computation is performed in the computer by an input subroutine. The parameter a_n represents the dollar cost, and b_n and c_n, the scientific and engineering manpower cost for contract effort and in-house effort, respectively, for each resource level of each task. V_τ then is the measure of effectiveness for the total Laboratory program and is to be maximized by choosing the proper solution set of tasks, where the use of the recommended allocation will result in dollar and manpower expenditures less than or equal to those made available to and budgeted by the Laboratory.

Since each task has six possible resource levels and only one level is to be chosen, the unitary constraint equations shown prevent the choice of more than one single resource level selection per task. For the Laboratory's 200 tasks, the actual matrix will have about 1200 terms in the first four equations and one constraint equation of six terms each for each task, resulting in a matrix of 204 rows and 1200 columns.

To cite Weingartner on this situation: "This model will select among independent alternatives those task resource levels whose total measure of effectiveness is maximum, but whose total resource consumption is within the budget limitation. The problem of indivisibilities is solved in the sense that the linear programming solution implicitly looks at all combinations of resource levels of tasks, not just one resource level of one task at a time, to select that set whose total measure of effectiveness is maximum. Furthermore, the upper limit of unity on each $X_{n-s} \cdots x_n$ guarantees that no more than one of any resource level of any task will be included in the final program. The omission of such a limitation would clearly lead to allocating the entire budget to multiples of the 'best' resource levels."

The computing program used is the CEIR LP 90, performed on an IBM 7094 computer. Programmers assigned to the RDE program in the Digital Computation group, Deputy for Studies and Analysis, SEG were Thomas Duvall and Lt. Robert Jurick.

Appendix C

The following are the management information reports and uses available from the RDE model:

1. Low-priority task list by Laboratory Divisions
2. Task nonselections for possible budget cuts
3. Recommended task allocation list for budget increases
4. System/Task Payoff packages: 12 advanced weapon systems
5. Information for quarterly input to Limited War support study
6. Identification of Laboratory task support to future systems Development Plan backup data. Areas in which other agencies (industry and government) are doing significant amounts of work
7. Input to the Laboratory. Automated management information system study
8. Prediction of planned Laboratory usage of current and future Laboratory and existing other agency facilities
9. Evaluation of Advanced Systems Analysis Group review of Laboratory task contributions to future systems
10. Preparation of Laboratory manpower versus contract dollar curve
11. Input to Laboratory manpower utilization studies.
12. Optimized fiscal year 1966 and 1967 Laboratory exploratory development program by task (computer runs)
13. Information availability for each task:
    a. Resource requirements—5 years
       1. Engineers—contract direction; engineers—in-house; funds —contract plus supplies and equipment
       2. Six possible resource levels (using in-house/contract mix) keyed to authorized ceiling man-years, half ceiling man-years, and twice ceiling man-years (three levels provided by computer interpolation subroutine)
    b. Rate of task progress for varying resource levels.
    c. Timeliness of task technology outputs with respect to AF Advanced Systems requirements (10-year time span)
    d. Advanced Systems and Laboratory technical goals supported by each task and level of the importance of this support
    e. Work required for each level of task progress and resources required to accomplish work
    f. Progress achieved with past years' funding
    g. Brief description of task state of the art
    h. Improvement afforded each advanced system supported by task
    i. Systems Management Office's coordination of important task contributions to systems
    j. Effect on the technical program of additions or subtraction of resources to or from the Laboratory's allocation
    k. Task cost effectiveness priority
    l. Optimal task resource allocation for given Laboratory resources

14. Tasks that contribute to the various sectors of the flight corridor
15. Relative cost effectiveness of new tasks as compared to the tasks in current Laboratory Technical Program
16. Cost of providing accelerated support to specific advanced systems
17. Cost of providing accelerated support to specific Laboratory technical goals
18. Tasks limited by technological progress
19. Relative importance of preferred advanced systems
20. Facility requirements summary
21. Task list flagged for management attention (5-year nonselection)

Planning Advanced Development

Howard A. Wells

"There is nothing so useless as working without a plan unless it's planning without doing the work." J. Mier

There is no convincing evidence that technological advancement occurs spontaneously, in spite of all of the folklore and controversy surrounding this subject. It is true, of course, that similar technological breakthroughs have occurred almost simultaneously in widely separated areas of the world. However, a common state of the art was available to each of the individual inventors or development teams involved. In addition, each was highly motivated either to attain personal prominence or to contribute to a well-ordered development plan. On the other hand, several studies conducted by government and private agencies indicate that technological advancement occurs at a more rapid rate when R&D is conducted in accordance with a carefully planned approach. (One such report is documented in Chapter 8.) The purpose of this chapter is to describe an explicit approach to the formulation of a plan for advanced development activities and then to illustrate how such an approach can be adapted either for a private enterprise situation or for government activity.

Advanced development is here defined as the development of hardware for experimental test purposes or for operational demonstrations. The resultant products are not intended to be used commercially nor for any other end use without further development.

In this situation, the major task facing the planner of advanced development programs is essentially that of selecting the most desirable programs for his particular purposes from among the large mass of possible programs. These programs are usually broken down into definable segments, sometimes called projects. Each project has specific costs associated with it as well as definable milestones or goals. These goals, rather than the projects themselves, are the raw materials to be evaluated by the advanced planner, assuming that the projects themselves are formulated by competent technologists who understand what is required in terms of time and resources.

There are two over-all classes of advanced development of interest to most companies and government agencies: The first is oriented toward specific end uses and is referred to as "objective-oriented" advanced development; the second is oriented toward technological advancement in general, which may progress in several directions at once. In fact, it may not be completely clear which direction really involves progress. For example, in the field of solid-state electronics one may have to decide whether it is potentially more beneficial to increase the heat-dissipation characteristics of the materials or to strive to increase the efficiency of a device so that less heat is generated. Even though the nonoriented development appears to be helter-skelter, quantitative methods can still be applied to assist management in planning this type of activity so long as general levels of technology can be established as goals.

In both cases, detailed planning can be accomplished only after a definitive forecast has been prepared. Several techniques for technological forecasting are outlined in other chapters of this text and referenced in the bibliography, but whatever technique is used, the end result should relate future time periods with distinct levels of technical achievement. This means that there must be some measurable parameter that is a useful indicator of progress in a particular technological area. Such parameters are most useful when they can be projected in the form of trend curves.

It should be stressed that there is a difference between a forecast and a plan. A forecast is an expression of opinion about some future event, often coupled with opinions concerning its likelihood of occurrence. Normally, it does not imply any desire on the part of the forecaster to bring about the event. That is to say, a forecast is an expression of what is likely to happen rather than what is a desire or goal for some future time period.

On the other hand, if overt action is taken to cause an event to occur, this becomes part of what is normally referred to as a plan. The basic difference here is that of desire or intent. Sometimes the dividing line is thin. One might create a plan by selecting from a group of alternative forecasts the one that most closely fulfills a desire for the future. The planner would then take measures to create the conditions under which the chosen forecast is likely to come to pass.

The Planning Process

The seven major steps in the process of development planning are outlined below to provide an over-all perspective. Several of these will be discussed later at length in order to clarify the most important concepts for understanding the use of quantitative methods The other steps are treated in greater detail in other chapters.

1. Define the planning period and the subject matter to be considered.
2. Describe the environmental conditions to be assumed for the planning period.
3. Identify the long-range objectives that establish the value systems to be used.
4. Establish specific short-range goals.
5. Project technological forecasts for each relevant technical area.
6. Obtain expert judgments concerning the utility, feasibility, and cost of each goal.
7. Select the most desirable projects to make up an "optimal" total program within the anticipated constraints, budgetary and otherwise.

Technical Areas

The Department of Defense has established a number of discrete program elements that may be useful as examples for organizing the advanced development programs. Since some of these program elements do not meet all of the criteria discussed below, the generic term "Technical Area" will be used here instead. Technical Areas should have the following characteristics:

1. Their scope should be precisely definable.
2. They should be mutually exclusive. This precludes the use of both discipline and function as bases for defining technical areas. For example, chemistry is so important to rocket propulsion that both chemistry and rocket propulsion cannot be defined as Technical Areas in this model.

3. Tangible, measurable results should be produced. A Technical Area is improperly constituted if there is no available mechanism for measuring progress or forecasting future results in terms other than the quantity of resources expended.

4. The results of each Technical Area should be identifiable in terms of a critical component of a commercial product, a weapon system, or a support system. Therefore, Technical Areas will not be alternatives to each other since each one is essential. For example, an aircraft designer must provide both a propulsion system and an airframe; he cannot choose one or the other.

Future Environments

The values associated with the future outcomes of any current activities are heavily dependent on the situations that exist when the outcomes actually occur. These future situations are often called scenarios in the jargon of the research and development planner. The scenarios selected for advanced development planning should be based on the most realistic forecasts available for each environmental factor that is expected to influence the outcomes of interest. Economic forecasting is important and should be included explicitly in every scenario. Other market factors must also be included. For example, if the organization is involved with military products, it will be important to obtain forecasts of the intensities of violence expected in military operations during the planning period. All forecasts should be combined into at least three complete scenarios: a most likely, an optimistic, and a pessimistic one with respect to the expected impact on over-all operations. If no explicit forecast is made, the inherent assumption is the continuation of the status quo.

The next step requires highly abstract value judgments. The significance of these judgments is such that they probably should be made at the highest level of responsibility. An estimate must be made of the likelihood of occurrence of each scenario (or of a real situation sufficiently similar to it for planning purposes) and of the consequences to the organization if it does occur. Multiplication of these value judgments for each scenario will provide an index of the relative emphasis to be placed on planning. It is the method selected for this combination because the emphasis should go to zero if either the likelihood or the consequences were to be judged as zero (see Table 6.1).

Table 6.1   Emphasis on Preparation for Various Environments
(hypothetical example)

Type of Environment	Likelihood of Occurrence		Consequences if it Does Occur		Relative Emphasis
I	0.4	×	8	=	3.2
II	0.4	×	5	=	2.0
III	0.2	×	10	=	2.0

Universal Decision Factors

A very large number of decision models have been studied by the author over a period of eleven years in government, industry, and the academic community. These models have embraced every segment of the R&D spectrum from the most fundamental research through operational development. In every instance, the factors included as major elements have fallen into three general categories: utility, feasibility, and cost. Sometimes one of these categories has been omitted, and consequently the models have been considered deficient by other practitioners. If these three factors could be expressed as single-valued quantities, the product desirability could be estimated easily. However, each is composed of a great many subfactors and also varies considerably over time (often in an unexpected manner) as forecasts are projected further and further into the future. The problem facing the planner at this point, then, is how to consider explicitly all of the subfactors involved in the decision and how to express their relative importance.

These factors can either be treated in their most abstract form or they can be structured in a hierarchy of subfactors. Others have referred to similar decision trees as "relevance trees."[1] The term relevance, however, appears misleading since it does not distinguish between a mere interrelationship and a relationship structure that shows some measure of importance or value. Adding to the confusion, some users of "relevance trees" have included feasibility concepts and even cost concepts in their structures.

[1] Cetron, M. J., Martino, J., and Roepcke, L., "The Selection of R&D Program Content—Survey of Quantitative Methods." *IEEE Transactions on Engineering Management,* EM-14, March 1967, p. 6.

Most factors and subfactors depend heavily on technical estimates and management judgments. The most productive approach to this situation is to divide the problem into those segments that can be supported by measurements or quantitative data and others that must be handled by using the judgment of responsible individuals or groups of experts. The availability of data or expert judgment can play a very important role in determining the level of abstraction for a particular planning exercise. The selection of an appropriate level of detail also depends on the perspective of the user of the model, the amount of time and resources that can be devoted to the use of the model and the acceptance or impact of the model's output.

The expression of subjective judgments in quantitative terms that are useful in planning models is not yet an accurate science. The most precise approaches, such as that of Churchman and Ackoff,[2] are generally too cumbersome to be used by day-to-day practitioners. The usual approach is to compare one's feelings about a matter against a list of adjectival ratings that have preassigned values on a scale—usually from 0 to 10 or from 0 to 100 percent. Table 6.2 illustrates one such scale that was used in the allocation of resources to a complex of government laboratories for two years.[3]

Objectives and Goals

All organizations have primary service objectives. In industrial concerns, these may take the form of providing a service to the customer, such as transportation, food or housing. In the case of a government agency, they may be broad social goals, such as national security, public health, or the welfare of the indigent.

Goals of specific advanced development programs may have certain inherent values of their own, but their major value normally derives from their contributions to the primary service objectives of the parent organizations. These goals are easier to evaluate if they are expressed in terms of items that have utility such as commercial products or military weapon systems. In general, each goal contributes to several objectives at the same time, and the nature of its contributions usually varies as a function of the environment. An evaluation matrix such as

[2] Ackoff, R. L., *Scientific Method: Optimizing Applied Research Decisions,* New York: John Wiley & Sons, 1962.
[3] Wells, H. A., Cannon, J. R., and Oakes, Carl L., *The Wright Air Development Division Effort Allocation Guide,* Wright-Patterson AFB, Ohio: Plans Division, WADD, June 1959.

Table 6.2   Quantifying Subjective Judgments

Adjective Rating	Numerical Rating (Percent)
Essential to attainment of design mission capability and will permit revolutionary improvement of performance beyond the design mission capability	100
Essential to attainment of design mission capability and would provide adequate performance for the design mission capability	80
Essential contribution toward attainment of design mission capability but would provide performance significantly less than desired for the design mission capability	50
Not essential to attainment of design mission capability but would permit small improvement beyond design mission capability	30
Not essential to attainment of design mission capability but would provide economy and/or convenience to the design mission capability	20
Negligible Improvement	0

the one shown in Table 6.3 may therefore be helpful. It is important to note that each evaluation must be made for a specific point in time, such as some future fiscal year, because the value varies as a function of time. Figure 6.1 shows the general shape of the variation in value of the goals with time. The use of such a standardized "product value profile" will permit a total cradle-to-grave evaluation of a new product line based on a detailed analysis of only one or two points during the product lifetime.

Trend Analysis

Once the value of the product, or goal, has been established, then each technical area related to that goal can be assessed. Those technological areas where progress is needed to attain the performance characteristics of the product are identified, and their relative importance is assessed in terms of their contribution to the over-all success of the product. Thus the total value of the product can be allocated, as it were, to each of the technical areas.

Table 6.3   Estimating Product Utility

Product Contribution Table for Fiscal Year ___						
			Product Number			
	1	2	3	4	5	6
Environment I						
Profitability						
Gross sales						
Product balance						
Image						
Profitability						
Gross sales						
Product balance						
Image						
Environment III						
Profitability						
Gross sales						
Product balance						
Image						

Admittedly this is not a precise process since there are trade-offs involved among the technical areas. For example, a better laminar flow-control device for a specific airfoil design of an airplane would permit the attainment of the performance characteristics desired using a lower-powered engine while, on the other hand, a higher-performance engine may permit the same over-all system performance without the new laminar flow-control technique. Figure 6.2 illustrates how the total value of a new product, such as a short take-off and landing transport aircraft, may be allocated to the several technological disciplines required to attain the needed performance characteristics.

Figure 6.3 depicts one approach to the assessment of utility of an objective-oriented advanced development program through a trend analysis. The star represents the state of the art that will be required at a future date to attain the goal. This goal may represent some weapon system capability in the national defense context or perhaps a new commercial product in an industrial situation.

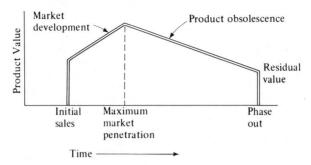

Figure 6.1 Projecting a Product Value Profile

Each relevant goal is thus plotted graphically on trend charts for each technical area, to indicate both the amount of advancement needed and the time element. If the goal falls on or below the trend line, a continuation of the past rate of progress will be adequate, but if it is clearly beyond the range of the expected progress, then one of two courses of action must be taken: either the requirement must be relaxed and the performance penalties implied must be accepted; or unusual effort must be expended to accelerate the expected rate of progress to overcome the forecast deficiency.

If an advanced development project is successfully completed, thus advancing the state of the art sufficiently to satisfy a particular product, it is also possible, even probable, that technological advancements will

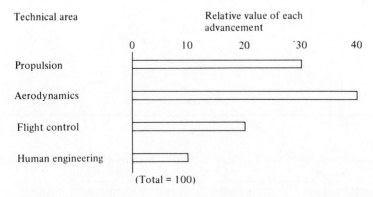

Figure 6.2 Contributions of Various Technologies toward Evaluating a New Product

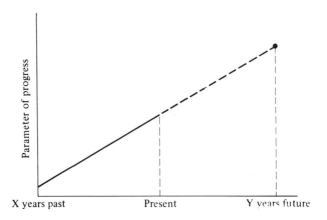

Figure 6.3   Forecasting Technological Needs

be made at the same time that will satisfy other products. Therefore, the total utility of the advancement will be the sum of the values of all contributions made toward attaining performance requirements of all the products known to be affected by that particular technology.

Figure 6.4 shows three possible forecasts for a given technical area: Position 1 represents the state of the art two years in the future, if no

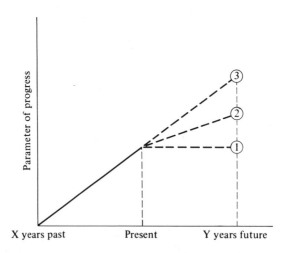

Figure 6.4   Alternative Technological Forecasts

further progress is made. Position 3 represents a continuation into the future of the rate of progress that has been experienced in the past years. Position 2 is some level of technology between these two.

Position 1 may be interpreted as the result of the maturing of a particular technology. For example, a few years ago the technologists in the area of miniaturization of vacuum tubes had very little room left to make progress. Their progress trend might be said to have been "saturated." However, the trend of miniaturization of electronic components in general was able to continue because of the introduction of solid-state devices. This would indicate that a trend such as that resulting in position 3 was superimposed on a maturing trend.

Position 1 could also be the result, of course, of no resources being applied to the research area. Differences such as these in the forecast of technological progress trends can in themselves constitute a measure of the utility of certain work. For example, if it becomes known that a competitor can expect to be in position 3 y years in the future, and if we are presently on a trend that would lead us to position 2, the difference between these rates of progress becomes very significant. In fact, this type of analysis is probably the most explicit approach available in the case of nonoriented advanced development.

When one compares several areas of technology it is usually impossible to find a single parameter of progress that is common to all of them. One method of relating competing organizations on a consistent basis from one technology to the next would be in terms of the years required to attain a certain lead or to overcome a certain lag. For example, if we are at position 1 and our competitor is at position 3, we lag the competitor by y years. A similar analysis for other technologies would give us a way of expressing how far ahead or behind our competitor we are in each case.

So much about utility. Another major factor in evaluating advanced development is feasibility. Feasibility is usually expressed in terms of the probability of success. This is necessarily a subjective judgment that can be expressed on a scale from 0 to 1.0. If we approach a condition of saturation in which our forecast indicates that the best we can possibly do is to attain position 2 of Figure 6.4, then a goal that requires us to be in position 3 x years from now is less likely to be attained than one that requires us to be between positions 1 and 2.

In addition to the direct question of technological feasibility, it has already been suggested that the shape of the trend curves may be influenced by the amount of resources applied. Thus, the attainment of position 3 will normally cost more than that of position 2. Of course, position 1 costs nothing because we are already at that level of technology. In general, an average annual cost can be associated with each slope shown in Figure 6.5, and a total cost can be estimated for each level of technology. The relationship of progress to cost has never been observed to be linear; it should therefore be treated cautiously, particularly when attempting to accelerate progress.

We have now indicated methods of associating a utility, a feasibility, and a cost with each increment of technological progress that might be represented by an advanced development project. These three factors must be treated together in association with each increment of technology. In some cases there may be several alternate approaches that can be represented by separate projects oriented toward the same goal. The utility, feasibility, and cost should be assessed for each project. A comparison will then help in selecting the most desirable method of achieving a given level of advancement.

If multiple approaches are funded to attain a certain level of technology, the utility of the goal is not increased at all, although costs may be increased considerably. Feasibility will be increased also, but probably far less than costs. Thus, the over-all desirability of a multiple approach method must be compared with the desirability of each single approach. The degree of desirability is calculated by multiplying the number that expresses its total utility by the feasibility and dividing this product by the total costs. The result is then compared with those of other technological advancements.

If this method is used to allocate advanced development resources in any specific organization, such as a government agency or a private company, it is very likely that certain research projects will not be supported because of a shortage of resources. In such a case, one must reevaluate the impact of each allocation to determine whether certain projects that are critical to a particular product may have been eliminated or stretched out because of inadequate funding. The utility of the affected product must not be included in assessing technological areas if it is not possible to achieve the performance required. Each time this happens, a complete reassessment of all advanced development programs involved may be required, particularly with respect to its utility.

Planning for Private Enterprise

The planning processes in a manufacturing company in a highly technical industry serve to illustrate the use of quantitative approaches in the private sector. The results reported here are taken from an actual planning cycle in a firm in the aerospace industry. Certain descriptors and numbers have necessarily been abridged to protect the privacy of the company involved. The problem analyzed is that of selecting products to be developed by the company, all of which will be based on the results of successful advanced development.

If industrial companies wish to exert technological product leadership, they must forecast the feasibility of attaining various levels of technology not only for themselves but also for their potential competitors. Usually, forecasts are required for a large number of seemingly unrelated technologies. This is obvious in the case of a complex product such as a major military weapon system but even for a fairly simple product forecasts must be made concerning technologies that could produce competing products. Many nontechnical forecasts are also required to establish the environmental assumptions concerning the future characteristics of the market and of the individual company.

Many companies that lack the technical depth to conduct forecasts completely on their own can participate with trade associations and government agencies to obtain them. For example, during the past ten years the U.S. Air Force has carried on several massive technological forecasting exercises, all of which involved industrial participation. These were intended to provide the basis for planning decisions concerning the advancement of broad technologies through exploratory development, advanced development demonstrations to establish the feasibility of some specific technique, and the engineering development of major weapon systems. Two of the problems encountered in most of these exercises were the very human tendencies to forecast fields of greatest familiarity and to emphasize the criteria most favorable to preconceived notions. These problems were minimized where a planning guide of some type had been established at the outset, providing at least a check list to assure that all relevant criteria were thoroughly and objectively considered.

The product mix to be evaluated should include all of the current product lines as well as potential new products. It is usually possible to forecast periods when some of the present products are likely to become obsolete. This possibility should always be considered, even for the shiny new products just introduced. A preliminary estimate of expected availability dates should be made for each new product. This estimate will be refined during the course of the planning exercise. The planning period should be long enough to encompass the expected lifetime of most of the potential new products as well as all current product lines. A shorter planning period is apt to penalize new products in favor of established ones.

For purposes of our exercise, three scenarios were selected: economic recession, status quo, and economic inflation. The major company objectives were profitability, gross sales, product balance, and company image. Several company officers were interrogated privately to determine their opinions concerning the relative importance of these objectives in each scenario. The consensus was synthesized in a matrix similar to the one shown in Table 6.4. These ratings are made on a scale of zero to ten, where ten represents the most important objective under the conditions represented by the scenario under consideration. Combining these judgments with the relative emphasis considerations described earlier permits an over-all assessment of the "expected value" of the company objectives. The table of expected values shown in Table 6.5 are obtained by multiplying the values from Table 6.4 by the appropriate relative emphasis for each environment from Table 6.1. Of course these objectives are highly aggregated and can be treated at their most abstract level or as composites of a great many components. Although most people in a company are concerned with the components, someone in the top echelon must think in terms of the aggregates.

All components of the first two objectives are easily quantifiable by means of measures such as dollar value of sales, percentage increase in sales, return on investment, or pretax return on sales. On the other hand, the other two objectives are highly dependent on management judgment. For this example, "product balance" is defined as that mix of product lines that assures the company the greatest degree of corporate stability in the face of a changing environment, at the same time exploiting current and projected competence, equipment, and facilities. "Corporate image" is even more subjective because it depends on a second-order judgment—management's judgment of how others view the company. It relates, however, to a few quantifiable factors

Table 6.4   Environment Versus Objective (hypothetical)

Company Objectives	Environmental Projections		
	Environment I	Environment II	Environment III
Profitability	8	10	8
Gross Sales	10	5	2
Product Balance	2	8	10
Corporate Image	5	10	8

Table 6.5   Expected Values of Company Objectives

	Expected Value in Environ- ment I	Expected Value in Environ- ment II	Expected Value in Environ- ment III	Total Expected Values
Profitability	25.6	20	16	61.6
Gross sales	32.0	10	4	46.0
Product balance	6.4	16	20	42.4
Corporate image	16.0	20	16	52.0

such as product quality, contract performance, and degree of technological leadership, as well as such intangibles as the effectiveness of advertising and public relations.

The planning structure is now sufficiently complete to permit the estimation of the utility of each product at a given point in time (e.g., for a selected fiscal year). This is most easily accomplished through the use of a table that indicates the contribution made by each product to each of the company objectives in each environment for a particular year (see Table 6.3). The product with the greatest contribution is assigned some arbitrary value, such as ten on a scale of zero to ten. Every other product is then related to it. A product contributing half as much is assigned a five, one tenth as much, a one, and so on. This is strictly a weighting process rather than a ranking, and a value of ten can be assigned to all products if there is no difference in their contributions.

The next step is the assessment of the marginal contribution of each product to each objective and environment, using the values assigned in the previous step as a rough guide. This marginal contribution is very sensitive to the product mix. It would be very helpful at this point if the planning group already knew the mix that will be selected by the model. However, in the absence of that information, an assumption must be made. It may for instance be assumed, as a point of departure, that all products under consideration constitute the product mix. A judgment should then be made concerning the degree to which each corporate objective would be satisfied in each environment. This should be expressed as a percentage of attainment of the objective. For example, if the corporate objective were a profitability of 25 percent before taxes, and if a certain product mix were expected to produce a profitability of only 20 percent in environment 1, the percent attainment would be 80 percent.

One product at a time is then removed from the product mix; new judgments of percent attainment are made for each goal; and the decrease in percent attainment is taken as the marginal contribution of product A to the objective in the environment considered. Any increase in attainment that may occur when a product is removed from the mix should be expressed as a negative marginal contribution. When all marginal contributions have been assessed, the utility of each product in the specified fiscal year is established by first multiplying the value of each objective in each environment (as calculated earlier) by the marginal contribution of product A to that objective and environment. All such products for product A are summed to obtain its total marginal utility in fiscal year y. Similarly, the marginal utilities of each product in fiscal year y are calculated.

This computation of utility at one point in time can be very misleading if it is used as an estimate of the total utility of each product. Ideally, the marginal utility of each product should be computed for each year of its lifetime and summed over its lifetime. Since the vast number of discrete judgments required for such a process rules out this approach, the total lifetime utility of each product can be estimated by using standard profiles of value, as discussed earlier. The most useful profile probably looks something like a child's drawing of a rooftop (see Figure 6.2). Utility normally increases as a step function in the year during which the product is introduced and continues to grow until the point of maximum utility is reached. This can be the point of maximum market penetration or the point at which some competitive product begins to replace the old one. Then a steady decline occurs until the product is phased out or removed from the market. This phase-out slope is often not as steep as the initial rise in utility because of a tendency to hang on to old, familiar products long after they should have been discontinued.

Such a simplified product value profile can be completely defined if its height at any point of the product lifetime is computed by the marginal utility calculations described earlier and if estimates are made for the date of initial sales, date of maximum utility, date of product phase-out, rate of increase in utility during market development, and rate of decrease during obsolescence. Thus, the area under the product value profile curve (or the annual summation of the utility of the product over all of the years in its lifetime) represents the total marginal utility of the product.

Product utilities or values are often discussed without explicit provision for the fact that it may not be feasible to market a product with the technological attributes described during the planning period or to meet the delivery time specified in the plan. Since a delivery schedule had to be assumed for each new product in the early phases of the planning process, the most useful criterion of feasibility may well be the probability that the assumed schedule can be met. The estimate of this schedule feasibility usually requires a technological forecast for each identified problem area and a method of estimating the time required for all of the many activities that can be grouped under the heading of "acquisition phase" (e.g., engineering, tooling, and manufacturing). The development of a new product can be divided into three phases: advanced development, acquisition, and product delivery. Since methods of planning the acquisition phase are fairly well known and in common use, it is sufficient to say here that three time estimates concerning this phase will be obtained from the responsible personnel: optimistic, most likely, and pessimistic.

Taking one problem area at a time, the technological obstacles must first be identified. The planners can then make estimates of the most likely, the longest, and the shortest time that will be required to solve each problem. By the use of PERT-type procedures, the expected time to overcome each problem can then be calculated. The problems are usually grouped in such a manner that they are not sequentially linked. The longest expected time to solve any one problem can then be taken as the time to complete the advanced development. Added to the expected time required to complete the acquisition phase, this gives the expected time to the first product delivery. The feasibility can then be expressed in terms of the probability that delivery will be made during or before each fiscal year.

Once the product characteristics and time estimates have been described in sufficient detail and the utility and feasibility judgments have been made, it should be possible to estimate the cost of delivering the product in the quantities predicted by the market forecasts which provided the basis for the utility estimates. This estimate should include total costs from the present time until product phase-out. For new products, this will include costs for R&D, for market development, for product acquisition, and for field service, all amortized on a unit cost basis.

Even if it appears impractical to project year-by-year costs for products that are to be developed several years in the future, it should be possible to use standard cost curves associated with classes of similar products, so that product costs are at least treated with a consistent level of ignorance. It would be unfortunate if one future product were favored over another purely on the basis of cost estimates when the costs of both were equally unknown. This can happen, however, if different groups make independent estimates without the use of standard costing methods.

The product planning group is now in a position to calculate the value (total marginal utility), the expected value (total marginal utility multiplied by feasibility), and the desirability (expected value divided by cost) of each product. Products can now be selected in order of decreasing desirability, intermixing current products with potential new ones until a limit is reached (e.g., funds, manpower, equipment, or facilities available in a specific year).

Up to this point the model can be handled manually unless a large number of products are included. However, even with a small number of products it will be very useful to have a computerized linear programming model available to test whether an optimal product mix has been selected. Such a model can test every possible product mix in groups of nine or ten without excessive computer time.[4] A situation is occasionally found in which the most desirable product consumes such a large portion of some critical resource that it displaces several others, the sum of whose desirabilities is greater than that of the more expensive product. Thus, the concept of marginal desirability is shown to be very useful, even though it is usually too complex to implement manually.

Once a product mix has been selected with the appropriate resource constraints, the total contribution of all selected products to each objective can be calculated for each future year. This analysis will usually indicate that certain objectives may not be completely satisfied while others are exceeded. An additional feature can be added to the model to halt the addition of products to the mix once preselected levels of attainment are reached for any or all company objectives. However, this usually makes the procedure so complicated that it becomes too difficult for the users to follow manually. It has been found that product planning guides will not be used at all unless they are so simple that the least sophisticated member of the product planning group can reproduce its essential features with pencil and paper.

Even without this extra sophistication, however, the product planning guide does permit the selection of optimal product mixes. Also, it provides management with a device that can assess the value of the selected product mix with respect to each company objective and policy

[4] Rae, R. H., "A Systems Development Planning Structure," Cambridge, Mass.: Abt Associates, Inc., January 1966.

and determine the over-all value of each product to the company, reducing most of the tendency toward emotional suboptimization. It can also serve an important role by indicating the impact of various policy decisions and the effect that variations of each type of resource constraint have on the total value of the product mix.

Development Planning in the Public Sector

Quantitative methods are just as important to the planning processes of educational institutions, nonprofit agencies, and government bureaus as they are to profit-oriented private enterprise organizations. The Federal budget is carried to a far larger number of significant figures than the budgets of most private organizations. On the other hand, many governmental goals are more difficult to pin down than profit. But corporate goals can be elusive also; self-perpetuation or status for the owners are more intangible than the major goals of some government agencies.

Most organizations in the public sector have definite long-range objectives against which quantitative goals can be formulated. Such goals and objectives are being prepared by the White House National Goals Research Staff.[5]

Since the national defense establishment is one of the largest and most complex of our public agencies, it has been chosen to illustrate the application of quantitative methods of development planning. The techniques are equally applicable to any other public agency.

The results reported in this section of the text are taken from an actual planning exercise, conducted by the organization responsible for planning all research and development for one of the military services. The three general scenarios used were general war, limited war, and counterinsurgency. The military functions established as capability objectives were intelligence, offensive firepower, defensive firepower, and logistics. All of the weapon systems then available or projected as future candidates for development were evaluated with the same general procedures as those discussed here. Optimal force structures were thus postulated to satisfy each objective. The new weapon system candidates that were included in these force structures were then established as planning objectives for the advanced development planning cycle.

[5] Nixon, Richard M., Press Release, Washington, D.C.: The White House, July 13, 1969.

Table 6.6 illustrates the types of technical areas that are typically used in military development planning. Progress trends were plotted for each area and the relevant planning objectives were plotted on each of them in the manner shown in Figure 6.4. As an approach to the assessment of the utility of the technological advances plotted, the effect on mission performance, M_{eo}, was defined as the extent to which the indicated advances in the technical area e will improve the ability

Table 6.6   Technical Areas of a Typical Military
            Development Program

1	Special-purpose materials
2	Materials applications
3	Protective materials and processes
4	Materials phenomenon and experimental methods
5	Load-bearing materials
6	Deceleration-device techniques
7	Structures
8	Astro/aerodynamics
9	Escape
10	Vehicle environmental protection
11	Flight control
12	Secondary power
13	Fuels, lubricants, and propellants
14	Rocket propulsion
15	Air-breathing engines
16	Personnel
17	Human engineering and training
18	Training devices
19	Habitable environment
20	Computer techniques
21	Navigation and guidance
22	Surveillance techniques
23	Reconnaissance-imaging
24	Reconnaissance-identification
25	Atmospheric reconnaissance
26	Communications
27	Electromagnetic vulnerability reduction
28	Electromagnetic countermeasures
29	Electromagnetic reconnaissance
30	Vehicle defense
31	Electronic components
32	Electronic design techniques
33	Radome techniques
34	Weapon fire control
35	Vehicle vulnerability to nuclear weapons
36	Support equipment techniques

of planning objective o to perform missions for which it is intended
or to which it is expected to contribute. The most precise way to
establish this factor is to estimate the percent degradation in the expected effectiveness of the planning objective in case the indicated
advancement of the technical area is not realized.

If the effectiveness of the planning objective (candidate weapon
system) is degraded to the extent that the force structure is just as
effective without the planning objective, the value of M_{eo} is 100 percent; if no degradation results, M_{eo} is zero. Of course this approach
requires advance knowledge of the operational concept of the planning
objective and of the over-all improvement in effectiveness it is expected
to make to the total force structure. If this approach is too cumbersome,
simplifying assumptions may be made to relate its expected effectiveness to performance parameters such as speed, altitude, range, and so
on, that can in turn be related to advancements in specific technical
areas. A third, and least satisfactory, approach is the use of adjective
scales such as shown in Table 6.2.

The utility or military worth w_{eo} of making the progress in e required
to attain o is simply the product of the effect on M_{eo} multiplied by the
desirability d_o of o.

In some cases the technical progress required to satisfy one planning
objective will also satisfy several others. The value of that increment
of progress is the sum of the values of the contribution to all planning
objectives. This is shown as

$$w_e = \sum^{M} (M_{eo})(d_o),$$

where M is the total number of planning objectives supported by e.

The next step required an estimate of the cost to the nation and to
the agency involved to achieve the historical progress shown. The
acceleration A_{eo} required in e to attain   the capability called for by o
was then estimated by plotting the trend that would satisfy the objective and comparing the angles with respect to the horizontal of the
new trend line and the original one (see Figure 6.5).

An estimate was also made of the total resources that would have
to be applied to each technical area to maintain the historical rate of
progress and to accelerate it by the degree needed to achieve each
planning objective. The historical national average annual costs H_e in
each area should be a dominant factor in this estimate, but any expected areas of diminishing returns should also be taken into account.
An estimate should also be made of the share of the total national
effort N_e in each technical area that the agency should expect to carry
if the indicated acceleration is to be achieved.

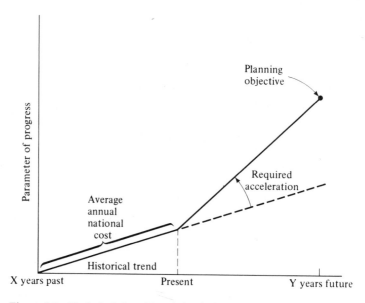

Figure 6.5   Technical Area Trend Analysis

The average annual cost c_{eo} to the agency of making the progress in any given technical area required to attain the capability of any given planning objective is the product of H_e the acceleration A_{eo}, and the agency share of the total national effort N_e. This is expressed mathematically as $c_{eo} = (H_e)(A_{eo})(N_e)$.

The cost c_{eo} is converted to total agency cost C_{eo} by multiplying by the number of years y_{eo} from now to the target year. Thus, $C_{eo} = (c_{eo})(y_{eo}) = (H_e)(A_{eo})(N_e)(y_{eo})$.

Experts in each technical area then made estimates of the probability of success in terms of the technical feasibility F_{eo} of reaching the state of the art called for by the time indicated by the planning objective. This judgment was of course dependent on the resource considerations already discussed.

Desirability of Advanced Development Programs

Explicit consideration of each of the factors discussed so far should be helpful in the development planning process, even if nothing more formal were attempted. However, the factors can be combined in the following manner to produce an over-all figure of merit for each technical area, goal, or increment of technological progress.

The desirability d_{eo} of achieving the progress in e needed to meet the requirements of o is the product of the probability of success f_{eo} and the military worth w_{eo} of making the progress in e required to attain o, divided by C_{eo}. This can be expressed as

$$d_{eo} = \frac{(W_{eo})(f_{eo})}{C_{eo}}.$$

This equation is then expanded so that all primary factors considered so far are displayed:

$$d_{eo} = \frac{(M_{eo})(d_o)(f_{eo})}{(H_e)(N_e)(A_{eo})(Y_{eo})}.$$

In a real-world planning exercise, advanced development projects are selected in the order of their desirability until a resource constraint is reached. Although the actual computations involved in planning models such as this are usually quite simple, it is useful to have a computer so that one can obtain an immediate calculation of the impact of new data or changes in judgments, in real time if possible. This permits the person making the judgment to adjust his thinking if the problem is more sensitive to a particular factor than he expects. This also helps to minimize over-reaction to dramatic pieces of information or to emotional elements of the problem. It should be emphasized that the computer, and the entire planning model for that matter, is only an aid to the planners' judgment, not a substitute for it.

7
Allocating Resources to Projects

Jacob N. Johnson

"The most significant impact of science on our technical systems will come from better methods for studying and laying out what choices really exist, and for differentiating between what we know and what we can merely guess." F. R. Kappel

While the over-all responsibilities of a manager of technology are similar to those of a manager in almost any area, the emphasis in his job is fundamentally different. In general, he must plan, organize, schedule, coordinate, and control. His success in discharging these responsibilities effectively depends upon many factors, but particularly upon the degree to which he plans the availability of needed resources and schedules their allocation among many concurrent work projects.

Programming the availability and optimum use of resources in conducting R&D activities continues to be a particularly difficult task, especially with regard to cost and time. The principal reason for this is the nature of the resources used and products developed. Depending upon the objective to be achieved, the R&D product may range from an intangible idea to the development of an immense prototype machine that will be the basis of models used in mass production. In nearly all cases, however, the principal resource is human intellect trained in many diverse scientific disciplines, and the technical equipment needed to support the work of those disciplines. Many feel that these factors of production are much more difficult to identify, control, predict, and measure than other resources in government and industry.

This chapter will identify the features of the R&D manager's resource allocation problem and outline an approach to planning this vital job. It will also discuss some of the practices of R&D management which all too often enlarge the allocation problem instead of helping to solve it.

Planning

Planning has been defined simply as thought in advance of action. To be effective, it must result in a method or approach that begins with a clarification of objectives and then clearly identifies the organization's needs. The planner must determine the most advantageous course of action in terms of policies, other programs, resources, and goals.

The ingredient of this definition that is most often missing from R&D planning is the complete consideration of resources and other programs. R&D projects are frequently planned on the basis of time and money alone. Because of the difficulty in forecasting their necessity, availability, and individual contribution, the special types of men, material, and equipment needed for a project are not given sufficient individual and explicit consideration. Moreover, even when such consideration is given, the potential conflict with the resource demands of other current or planned projects is often overlooked.

Experience shows that the failure of R&D management to face the resource allocation problem at the planning stage can lead to many problems in subsequent phases of a project. Indeed, it can easily affect the entire competitive position of the company. It is equally clear that if the resource problem is to be adequately considered in the plan, a system must exist whereby the R&D manager can identify all his resource needs and determine at any point in time the disposition of the resources at his disposal. The search for such a management tool is widespread and intense.

Organization

Research and development work has traditionally been organized into projects and subjected to what has become known as project management. As shown in Figure 7.1, this type of organization is characterized by the following:

1. Each project is divided into phases, such as literature search, basic research, development, experimentation, and so on.

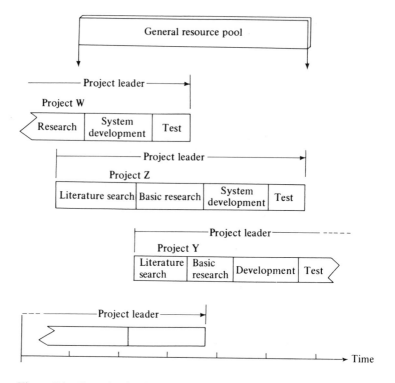

Figure 7.1   Organization by Project

2. Work in each phase is performed by small groups of specialists.

3. Each project is administered by a project leader who is responsible also for providing various support personnel and equipment.

4. Resources needed by each project leader are allocated from a common pool.

Although this form of organization is theoretically sound and indeed is used in many areas other than R&D, numerous difficulties may arise during its implementation. For instance, because not all resources are under the direct control of the project leaders, the latter cannot really be given complete authority and responsibility for the projects. For the same reason, over-all priorities must be established for the resources to prevent conflicts among the project leaders. Finally, the allocation of support activities must be carefully timed among all projects.

These and other problems have stimulated search for improved approaches to coping with the over-all **R&D** management problem. One notable product of this search is the "functionally phased" organization developed by Roman.[1] As illustrated in Figure 7.2, the essence of his approach is what may be called the "functional leader" who supplants the project leader and is responsible for his function within all projects. The man responsible for literature search, basic research, and so on, is given complete control of all the company resources applicable to his particular function.

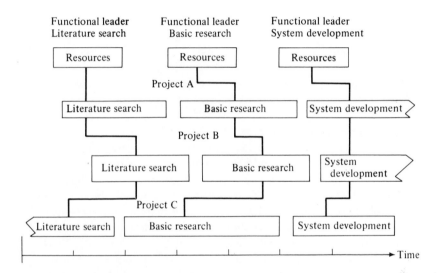

Figure 7.2   Organization by Functional Area

This type of organization can have many advantages over the usual project management approach. It recognizes the need to organize by project, but overcomes potential conflicts among project leaders by giving the functional leaders authority and responsibility that transcends any particular functional area of all projects. In effect there can be no leadership conflict, because one leader is not concerned with the activities of another; there can be no competition for resources, because those assigned in one area are specialists in that area alone and are not applicable to another.

[1] Roman, D. D. (discussed in course: R&D in the Total Organization, November 1965).

The over-all management function becomes easier, because project responsibility is passed from functional leader to functional leader as the project advances from phase to phase. To overcome potential problems during each transition, a system for work measurement and reporting must be set up to allow the functional leader to know precisely the status of a project when it enters and when it leaves his area of responsibility. Regardless of the type of R&D organization, decisions must continuously be made concerning the allocation of scarce resources to the numerous jobs to be performed.

Control

Churchman has described control as "the process of deciding when to test for accuracy and what corrective action to take when it is decided that the accuracy requirements are not met."[2] Too often, measurement of accomplishment in R&D work is difficult because of the absence of specific and discernible milestones in different phases of the work. In the basic research phase, for example, it is almost impossible to measure progress, particularly when the product of the phase is to be a new technique or some new body of technical knowledge. In such cases, the breakthrough could come near the beginning of the phase or on the last scheduled day. If the project leader is asked about progress, his reply is typically that the work is on schedule. It is not until the phase, or project, is nearing its completion date that it becomes apparent that a significant delay will be incurred.

This should not imply that a requirement for control is not recognized by R&D management. Rather, the control job is often slighted. One avenue to improvement might be a control system based on resource allocation. The fact is that progress in a great many R&D jobs is more dependent upon the resources of men and support equipment than upon the time apportioned or money expended. Another aid to control could be the functionally oriented organization of Figure 7.2. This would shift to managers with responsibility for a limited part of a great many projects instead of all parts of just one project. Certainly the functionally oriented organization approach would tend to minimize the inclination of project leaders to continue work on projects that may be essentially completed or have become nonfeasible for technical, financial, or other reasons. It is hard to expect a man to end his own job and break up his organization voluntarily.

[2] Churchman, C. W., *Prediction and Optimal Decision*. Englewood Cliffs, N.J.: Prentice-Hall, 1961, p. 128.

Communication and Coordination

Communication and coordination are closely related and may even be synonymous when considered from a resource allocation problem standpoint. Communication is the transfer of information or ideas between individuals or groups for purposes of mutual understanding and motivation for action. Coordination goes beyond the process of achieving effective communication and is the process of achieving a goal most efficiently. If communication breaks down, so does coordination, and the chance for reaching an organization's objectives dies.

In R&D management the problem of communication and coordination is significantly more complex than in other fields. People working on a "breakthrough" project may have to create new terminology to describe their findings. Moreover, R&D projects involve many sets of unusual or specialized terminology. Within a corporation or even within one project, numerous strict disciplines may be involved, each of which has its own special jargon. The equipment required is similarly specialized and difficult to describe. The product usually is not an easily visualized physical item, but new ideas and concepts.

The results of R&D work are particularly difficult to communicate. Paradoxically, even when the languages of physics, mathematics, engineering, and statistics use the same words, the implications of the words mean different things to different specialists. The point is that managers cannot work closely enough with all technical activities in a project to be expected to know all of the terminology involved. And various managers may also have divergent academic backgrounds, thus adding to the complexity of communication and coordination between them.

Finally, the type and detail of information required by each level of management varies. For instance, a project leader should not be too concerned with long-range availability of funds; top management should not be directly concerned with individual work assignments within a project. A design of R&D communication must be found that transmits the degree of detail needed by the various strata of management involved. If proper degrees of detail are not observed, unnecessary or insufficient information may be communicated. Either situation compounds an already intrinsically complex problem.

Multiple Project Environment

Since project management is the usual situation in R&D, most procedures for improving resource allocation have been tied to this type of organization. The project concept ties the allocation of money, machines, and men to the accomplishment of one specific task, and each task has its own objectives of a completion date and expected results.

One dynamic approach is to break down a project into its various parts, or activities, and to associate resource requirements with each activity. PERT, CPM, and other similar systems are used to show the relationship between activities in a time continuum and have become key tools used to implement this approach. Another approach is to consider the total resources needed to complete a project as a static requirement. Here management must solve the traditional decision theory problem of selecting a mix of projects to yield the highest expected total value. A more rudimentary view of the situation that actually exists in R&D work is that numerous projects and activities within each project compete simultaneously for a common pool of resources, as illustrated in Figure 7.1. This then will serve as the basis for the methodology that follows.

Factors to Consider in Model Design

Economic factors involved in resource allocation may be clearly defined and evaluated in the light of competition for resources to perform work. Our objective, then, is a practical procedure for obtaining these economic factors and utilizing them in an allocation model. We will concentrate on three economic factors that have a particular bearing on the allocation of resources among multiple projects. They are opportunity costs, saturation costs, and inefficiency costs.

The first major problem is the evaluation of opportunity costs for individual resources or projects. Value is by its very nature a relative term. The question is always: what are the alternative opportunities in terms of cost, profit, product, and so on, for whatever item is being evaluated. The alternatives must be measured in relation to future opportunities, not past events. Clearly, there must be a way to measure the future cost incurred or the profit received from one alternative against those which would have occurred under another course of action or inaction.

The importance and impact of the study of opportunity costs are stated well by Miller and Starr: "A large number of important decision problems involve the allocation of resources to various activities in such a way as to maximize profit or to minimize costs. Typically, there are a number of things to be done and there are not sufficient resources available to do each of them in the most effective way. The decision problem, then, is to assign the things that must be done in a less-than-optimal way means that opportunity costs arise and suggests that one method for finding the best allocation would be to minimize these opportunity costs."[3]

For the second problem, the term "saturation function" is used to describe the nature of the input-output relationship in the application of resources. It resembles the analysis of the "production function" for economic problems in production, a subject often discussed under headings such as the law of variable proportions, or the law of diminishing returns.

An expression of the saturation function, therefore, could be $Y = f(X_1, X_2, X_3, \ldots, X_n)$, where Y refers to the specified output as a function of the various input resources specified and unspecified. The most elementary form of saturation analysis is the single factor-resource relationship expressed as $Y = f(X)$. However, since Y will be the result of combining the input resource X (e.g., men) with other factors (such as money, materials, management, etc.), the functional relationship may be expressed more appropriately as $Y - f(X_1/X_2, X_3 \ldots X_n)$. The slant bar indicates that the input resources to the right are regarded as fixed in the analysis, the resource to the left (X_1) as variable.[4]

It should be noted that for this study the input factors would be resources; the output factors may be project objectives, such as completion time, or other values, such as profits or penalties. Figure 7.3 presents several hypothetical saturation cost relationships. The one marked "Lateness Penalty" shows that in different situations the applications of resources can have drastically different cost results.

The third area to be covered, as we get deeper into the problem of constructing an allocation model, is inefficiency cost. We will often be dealing with three types, associated with productivity, availability, and utilization. These costs are directly linked to the individual activities of the projects and to the various levels of resources allocated to them. Let us briefly consider each of these inefficiency costs:

Productivity. One activity of a project may clearly be completed faster by the allocation of additional resources. However, as these

[3] Miller, D. W., and Starr, M. K., *Executive Decisions and Operations Research.* Englewood Cliffs, N.J.: Prentice-Hall, 1960, p. 400. A similar discussion is presented by Churchman, C. W., *Prediction and Optimal Decision.* Englewood Cliffs, N.J.: Prentice-Hall, 1961, p. 332.
[4] A full discussion of this can be found in Spencer, M. H., and Siegelman, L., *Managerial Economics.* Homewood: Richard D. Irwin, Inc., 1964, pp. 258–59.

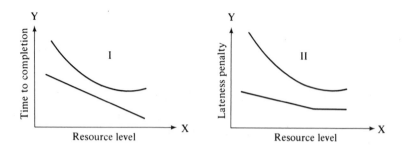

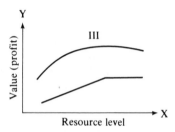

Figure 7.3   Project on Activity Saturation Cost Relationship

additional resources are applied, a proportionate advantage is not always attained. For example, if it is determined that four economists can perform a specified study in eight weeks, it should not be assumed that eight economists could perform the same study in four weeks. Productivity cost is thus the additional cost incurred when the addition of resources does not produce a proportionate increase in productivity. Good estimates of these costs can assist management in making many important resource allocation decisions that seem obvious but have hidden problems.

Availability. When additional resources are allocated simultaneously to numerous activities (to decrease project completion times), unit resource costs will usually go up because of the additional demand. These higher costs can be expressed as premium or overtime charges. Too often, these costs are not accurately computed in advance; this makes it impossible for management to manipulate the allocations of resources to reduce total project costs.

Utilization. This cost relates to the level of resource allocation for each activity and the worth of increments of allocation. The addition of resources to an activity often results in only partial usage or even total idleness of these resources. For example, to increase equipment testing effectively may require two additional engineers to be assigned to a project. If only one were assigned, little additional contribution may be made. On the other hand, if three men were assigned, one may really be idle and costs unnecessarily increased.

Development of the Model

"For the solution of most important business problems, four things are required: models, concepts, analytical process, and data."[5] In general, this statement is an accurate guide. The remainder of this chapter will show how various factors can be brought together for an effective resource allocation system. Particular emphasis will be placed on the comparatively new techniques for defining work by activities with resource requirements in a time continuum. While the discussion will be essentially an overview, sources of detailed information on specific techniques are listed in the footnotes.

Directed Graphs

The identification of individual work tasks (activities) and the time dependencies of activities can be combined to form what is called a directed graph or network. The general idea can be stated as follows: "While certain activities are independent of one another, there will, in general, be certain essential dependencies, with respect to time, which take this form: Activity a_1 must be completed before activity a_j can be initiated. If all such time dependencies are given, they can be conveniently summarized by a directed graph. Each arc represents one activity, and each vertex is called an event and represents a point in time."[6]

Numerous management techniques such as CPM, PERT, and RAMPS use the directed graph or network for analysis and data representation.[7] The network serves as a useful tool for management at all

[5] Koontz, Harold (ed.), *Toward A Unified Theory of Management.* New York: McGraw-Hill Book Company, 1963, p. 176.
[6] Busacher, R. G., and Saaty, T. L., *Finite Graphs and Networks: An Introduction with Applications.* New York: McGraw-Hill Book Company, 1965, p. 129.
[7] Stilian, G. N., et al., *PERT: A New Management Planning and Control Technique.* New York: American Management Association, 1962, p. 61.

levels and provides a comprehensive and intelligible display or work organization in a time continuum.

While network analysis was originally developed for large programs, it can be used as a simple and effective business technique where operations are on a smaller scale. The great value of network analysis is that it permits the selection of different routes to pursue, together with some estimate of the future hazards. In a multiple project environment, the network is an instrument for representing one project, but the total allocation system would consider multiple projects and thus many networks.

Critical Path Computation

In the ideal network of activities and events, each activity consumes a known and constant amount of time. In practice, the activity duration will frequently vary and could be governed by a probability distribution. The sum of the activity times along a particular path through the network represents the total time consumed by that path for project completion (Figure 7.4). The longest path (in terms of time) from the starting event of the project to its concluding event is the critical path, and its duration is the minimum time needed to complete the entire project.

For management planning the most important activities are those one or more critical paths, since any problems arising from them will hold up the whole project. The noncritical activities in the network have scheduling flexibility. The extent of this flexibility is called activity slack time. Critical path computation can be performed manually for networks of up to a few hundred activities and can be calculated efficiently for networks of practically any size by small computers.[8, 9]

Project Value Functions

Associated with each project is an objective completion time which will be used for the computation of an adjusted activity slack, to establish activity importance. In addition, a project value function must be given to provide a relative worth between projects. The value function may represent the return for completing a project, such as the

[8] Miller, R. W., "How to Plan and Control with PERT," *Harvard Business Review,* March–April 1962.
[9] Hansen, B. J., *Practical PERT, Including Critical Path Method.* Washington, American House, 1964.

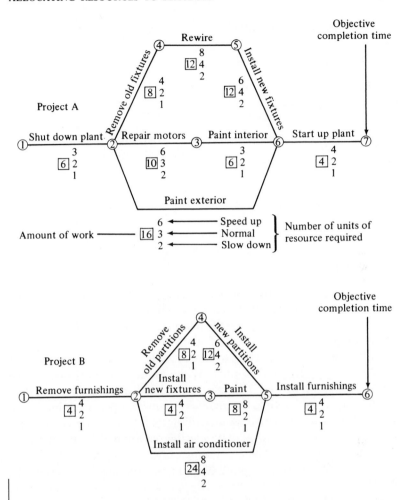

Figure 7.4 Multiple Project Concept, with Estimated Amount of Work, Alternate Resource Levels, and Completion Time

present worth of the chain of annual profits. It could represent the contractual penalty to be incurred in the event of project slippages (Figure 7.5).

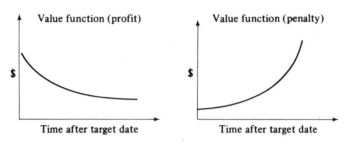

Figure 7.5   Project Value Functions

Basics of Allocation

As just explained, activity scheduling flexibility in the time continuum is represented by slack. When slack is combined with the project value function, it constitutes a guide for major decisions on resource allocations. In general, the amount of work for an activity is derived by multiplying the number of unit time periods required to complete an activity under normal conditions by the number of units of resource applied per time period. The unit time period may be an hour, day, month, or any unit of time that defines the smallest period within which work will be scheduled and resources allocated. In networks the amount of time required for any activity can be determined by dividing the resources assigned into the amount of work.

To provide for the possibility of doing the job faster or slower than normal, alternate levels of resource application can be provided. The first may be a resource level under accelerated work conditions (speedup); the second may be a resource level under relaxed or extended work conditions (slowdown). The work efficiency at other than the normal rate is introduced to account for the absence of precise linear relationships. Figure 7.6 shows examples of alternate resource levels.

The levels of resource utilization provide great flexibility in manipulating the time and resource requirements of each activity to meet resource availability levels. The same flexibility extends from the activity concept to the project concept where the speedup, normal, and slowdown rates allow the system to adjust work accomplishment rates to meet project completion deadlines.

As shown in Figure 7.6, project A could be completed in as few as 9 time periods at the speedup rate, or as many as 32 time periods at the slowdown rate. At the normal rate, the project could be completed

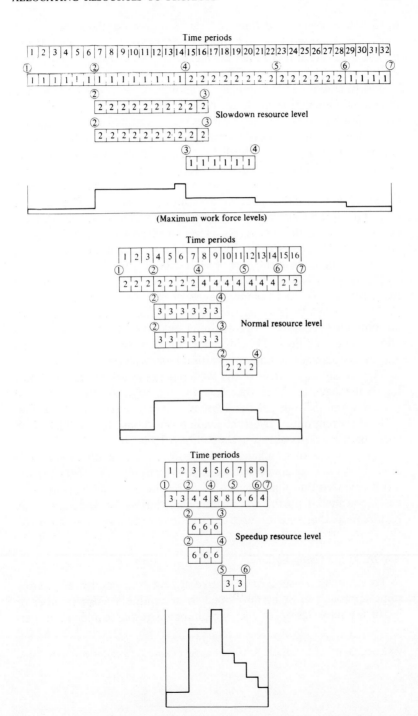

Figure 7.6   Effect of Resource Levels on Project Completion Time

in 16 time periods. Note that each rate requires a different peak work force. The total work force required reaches peaks of 20 men during period 5 at speedup, 10 men during period 8 at normal, and 6 men during period 15 at slowdown rates.

The time required to complete an activity is determined by the level of resource allocation made to the activity. Examination of possible combinations for allocating resources in an extremely limited situation shows the complexity of the over-all problem and brings into focus this statement by Karger and Murdick: "The need for better ways of allocating resources in research and engineering projects has grown as these projects have become more complex and costly. For defense contracts, time is often the most critical factor—not the dollar cost. The manager of a large project today must be able to follow rapid changes in progress, costs, schedules, delivery dates, etc., in order to guide an 'army' of engineers and scientists towards successful completion of the project. Intuition is helpless in the face of such complexity."[10]

Going on to Table 7.1, we have a single activity with an amount of work equal to six and resource levels of one, two, or three, with six time periods available for accomplishment. The amount of work must be completed accurately. In this simple example there are seventy-one allocation possibilities. This illustrates the complexity of the problem and the inadequacy of human intuition in solving the problem.

The remaining element of the system is the resource pool. At some higher management level, specifications will be set for the quantity of resources and the time periods available. In most cases, normal availability and premium or overtime availability should be provided. And corresponding costs of resources will be calculated.

For purposes of simplicity of discussion and of analysis, only one type of resource is being discussed here even though in a real situation it is recognized that numerous types of resources would be simultaneously considered during the resource allocation. Each activity may require more than one resource or, in other words, a team of resources.

Adding Value Computations

To establish a useful quantitative system for resource allocation, some approach must be developed to determine a value number or factor for activities or for each simultaneous resource allocation. Per-

---

[10] Karger, D. W., and Murdick, R. G., *Managing Engineering and Research.* New York: The Industrial Press, 1963, p. 223.

Table 7.1   Form for Time Allocation of Amount of Work

Resource Level	Allocation						Possible Combinations
	Time Periods						
	1	2	3	4	5	6	
1	1	1	1	1	1	1	1
2	2	2	2				20
	2	2		2			
	2	2			2		
	.	.	.				
	.	.	.				
	2		2	2			
	2		2		2		
	.		.	.			
	.		.	.			
3	3	3					15
	3		3				
	.	.	.				
	.	.	.				
1 and 2	1	1	2	2			17
	1	1	2		2		
	.	.	.		.		
	.	.	.			.	
1 and 3	1	1	1	3			18
	.	.	.	.	.		
	.	.	.		.	.	
					Total	71	

Resource Allocation Combinations For One Activity

haps the most practical approach is to equate each factor to a dollar figure so that comparisons can easily be made between the project objective values.

One computational approach would be to consider all activities eligible during one time period in a combined manner, perform a resource allocation, and evaluate the allocation based on criteria such as network parameters plus resource availability data. Another approach would be to evaluate each individual activity during the time period in terms of the same criteria, and allocate resources according to these activity values. Figure 7.7 shows examples of combined and individual evaluations. Advantages and disadvantages exist for each method, but the second approach will be used in this discussion.

Four resource allocation criteria will be briefly discussed; they are work continuity, number of activities, look ahead, and activity slack. The purpose of the work continuity criterion is to assure that activities are not interrupted. Certain activities may, for example, have high start-up costs; others might involve work on perishable goods which would be ruined if work were interrupted. An interruption penalty

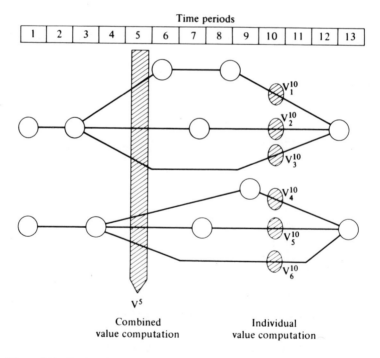

Figure 7.7   Evaluation of All Eligible Activities Combined versus Evaluation of Individual Activities

function could be specified for the activities, with the start-up cost and cost per time period of interruption given for inclusion in the computation of the activity value.

The purpose of the number of activities criterion is to allow widespread work at the expense of fast project completion. Its result is to use slowdown levels of resources or to spread resources thinly over many activities. A possible value statement of this criterion would be to give added value to the activity slowdown level.

The look-ahead criterion is an attempt to provide short-range protection against working into a bottleneck. The value determination should be based upon the resource demands contingent upon completion of the activity. For example, priority should be given to an activity upon whose completion heavy resource demands are waiting.

The slack criterion is intended to give value to allocating resources to those activities with smaller or no slack, thus assisting in reducing project delays. The value of the slack criterion may be directly related to the objective completion time and project value. Resource allocations would be made at any cost up to the corresponding project value, because an over-all saving would be possible within the described value framework.

All of these criteria are based on general management objectives, so that resource allocation may vary among situations and could even change during the initial proposal time span of the allocation to a specific project. They could be applied in combinations or as relative weights so that the final value computation would reflect management objectives. Management objectives may range from project completion at the earliest possible time to minimization of costs or minimum idleness of resources.

Methods for Model Solution

Several approaches could be proposed for determining the "best" resource allocation, but each method would have its own practical limitations. No attempt will be made here to present an exhaustive survey of possible methods or to evaluate the worth of all the methods. Only a few of the most universally useful approaches will be presented.

In most complex situations mathematical programming is the best approach. The situation is well and briefly put by Ackoff: "Mathematical programming refers to techniques for solving a general class of optimization problems dealing with the interaction of many variables, subject to a set of restraining conditions. Such problems are called allocation problems and arise when: a) There are a number of activities to be performed and there are alternative ways of doing them, and b) Resources or facilities are not available for performing each activity in the most effective way. The allocation problem, then, is to combine activities and resources in such a way as to maximize over-all effectiveness." [11]

The most important mathematical programming technique from an actual application standpoint has been linear programming, which can be described as follows: "When linear input-output relationships are assumed, together with a linear objective, e.g. profit or cost function, optimization involves solving a linear-programming problem. The assumptions of linearity for the constraint sets are frequently justifiable in practice." [12]

To formulate the LP model for a single time period and single project, it is necessary to define these factors:

a_{ij} = the number of resource units required to perform one unit of work on activity j where $j = 1, \ldots, n, i = 1$ for normal resources, and $i = 2$ for premium resources;

x_j = the specified amount of work to be performed on activity j with a lower boundary being the minimum work, upper boundary being the maximum work and where $j = 1, \ldots, n$;

c_j = the activity value as computed from previously defined criteria where $j = 1, \ldots, n$; and

b_i = the constraint on units of resource i available.

It is the purpose of the LP problem to allocate work x_j such that resource constraints are not exceeded:

$$\sum_{j=1}^{n} a_{ij} x_j b_i, \, i = 1, \ldots, n.$$

The lower and upper bounds on work performed must be satisfied, and the activity value function is maximized:

$$\sum_{j=1}^{n} c_j x_j \text{ (maximum)}.$$

[11] Ackoff, R. L. (ed), *Progress in Operations Research*. New York: John Wiley & Sons, 1961, p. 109.
[12] Saaty, T. L., *Mathematical Methods of Operations Research*. New York: McGraw-Hill Book Company, 1959, p. 165.

A broader model for multiperiod and multiple projects can also be formulated with additional considerations included. To facilitate the presentation, matrix notation is adopted. These factors are defined:

$A^t = (a_{ij})^t$ = the resource units required to perform one unit of work for time period t, $i = 1$ and 2, $j = 1, \ldots, n$;

$c^t = (c_j)^t$ = the activity value function for time period t;

$b^t = (b_i)^t$ = the constraint on units of resource i during time period t;

$x^t = (x_j)^t$ = the amount of work for activity j in time period t. Upper and lower bounds are specified for all time periods; and

$y^t = (y_j)^t$ = the amount of work on activity j carried over from period t to period $t + 1$.

The LP problem is to allocate work for all time periods x^t, $t = 1$, ..., T while observing resource constraints and such that the value function is maximum.[13] Figure 7.8 shows the LP table for this multi-period and multiple-project model without the upper and lower bounds on the variables.

Frequently, however, mathematical formulations of real work problems are not feasible. The solution of the mathematical statement may not be possible, may be expensive, or too time-consuming to be practical. Under such circumstances other approaches, such as heuristics, may be used to obtain problem solutions.

When applied to production problems, heuristic techniques lead to solutions by trying common-sense rules and procedures rather than setting up rigorous criteria. Heuristic results are usually not optimal; but, since optimal solutions are very difficult or impossible to find in some problems, heuristic solutions are very useful. "The strict definition of heuristics is literally that it 'serves to find out and encourages further investigation.'"[14]

A common sense set of rules and procedures could be developed for the resource allocation problem outlined. One simple procedure

[13] See Dantzig, George B., *Linear Programming and Extensions*. Princeton: Princeton University Press, 1963, pp. 55–60 for more information on the formulation of dynamic LP problems. Included are sample formulations of a single warehousing problem and on-the-job training problem. It is also noted that the size of the LP problem becomes large for dynamic situations.

[14] Bock, R. H., and Holstein, W. K., *Production Planning and Control*. Columbus: Charles E. Merrill Books, 1963, p. 12.

C^1		C^2		•		•		•		C^T	= z(max.)
X^1	Y^1	X^2	Y^2	X^3	•	•	•	•	•	Y^{T-1} X^T	
A^1											$= b^1$
$-I$	I	A^2									$= b^2$
		$-I$	I	A^3							$= b^3$
					•						•
						•					•
							•				•
										$-I$ I A^T	$= b^T$

Figure 7.8   Matrix for Multiperiod and Multiple Project Allocation

might be to start with the first time period and allocate available resources to activities at normal levels, beginning with the activity having the highest value, as computed by criteria described earlier, and then proceeding to each lower valued activity in turn. The full procedure would be to go on to the next time period, apply the same rule, and continue until all projects have been completed.

This method can be beefed up by adding more sophisticated allocation rules. Logic could be included concerning the application of speedup or slowdown resource levels to provide additional responsiveness to important management objectives. Rules could be included to consider the actual values of interrupting activities or for computing the value of allocating premium resources to shorten project durations. The rules could be refined to include logical or mathematical functions utilizing the activity values obtained.

Applications of the Model

This section will present procedures for applying the allocation of resources technique among multiple projects. The key point in this effort is that alternative management strategies may be inaccurately evaluated if resource constraints and costs are not taken into account accurately. For example, some strategies may require more resources than are available, or they may use premium resources extensively without proper consideration of the costs involved. Inaccuracies in allocations are prone to occur in complex situations, such as in the dynamic multiple-project environment of large R&D laboratories, or because human intuition is inadequate for simultaneous consideration of a series of multidimensional interactions. Therefore, the analysis in this chapter assumes the availability of a computerized tool having the characteristics described earlier. Such a tool is capable of performing the analysis described here.

Since we are concerned with differences between allocations, the *degree* of optimality is not of major importance. Instead, the observance of resource constraints and costs are considered of major importance in determining the economic aspects to be considered. In the situation examined, the proper value functions are assumed to be known, resource costs are considered as known and constant, projects must be defined, and project management objectives are considered definable within established criteria.

For example, if the aim of a decision maker is to maximize cash on hand at the end of a specified period, then a simple meaning can be given to the "best" action for him to adopt. No value considerations would be involved in the problem, even though the methods of finding an optimal decision under such circumstances may be difficult. However, no business firm tries solely to maximize cash at a specific moment in time. Instead, firms are often said to maximize profits or return on investment; but there is no clear way of defining those concepts that will satisfy the requirements of value measurements. The argument for this view is that in most cases we cannot define adequately the time over which profits are calculated. Opportunity costs are usually not included.[15]

Numerous presentations are available concerning the economic importance of opportunity costs, but their inclusion in practical economic analysis is rarely documented.[16] Where theory does exist, it can never be exactly applied in practice because we will always lack precise measurement of the future value of many activities.

For our purposes, the measurement of future value can be accomplished by finding expected future costs from resource consumption and by finding expected revenue from project value functions combined with the computed completion time of the projects.

One of the most important factors to consider is opportunity costs

[15] Churchman, C. W., *Prediction and Optimal Decision*. Englewood Cliffs, N.J.: Prentice-Hall, 1961, p. 50.
[16] Dean, J., *Managerial Economics*. Englewood Cliffs, N.J.: Prentice-Hall, 1951, p. 122; Spencer, M. H., and Siegelman, L., *Managerial Economics*. Homewood: Richard D. Irwin, Inc., 1964, p. 305.

for project or alternative strategies with many projects. To state a hypothetical problem: A manufacturer has four products developed and ready for marketing, each requiring major plant construction. A project is defined for building each plant, and a fixed pool of resources is available. The expected revenue function is known for each product. The decision problem then is to select the products to be introduced. Two strategies are possible; the resource allocation for each is contained in Table 7.2. The opportunity costs between strategies can be determined from the allocation data computed. For instance, the profit advantage of *B* over *A* is 3 million dollars. Thus, in this case, strategy *B* would clearly be the more desirable. In actual practice, of course, there would be many more strategies to consider, since there are many other possibilities for project mix.

Another major factor is the saturation function; here the discussion is based on an actual study,[17] which consisted of 22 projects representing facility installations with durations of 1 to 10 months. A time continuum of one year was used and 12 resource categories representing special skills and equipment were available. The primary objective of management was the continuous utilization of all resources. Penalties for late completion of projects were specified by contractual agreement or expected loss of revenue.

The most critical resource was selected for parametric study. The available amount of this resource was variable while that of all other resources was constant. Resource allocation was performed for each variation in the critical resource availability and the resultant total periods of project delay were recorded together with the total penalty. Figure 7.9 shows these figures and relates incremental increases in penalty cost to incremental changes in resource availability. By the same procedure, the saturation functions were determined for other resources and for sets of resources changed simultaneously. The output function for costs could also be found by accumulating normal and premium costs for the resources consumed.

The productivity cost for alternate resource levels for each activity can be computed before allocation by multiplying the resource cost by that incurred due to reduced productivity. Inefficiency costs can be computed by accumulating the additional costs for each activity for the actual allocations performed. The data could also be presented by activity so that projects, or portions of projects, with excessive loss in productivity can be identified.

[17] Performed jointly by the Detroit Edison Company and the author. Lloyd Coombe, Director of Research, Detroit Edison, served as coordinator. Values used in this paper are fictitious to protect confidential information.

Table 7.2 Opportunity Costs for Alternative Resource Allocation Strategies

| Project | Strategy A | | | | Strategy B | | | |
| | Completion Time (Months) | Cost | Revenue | Profit | Completion Time (Months) | Cost | Revenue | Profit |
		(Millions of Dollars)				(Millions of Dollars)		
I	6	50	55	5	5	60	64	4
II	7	40	44	4	6	38	42	4
III	9	30	36	6	–	–	–	–
IV	–	–	–	–	8	35	45	10
Totals		120	135	15		133	151	18

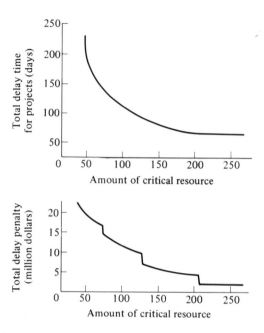

Figure 7.9 Project Performance Determined by Parametric Resource Allocation

Total availability costs can be computed for all projects by multiply-ing and accumulating the resource premium cost by the premium units used. These premium usage costs could also be computed for each time period for all projects. No information is available for identifying premium usage with individual projects or activities.

Finally, utilization costs for each activity prior to resource alloca-tion can be derived by computing the difference between the costs of performing an activity at the normal resource level and those at other resource levels. After the resource allocation is made, the actual utiliza-tion cost for each activity is the difference between the cost at resource levels assigned and that at normal levels.

Contributions to R&D Management

The planning of R&D activities can be improved by the use of any of the techniques discussed, since all of them require a manager to quantify work requirements and arrange these requirements logically for the anticipated work program. Gantt charts and networking methods relate time and work and provide a beneficial cost framework. However, there is a potential problem area: Without careful evaluation, results can also be misleading, since test facilities and other critical resources may be scheduled for simultaneous use by numerous other projects. Further, management may be carried away by apparent ways to compress schedules in the time continuum and will naturally plan accordingly—without due regard to other factors.

The truth is most R&D work contains a large element of uncertainty and the lead times needed to start and stop projects make it necessary to consider the availability of critical resources carefully. The rapid changes that often occur in the technologies in use also make it necessary to have a quick and accurate method for the reallocation of resource utilization. For these reasons, a system that explicitly represents resources in a dynamic work environment is essential for adequate planning. While participation in such a system by all levels of management is important, one central group without responsibility for work accomplishment may often be the best way to perform the computation and coordination involved in work planning and scheduling.

There remains another level of consideration of the allocation models presented here. In many cases, corporate organization has been disrupted by the advancement of quantitative methodologies. For instance, using these techniques usually means crossing previously well-established organizational lines. Staff people also gain new control, importance, and information. Interfaces of work between organizational groups are explicitly located and all of management is given an overview of various operations. When schedules are not met, responsibility can be pinpointed. These results may be good, but they do cause problems. Managers may be reluctant to cooperate in the implementation of new quantitative methods.

But if these obstacles can be overcome, it is possible to create an organization in which a central master scheduling group benefits all levels of management. This group can assist the functional managers (operational management) in scheduling and utilizing resources under their control and can prevent false placement of responsibility for poor performance. The most satisfactory way to achieve this goal is usually to set up an organization something like that shown in Figure 7.10. The master scheduling staff should work with top management and functional managers on planning, and with functional managers in work scheduling and control. It should be emphasized that the master scheduling group is a staff organization that *assists* management in scheduling, controlling, and planning.

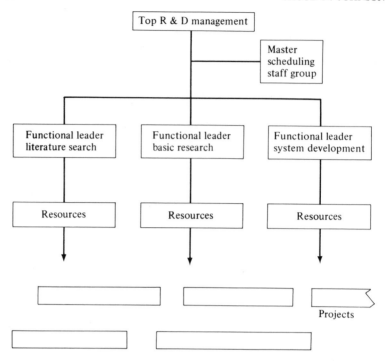

Figure 7.10   Functionally Phased Organization with Master Scheduling

Improved control has been a valuable result of the techniques discussed. They allow work measurement to be associated with specific identifiers, such as a network activity or bars of a Gantt chart. Milestones can be located and periodic evaluations are made possible. But used alone, those networks and Gantt charts are geared to after-the-fact decisions rather than a real-time or predictive approach. Overcontrol may be a danger since the principal consideration is time control rather than resource control.

The functionally phased organization supported by a resource allocation model can help overcome these drawbacks. It helps bring the time continuum into view by its determinants—resource consumption and work accomplishment. Despite the difficulty of measuring work accomplishment in R&D, the relationship between progress and resource usage seems to be more accurate than the relationship between progress and elapsed time.

8
Estimating Funding Levels

Raymond S. Isenson

"Our hindsight is better than our foresight by a darnsight." Anon.

Few matters can be more perplexing to management, whether government or private, than establishing the over-all size of a research program in science and technology. Despite this fact, the available literature offers little or no guidance for setting up a total R&D budget. In the other chapters of this book we have usually assumed that the total budget available to the planner had been established by some higher authority, and we then proceeded to discuss the resource-allocation task. The intent of this assumption was not to beg the question but to clearly differentiate between the two problems involved, establishing resource level and allocating resources, where the planning technique did not inherently address both matters as a joint or common problem. The primary exception was described in Chapter 3. There the application of marginal utility concepts to planning and resource allocation was addressed, and the two planning jobs became intertwined.

The present chapter considers the establishment of an over-all level for a research program. The objective is to demonstrate that a meaningful, analytical approach can be taken, that identifiable and measurable guides are available to the planner who wishes to avail himself of them.

The value of being able to define and justify a level of expenditure for an organization's research budget analytically is self-evident when one considers the stakes involved. The U.S. budget alone included about $5.2 billion in 1966 for federally funded basic and applied research.[1] In addition, the private sector, while actually performing the major portion of the research for the federal government, furnished some $2.3 billion from its own resources. In some industries, up to 3% of net sales went into the R&D effort. Thus, from the point of view of the federal government, approximately 6 to 7% of its total budget has been involved in research; for industry, a very significant portion of its profit margin has been invested.

Research in science and technology is undertaken by a corporation or, in the case of government, by an agency in order to satisfy some other objective of the organization. On the surface this would appear to be a childishly self-evident statement. Yet too often this fact is ignored as the underlying guide to establishing the R&D budget. The important thing is a recognition that research is not in general an end unto itself. Accepting this fact makes it necessary to consider how research results can be expected to affect the product line or services offered, and how these products and services will interact with the market. Knowing the demands that will be made on the market place and having some understanding of the amount of research requisite to satisfying these demands, the planner can establish his research budget. At least, he can be in a position to propose various budgets to top management and define the likely advantages and disadvantages of each.

The importance of having succinctly stated corporate objectives as inputs to the planning processes has been stressed repeatedly in the preceding chapters. Nowhere is the requirement for such statements more important than for the task of developing the over-all research budget. In fact, for this purpose perhaps more than for any other purpose, a very complete understanding of all short- and long-range corporate objectives is self-evident and there is a good likelihood that these goals will be readily recognized and made available to the planner.

It is for the longer time frame that the greater risk exists of overlooking objectives or underestimating the magnitude of the requirements imposed by these objectives. For example, larger organizations, trade groups, and federal agencies will find it necessary to fund graduate research in the universities merely to insure future availability of the proper number and kind of trained scientists. Although it can be argued that such training is more properly a personnel than a research function, the costs are true research costs, and management is given a

[1] "Federal Funds for Research, Development, and Other Scientific Activities; Fiscal Years 1966, 1967, and 1968." National Science Foundation, NSF 67-19, 1967, p. 4.

more realistic picture of the organizational expense structure when this training is reflected as a cost of the research program.

As a further example, capital equipment costs and facility costs associated with research along with the lead times required for their acquisition have increased rapidly through the years. In many cases it will be desirable to anticipate and fund for these expensive, long-lead-time items in a way that avoids overstressing the new capital-acquisition capability of the organization. These funds, too, are properly a cost of research. In the subsequent discussions it will be assumed that the planner is aware of all his organizational objectives and, in one way or another, accounts for them in his derived budgetary estimate.

Budgetary Bounds for the Corporation

In parallel with over-all corporate strategy and objectives, as well as the strictly technical factors involved, there are significant socio-economic factors outside of the organization that act as constraints on the size of an effective research effort. Frequently it will be these outside considerations, vague and hard to pin down though they may be, that will dictate the optimal budget level. Invariably they will dictate what should constitute the upper and lower bounds of the budget.

Whether one chooses to picture the interface between the organization and the market place in terms of classical economic theory or adopts a more Keynesian approach, to say nothing of Galbraith's [2] ideas on the New Industrial State, certain basic facts are clear. If the corporation invests too heavily in research, whatever "too heavily" may mean, and continues to do so over an extended period of time, this inefficiency will be reflected in lowered economic strength of the organization. Conversely, if the research investment, is, and remains, too low, eventual product or manufacturing process obsolescence will place the organization in a noncompetitive position. Many factors that are exogenous to the corporation will define "too high" and "too low." Thus, such measurable factors as the corporate gross sales or profit levels, important as they may be to management, cannot dictate the upper or lower bounds on the research program if the initially stated objectives of the organization are to be met. Of course, and this may frequently be necessary, corporate objectives may be lowered or

[2] Galbraith, J. K., *The New Industrial State*. Boston: Houghton Mifflin and Co., 1967.

eliminated in order to keep the requisite research program within the limits of the resources available.

If the assumption is made that the technical direction of the research program is adequate, it follows that the entire effort will be directed toward improvements in the corporate product lines, in preparation for new product lines, or toward greater efficiency in the manufacturing processes with which the organization is concerned. Then, in general, the existence of too expensive a research program will show up in either or both of two ways: The results of the research program will offer a high redundancy in solutions to the scientific and technical problems of the organization, all of which must be paid for but only a portion of which can be used. Or, if the research program is excessive but so directed that redundant solutions are kept to a minimum, other manifestations are observable. One, the organization is in a technological position to manufacture products that in number of types exceed the resource-dictated ability of the manufacturing arm or, two, it is technologically able to manufacture a product that is far different from or far ahead of functionally comparable products more familiar in the market place.

Where there ensues a potential for a product line in excess of the other capabilities of the corporation, there of course arises the possibility that patents may be obtained and sold. History suggests that such an escape is not likely to be particularly successful. In the other event, where the research program is so successful as to result in products that are markedly superior to and somewhat different in appearance or somewhat more expensive than functionally similar competitive products, the lessons of history are even more emphatic. The corporation will almost invariably find itself involved in a most expensive educational program, the cost of which, in a circular way, further increases the break-even selling price of the product, thus decreasing its marketplace desirability. As an aside, for this reason, particularly in those technological fields in which patent protection is of limited value, a corporate policy of "being second" is frequently observed, generally successful, and not to be disdained. At any rate, in any of these situations the existence of an inordinately high research budget and expenditure is (after the fact) obvious. More important, the examples demonstrate that even with otherwise good management the corporation can suffer from too great a research effort; the concept of an externally dictated upper bound for the research budget is a real and a meaningful one.

In a similar vein, the concept of a lower bound is equally valid although its existence may be subject to a considerable amount of concealing camouflage. There is the simple situation in which the corporation chooses to undertake a research program that in reality is inadequate to satisfy the organizational objectives. The most likely result is the gradual obsolescence of the product line or of the manufacturing processes. In a less obvious situation, it is recognized that the organization has options other than direct support of research. For example, it can elect to forego its own investigations, later obtaining patent rights or making license agreements to acquire needed new technology. Similarly, it can rely upon its vendors and suppliers to furnish the requisite advanced technology. In any event, the corporation that chooses to avoid direct research support is still going to pay for research, but here the payment will be indirect. It will be included in the prices paid to its vendors or stipulated in the contracts for licenses or patents. The matter of whether such an indirect method for the support of a research objective is more or less expensive than conducting one's own research is outside the scope of this discussion. The important matter is the recognition that these indirect expenditures are just as real research costs as the salary going to the corporate laboratory director.

There is another class of hidden research costs that only very infrequently is recognized as such. For example, at times the corporation that finds itself technologically obsolete will take recourse to an aggressive advertising program. The firm will try to convince the consumer that an older technology is better than the newer one offered by the competition. The widespread adoption of this tactic is readily appreciated when one thinks of the number of commercials lauding the virtues of "made by hand" and "every part carefully checked and assembled." Clearly this is a temporary solution. Eventually the consumer learns better, and the corporation is forced to pay for the new technology. It is unlikely that the deferred purchase of the new technology will result in lessening its direct cost to the corporation. Further, to the direct cost of the research results must be added the cost of the advertising that allowed the corporation, for a limited period of time, to defer the former investment.

The costs of these various alternatives to an immediate, adequate research program and, in principle, the upper and lower limits of these estimates can be viewed as the range of the lower bounds of an equivalent research program. If the corporation drops below the lower limit, choosing to forego both an adequate research program and the effective alternatives, in the long run it can expect to lose its market through product obsolescence. If, in accord with the earlier discussion, it drastically exceeds the upper bounds over the years, the corporation can expect to be forced to bear inordinate costs. In the long run only an expenditure rate somewhere between these bounds will be commensurate with the satisfactory achievement of the corporate objectives.

The consequence of failing to establish a budget between these bounds cannot be escaped by following a feast-or-famine strategy that funds research heavily for one or several years and then drastically reduces the funding level for a period of time. The expectation that bursts of effort will satisfactorily replace an essentially constant level of effort is not likely to be realized. At best the total funds expended will be about the same as the more constant program would cost. In most cases, however, the costs of a widely swinging level of effort will exceed the more level program by a wide margin.

The most obvious weakness of a sporadic funding policy is that during periods of retrenchment technical people will either be released or will resign because of the paucity of available funds. Then, when funds again become available, the corporation will be faced with an expensive recruiting task. Further, when the corporation develops a reputation among professional people of having an unstable research program, the better scientists and engineers can be expected to spurn employment opportunities offered. Those who do accept employment will normally insist on a higher-than-average wage as compensation for the risk of early termination. Then there is an added factor that may turn out to be far more damaging than merely increased costs, a factor that was vividly demonstrated by a research management study of the Department of Defense, Project HINDSIGHT.[3]

In examining the personal histories of scientists and engineers who had contributed most heavily to the new technology of use to the Department, the employment stability of these individuals stood out as a most significant factor. Moreover, it was found that the most effective scientist or engineer—in terms of the probability that he will come up with something that will be profitable to the organization—is one who has been in the company for a number of years. The modal point on the distribution curve displaying length of employment against probability of making a useful contribution occurs at between

[3] Final Report, PROJECT HINDSIGHT, Director of Defense Engineering, Washington, July 1967.

seven and nine years of employment. Clearly, if the professional turn-over rate exceeds 10% to 15% per year, it will be most unlikely that the peak performance of the laboratory will ever be achieved.

Budgetary Bounds for Government

The concept of an optimum funding level for research in science and technology is as valid for the mission-oriented departments and agencies of a federal government as it is for a private corporation. However, the factors defining the upper and lower bounds differ from those in industry. In the general sense, the price-oriented market place does not exist as an unforgiving taskmaster. In its stead, however, there are other very real constraints.

Research is supported by the federal government as a service to the people of the nation, in the hope that the results will serve the interests of that public: it may mean protection against disease, starvation, and threats of an enemy nation; or it may make available to the individual a more pleasant, intellectually stimulating life. In any case, the support of research must compete with other government services for a share of the tax dollar.

Because the power of the government to tax and the ability of the people to pay a tax are not unlimited, and because the services demanded tend to exceed what can be purchased with the tax dollar, there are allocation problems. Usually, one service is funded at a high level, at the expense of another that suffers a less than optimum level of support. In the short run, a government can underfund an activity or area of service without great difficulty. However, if a condition of unbalance continues too long, the government itself can be threatened. Consider the Watts riots and other civil disturbances for example. Many think they could have been avoided if social welfare activities had received some of the funds going into the space program or other federal activities.

If there are upper limits on R&D budgets because of other vital needs, there are also lower limits. The existence of this lower boundary is most evident in terms of military defense. Here, the research results of hostile nations provide a close analogy to the technological capabilities of a competitor in the industrial world. However, many of the options mentioned above still apply.

Certainly, smaller nations may be well advised to forego wide-ranging research programs, undertake only what they can readily afford, and buy their military technology from a major power. At times, even the largest nations may find it practical to buy certain research results rather than duplicate an accomplished research task.

Growth of Technology

In the preceding discussion the fact was demonstrated that the corporate or governmental research budget requisite to satisfying the organizational objectives would be, in the long run, bounded by factors exogenous to the organization. Additionally, certain examples were suggested of criteria that could be taken as manifestations that a previous research budget lay outside of or, by deduction, within these bounds. It is obvious that with hindsight one can judge the correctness of a previous budget. If it is found to have been clearly too high or too low, commensurate adjustments can be made to upcoming budgets.

Then, through a series of successive approximations over the years, an appropriate budget can be derived. There is no question that this can be done and, despite any other research-budget-establishing technique that is employed, should be done, at least as a check. However, it is an evaluation rather than a planning technique and is of little use in the absence of corporate or agency history or when an unusually dynamic situation is developing. In the latter cases and whenever else forward planning is required, consideration also must be given both to the nature of the growth of technology and to how the organization proposes to exploit advancing technology in order to satisfy established objectives.

One possible approach to the inclusion of these factors is presented in the following paragraphs. It is not suggested as the only or even the best one. However, it does take into account those considerations that appear to be fundamental to almost any research-budget-establishing technique that might be devised. In this light, independent of whether or not the planner chooses to accept for his purposes the details of the procedures, the attendant discussions will be of value. Much of the understanding upon which the technique is based was drawn from the findings of the Project HINDSIGHT study. Implementation of the planning technique involves the selection and manipulation of data made generally available in the National Science Foundation's publications on industrial R&D funding practices. The result is a suggested budgetary figure that can be expected to lie between the upper and lower bounds discussed previously. It should not be pictured as an absolute and final budgetary figure but a point of departure from which at least minor deviations can be made with some degree of relative safety.

To introduce the rationale for this technique, it is convenient to start with a discussion of some characteristics of the growth of technology. The primary objective of so doing is to demonstrate that the growth of science and technology is well described as a stochastic process.[4] In turn, the demonstration is essential, for it is this particular characteristic of growth that permits relatively abstract planning.

Without some reflection, it is unlikely that a stochastic process would be expected. This is true because the public fancy is usually caught by the epoch-making events in the growth of technology. The first demonstration of the transistorized radio, for example, far eclipsed all of the preceding advances in solid-state physics, metallurgy, crystallography, soldering and welding processes, etc. that made this advance possible. Nevertheless, these other, less glamorous, advances were part of the growth. They had to be made, had to be paid for, and more importantly, were accompanied by perhaps an even greater number of equally expensive but less productive scientific and technical investigation. In a completely qualitative sense, the foregoing sentences alone are enough to suggest the validity of the contention as to the stochastic nature of technological growth. For additional proof, recourse will be made to a somewhat more rigorous and quantitative demonstration.

A Quantitative Approach to Rate of Growth of Technology

Earlier literature[5] suggested, based upon purely philosophical derivations, that the rate of growth of knowledge in a scientific or technical field could be analytically described as

$$\frac{dK_i}{dt} = A{\cdot}p(c) \left(1 - \frac{K_{ia}}{K_{i\tau}} \right) N(t) \; [1 + bN(t)],$$

where

K_i refers to the state of knowledge in the ith field
A is a proportionality constant
$p(c)$ is the probability that a given investigator will make a significant contribution during the increment of time

[4] "Management Factors Affecting the Utilization of Research and Development Results." Springfield, Virginia: Arthur D. Little, Inc., Clearinghouse for Federal Scientific and Technical Information, AD-618 321, April 1965.
[5] "Technological Forecasting in Perspective," *Journal for the Institute of Management Sciences,* October 1966, pp. B70–83.

K_{ia} is the current level of the state of the art or state of knowledge in the ith field and thus the ratio $K_{ia}/K_{i\tau}$ describes the current relative state of knowledge

$N(t)$ describes the rate of growth in the number of scientists and engineers employed in the advancing of the ith and closely associated fields

b takes a value between 0 and $\frac{1}{2}$ as a function of the degree of freedom of communication among the involved scientists and engineers.

When originally developed, this model was presented as a means of describing the expected rates of growth in broad technical areas. It was intended as a tool for long-range technological forecasting at the higher levels of government. However, assuming that the model is also valid for near-term projections, its potential as a planning tool is evident. In this proposed role, in principle, the research manager, by manipulating factors affecting the parameters, could cause technology to advance at a rate of his choosing. Of the three variables that appear to be subject to some control—number of scientists, productivity of scientists, and level of communications—at least the first can be affected by changes in the research budget level. We have already noted that the second variable, productivity, is sensitive to stability of funding.

More important to the discussion at hand, however, is the fact that— again assuming short term validity of the model—it affords certain thoughts that are particularly germaine to the task of research-budget establishing. First, it states that the *potential* for growth of two or more sciences or technologies is equivalent if their current, relative states of knowledge are equivalent. Second, as already noted, it states that the expected rate of growth is proportional to the number of professionals employed in that field; which, in our society, is dependent in the end upon the interest of the consumer in that area. The manner in which use is made of these factors in the determination of the research budget level will be discussed later. Prior to that discussion attention must be given to a test of the short-term validity of the model. For this purpose recourse is made, once more, to findings of the previously named Department of Defense study.

In the study, twenty major items of new equipment were examined in order to identify recent scientific and technical advances that were clearly important to the operational effectiveness of the piece of equipment or to its relative cost effectiveness as compared to a predecessor equipment. In all, about 1000 significant discrete scientific and technical advances were identified. Some of these were found to be uniquely important to only one of the equipments studied; some, to two or more of the items. A separate investigation of each advance was undertaken in order to determine who had been the discoverers or inventors, what characteristics they had in common, who had funded the research, why the research had been undertaken, and similar information. Analysis of the collected information provided much of the understanding that is being made use of here.

Of the twenty equipments studied, ten had readily identifiable functionally similar predecessors. Included in these ten were such items as cargo aircraft, second-generation guided missiles, advanced computers, an artillery piece, and some conventional munitions. For each of these an "improvement factor," referenced to the predecessor item, was calculated to a first-order approximation. At the same time, note was made of the number of significant scientific and technical advances that appeared to be responsible for the assigned improvement factor and a measure was made of the relative sophistication of the predecessor. The criterion for the latter purposes was simply the cost per pound of the predecessor equipment, as delivered.

Returning to the analytical model for the growth of knowledge, we note that the factor relating rate of growth to current state of knowledge takes the form $1 - a/b$; that is, the first two terms of the expansion of $\exp(-a/b)$. This suggests that a logarithmic relationship will be found to exist between the number of advances identified in the HINDSIGHT study for each equipment and the "product improvement" factors that were calculated. In line with that suggestion, the data for the ten equipments were assembled and plotted as shown in Fig. 8.1.

The linearity of the distribution is of primary significance. Despite the fact that the identified advances were randomly distributed among 14 broad areas of science and technology, and despite the fact that the equipment studied included aircraft, missiles, computers, radar, some rather rudimentary artillery weapons, and high-sensitivity night-viewing devices, the plot seems sensibly ordered.

The parameters of the HINDSIGHT plot and those of the analytical model are not identical but they appear to be reasonably equivalent. For example: Each new contribution to science and technology is the result of the activity of people, and there is a clear, direct relationship between the number of scientific or technical advances (events) and the number of people involved. The normalized measure of product sophistication, dollars per pound, is a generally accepted approxima-

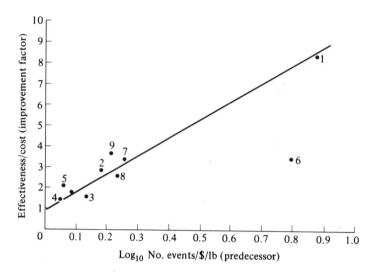

Figure 8.1   Relationship Between Improvement, Complexity, and Requirement for New Technology

tion and seems to be a reasonable analogue to the relative state of the art. Similarly, the product-improvement factor is philosophically comparable to an increased level of knowledge.

The remaining factors of the model—the probability that a given scientist will make a contribution during the time frame of interest and the communication factor—are not explicitly observable. We can note only that while they have not been demonstrably confirmed, they have not been denied. Fortunately, because they effect only the slope of the curve and not its shape, it is not important that they be validated.

The most significant finding is that the data do plot in a form suggesting a monotonically increasing equation, independent of the specific science or technology involved. This makes it possible to argue that one can determine the size of a corporate research budget without paying too much attention to the details of the research tasks to be undertaken.

The Roles of New Technology

Although most major corporations attempt to exploit new technological advances, there are great differences both among the corporations and frequently between the operating divisions of a given corporation in the manner in which it is used. At one extreme, there is little or no interest in changing the nature of the product. Science and technology are exploited primarily to improve manufacturing processes. The paper industry is a classic example of this situation. The intermediate consumer of the product, the printer or publisher, insists on a uniformity of product. He wants to be able to buy his paper stock from any of several manufacturers with confidence that he will not have to adjust presses or worry over the appearance of the printed product. Thus, the paper manufacturer is very limited in what he can do to his product. His opportunities for using improved technology are restricted to what can be done to processes; whether they be in the growing of the pulpwood, the processing of the pulp into paper stock, or the relative amount of hardwood pulp he can add to his mix and still meet the buyer's specifications.

Petroleum distillation plants for gasoline, fuels for engine and heating purposes, and lubricants are similarly limited. Here, again, the main thrust of the research program is toward process improvement, although some effort, particularly lubricant improvement, is directed at the end product. A similar situation obtains for most of the basic metal industries. In these cases, the length of time the product is essentially unchanged as a production-line item can often be measured in tens or even hundreds of years. However, in these industries, process life can be considerably shorter.

In other industries, of which the pharmaceutical is an excellent example, product-manufacturing lifetime can be quite short. With the exception of such staples as aspirin, the useful manufacturing life tends to be on the order of a few or possibly ten years. In advanced military equipment, a manufacturing lifetime of ten to fifteen years appears to be about average.

The food-processing industry is an example of one that is quite mixed, with some staple items unchanged for decades and others that fade fast as the public tastes change. Among relatively short-lived items, however, the processes involved tend to be quite unchanged, though products may seem drastically different.

Then we have the certain extremes, such as wood-furniture manufacturing that changes neither process nor product over long periods, or the electronics industry that shifts products and processes very rapidly. The recognition of differences in manufacturing lifetimes and process lifetimes not only makes clear that research budgets must vary widely among different types of manufacturing organizations, but also affords a key to specifying appropriate levels for each.

Planning Criteria

All of the preceding discussions lead to several conclusions. First, there is an optimum level at which research programs should be funded. For the corporation this level normally should be that amount necessary to maintain a slight lead over the competition. In a mission-oriented department or agency of the federal government, the competition might be a potential enemy, a crop disease, inadequate food production, or development of a cure for a virus. In industry the competition is industry. In at least the latter case, the "expected" rate of growth in the state of knowledge of those sciences and technologies upon which the corporate products and processes are based can be estimated. We have seen growth to be a function of the existing state of the art, the number of professionals involved in fostering its growth, and the freedom with which ideas are communicated within that group.

Second, the size of the research program needed to maintain a desired rate of growth is primarily a function of the existing state of the technologies of interest. The more complex and refined the product or process, the greater will be the effort required to achieve a constant rate of improvement. This of course doesn't necessarily mean that research budgets will continue to become greater and greater without end. It more likely means that rates of technological growth will slow down. In fact, some of the current talk about being on a "technological plateau" may be a manifestation of an implicit recognition of this phenomenon by the political segment of the nation. During the past few years there has been a leveling off of the total federal support for research and development (Fig. 8.2). Having seen that even a constant increase in the budget will not result in a constant rate of increase in "product improvement," the consequence of a leveling of the budget is, of course, obvious.

Third, the requisite research budget level is clearly a function of the product-manufacturing life or manufacturing-process life associated with the organization. This point leads directly to the further conclusion that the corporate or agency objectives must contain quantitative statements as to how soon a given product or product line is to be replaced or how soon a new manufacturing process is to be introduced. If the budget planner is allowed or required to introduce his own estimates regarding these factors and is not questioned by management in this regard, he, in fact, has implicitly established the corporate objectives.

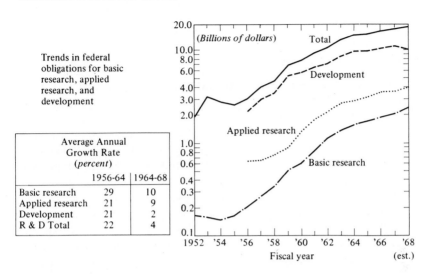

Trends in federal
obligations for basic
research, applied
research, and
development

Average Annual Growth Rate (*percent*)		
	1956-64	1964-68
Basic research	29	10
Applied research	21	9
Development	21	2
R & D Total	22	4

Source: National Science Foundation

Distribution of federal R & D obligations,
by character of work,
fiscal year 1967 (est.)

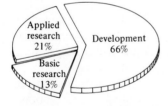

Percent distribution

Year	Research		Develop-ment
	Basic	Applied	
1956	7	22	71
1957	7	17	76
1958	7	16	76
1959	8	13	79
1960	8	18	74
1961	9	20	71
1962	11	21	68
1963	11	21	68
1964	11	20	69
1965	12	22	67
1966	12	22	66
(est.) { 1967	13	21	66
1968	14	24	62

Source: National Science Foundation

Figure 8.2   Federal Research, Development, and R&D Plant

The relationship between the second and third conclusions should
be obvious. The former provides a means for determining the effort
required to achieve a desired growth rate; the latter, for translating
corporate objective statements into terms of growth rate.

The Budget-Estimating Model

Having developed the major conceptual ideas, the next task is to array them into a form or a model. In turn, the model will be used to make the research budget estimates.

Fig. 8.3 shows the considerations and influences to be accounted for by the budget estimator. The flow is presented in an open-loop configuration, starting with the statements of corporate objectives and ending with the R&D budget. The obvious extension through research resource allocation, research performance, product design, manufacture, marketing, and a feedback path from marketing to new corporate objectives is deliberately not shown in order to avoid unnecessary confusion of the diagram. Additional feedback paths may exist. It is recognized, for example, that from time to time particularly exciting discoveries in the research laboratories may provide a direct feedback to corporate management, resulting in new objectives and impacting on the size of the research budget. Clearly, then, this is not a complete planning model but one designed to deal solely with the problem at hand, that of estimating the organization's research budget. Should the planner desire to expand the model so as to demonstrate the interfaces with other factors explicitly, the task is straightforward and relatively simple.

The organization's input to the model is its statements regarding corporate objectives. As already noted, it is essential that these objectives be stated in quantitative terms and that they contain indications as to when it is desired that the new product or service be marketable or when the new process is to be introduced; statements as to product or process lifetime of those currently in hand. The question arises, "Should the objectives also specify the degree of improvement required?" This is a good question and the answer warrants some discussion.

Earlier in this chapter we noted the danger attendant to attempts to introduce to the market a product that was too far in advance of competing items. In so doing, we implicitly acknowledged that a successful new product could be more or less advanced, relative to its predecessor, depending upon exactly how soon introduction to the market was to occur. Continuing in this vein: if the research budget and the program are maintained at a level that will keep the technological capability of the organization slightly ahead of that of the competition, it makes no difference when the new product is introduced. It will be slightly

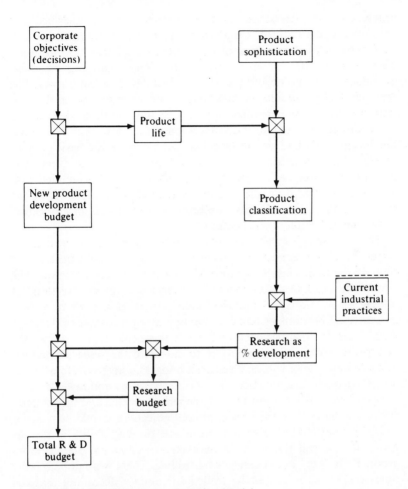

Figure 8.3   Research Budget Planning Model

better than another that is introduced simultaneously by a competing organization. Therefore, it follows that corporate management is in a position to specify the desired time of introduction without having to concern itself with what the state of the art will support at that time, in the full knowledge that its new product will more than likely represent the state of the art. It is not necessary to specify the degree of improvement desired. In fact, as will become apparent, this first planning procedure is not capable of treating with the situation in which the corporate objective specifies both time of release and degree of improvement. In a later section an alternative approach is described that does offer a potential for considering degree of improvement.

Returning to a discussion of the model, we see that the corporate objectives manifest themselves as decisions regarding product-manufacturing lifetime and the new product development budget. The research budget should be adequate to develop new scientific and technical ideas of the organization, to the point that these ideas can be incorporated into new product developments at low risk. Therefore, the development budget can be calculated solely on the basis of engineering time and material estimates for prototype fabrication. The decision regarding desired product manufacturing life is coupled with observations regarding the degree of relative sophistication of the current product line. This is purely a descriptive coupling resulting in a complex product classification.

The next step involves the determination of typical industrial research funding practices for products in the same sophistication/life class or the same classes as those of interest to the organization. The manner in which this is done will be described in the next section. At present we will note only that the funding practices so determined will be expressed in terms of research funding as a percentage of development. Then the planner need only apply this percentage factor to the new product-development budget to calculate the research budget. The resultant figure will be a research budget commensurate with the objectives of the organization and within the upper and lower bounds as described. If these resources are properly allocated and the research effort is well directed, the organizational objectives should be met.

If the total R&D budget is beyond the funding ability of the organization, it will probably be necessary to eliminate one or more products from the organization's future line. There is no potential for time stretch. Time cannot be traded for dollars. Recalling that the research budget was set so as to keep the corporation slightly ahead of the competition, it is obvious that any lower expenditure rate would result in a gradual falling behind in technological position.

Building a Data Base

At frequent intervals the National Science Foundation publishes tables of R&D funding practices of U.S. industry. These tables provide a primary information source to the research budget planner. From them he can develop quantitative estimates of the funding levels appropriate to his own organization. Because the tables are based on Census

Bureau surveys, the original sources of the data are disguised and a direct comparison between the planner's organization and a competitor is not possible. However, by analyzing the published data in terms of product sophistication and product manufacturing life or process life, the planner can develop his own keys to the tables. Table 8.1 lists the NSF product classification scheme.

Table 8.1   National Science Foundation Product Categories

Food and kindred products
Textiles and apparel
Lumber, wood products, and furniture
Chemicals and allied products
   Industrial chemicals
   Drugs and medicines
   Other chemicals
Petroleum refining and extraction
Rubber products
Stone, clay, and glass products
Primary metals
   Primary ferrous products
   Nonferrous and other metal products
Fabricated metal products
Machinery
Electrical equipment and communications
   Communications equipment and electronic components
   Other electrical equipment
Motor vehicles and other transportation equipment
Aircraft and missiles
Professional scientific instruments
   Scientific and mechanical measuring instruments
   Optical, surgical, photographic, and other instruments

Note was previously made that relative product sophistication could be measured in terms of dollars per pound. Although the concept may be surprising at first, a slight reflection on the common articles of manufacture encountered in daily life will offer quite convincing evidence for its general validity. With the primary exception of jewelry and objects of art, where the "value added" through manufacture comprises only a small part of the assessed worth of the item, the cost of manufacturing tends to vary directly with the relative sophistication or complexity of the item. Among items of such a nature that the measure holds generally true, there are still perturbations. One major cause for such perturbations is production quantity scales. Thus, although we would most likely agree that an automobile is technologically more sophisticated than, say, a small sailing boat, naive comparison made on the basis of dollars per pound would be contradictory. Clearly this cost-per-pound comparison basis does allow room for error. Nevertheless, it is believed that the planner can make the necessary adjustments to his collected data in order to work around this problem. Continuing with the same example, if it were found to be necessary to compare the two, one properly should think not of the mass-produced auto costing 2–3000 dollars but of the custom-fabricated vehicle that costs 18–20,000 dollars. In each case, then, he is looking at items with a more nearly common manufacturing and distribution approach.

Perhaps a more discomforting problem will arise from the difficulties in assessing a precise manufacturing cost. Despite the greatest pains in the cost-accounting department, the setting of an exact production cost is a virtual impossibility in most cases. Such matters as depreciation rates on capital equipment, allocation of general overhead expenses, the routine maintenance requirements for each piece of equipment, the cost of work stoppages caused by machinery breakdowns, combine to complicate the assessment. Despite the discomfiture that this problem may cause the planner, it is not particularly serious. At the very worst it will be necessary for him to estimate a spread in costs, an upper and lower limit, and then to see if these limiting cost figures will result in significantly different research budget estimates. In most cases they will not.

Unfortunately there are also difficulties in assessing precise product or process lifetimes. It is unusual to find a sudden change from one item to a completely different one with the same functional or use characteristics. Generally there is a gradual transition from one version of a product to another and it is only after a great number of changes that comparison between a currently manufactured model and a previous one is describable as a "complete change."

The same situation tends to be even more true for process lifetime. Automatic assembly may be replacing manual assembly; dip soldering may be replacing hand soldering; automatic control may be replacing an operator on a lathe—but what point in time is assessed as the transition point?

In practice a solution to this doubly described dilemma has been found. For both manufacturing life and process life the problem can be reduced by adopting the concept of "half-life," that is, the length of time at which about a 50% change has been introduced. Although philosophically this would appear to be no less difficult an assessment to make, experience shows that it is psychologically more acceptable to the engineering personnel upon whom the planner must call to make the judgments.

Circumventing these and similar real or imagined difficulties as best he may, the planner must extract as much of the National Science Foundation tables as apply to his purposes. The interesting portions of the tables, obviously, are those concerning products with sophistication and manufacturing lifetimes that closely match those of his organization's products. The results will constitute his planning data base. In the following section further attention is given to the details of this task.

The Planning Procedure

In accord with the planning concept proposed in this chapter, estimating the research budget consists of describing the "product line" of the organization in light of the criteria outlined above and then determining, with the help of the National Science Foundation tables, an appropriate funding level for each item in the line. A technique for accomplishing the job is presented here. One major digression from the previously presented model, a complicating digression, will be made. In this technique the assumption that a separate development budget has been previously developed will not be made. Thus, demonstration is made of how the total R&D budget can be estimated and then how it can be divided into the two major components. Obviously, where the development budget is "given," the research budget is calculated separately and added to the former for the total R&D budget; it is not taken from the development budget. With regard to the particular technique suggested, it is only one of many that are possible. Undoubtedly any other user of the general approach to research-budget estimating that has been described in this chapter will develop variations to satisfy his own situation better. The important thing to keep in mind is that whatever detailed technique he chooses to adopt, it must be based on logical and pragmatic grounds. Research and development budget planners may never be able to eliminate emotional considerations entirely, but this should remain as a cardinal target of their efforts.

The initial step in the planning procedure is to classify each of the products in the organization—whether the company's operating division, laboratory, agency, and so on—in terms of relative product sophistication, manufacturing half-life, and process half-life. At the same time the planner notes the dollar sales volume for each product—either current or projected.

Where a number of products have the same sophistication and half-life factors, they can be considered together and their dollar sales totaled. Where two products have one or two factors in common, but not all three, they must continue to be treated separately.

How closely must the factors agree before the products can be classed as "essentially the same"? It was noted earlier that despite the greatest of pains in the cost-accounting department, the listed production cost of an item is generally imprecise. Further, mass-production techniques and other economies of scale serve to deflate the calculated relative sophistication factor for the affected products. The planner must take the impact of these disturbances on his calculations into account; that is, estimate the error in his estimates. Where the difference between the factors associated with two or more products is less than the estimated error, the products can safely be held to be "essentially the same."

This apparently cavalier treatment in the groupings of products is permitted by the coexistence of two facts. First, the spectrum of possible sophistication factors across all classes of manufactured items is quite great. Among the less sophisticated products, such as writing paper or gasoline, values on the order of a few pennies per pound are found. At the other extreme, among items such as missile guidance systems, factors of hundreds of dollars per pound are not uncommon. Therefore, the spectrum of possible sophistication factors covers about three orders of magnitude. At the same time the portion of the total R&D budget that is apportioned to research in science and technology varies roughly between 3 and 60 per cent. Thus, a great deal of tolerance can be permitted in assessing of sophistication factors and the half-life factors.

Examination of the National Science Foundation data reveals that it is presented in tabular form, in accord with a significant number of variables. The particular tables of interest here are those labeled "Funds for R&D performance as percent of net sales in R&D-performing companies, by industry and size of company." In these tables the planner identifies those industries whose products are most similar to his classifications. Unfortunately, the first time the planner uses this procedure it will be necessary for him to assess technological sophistication factors and half-lives for each of the product categories listed, later rejecting those that have little comparability with his own. As we have seen, however, the required precision of these estimates is not too great. While different planners might be prone to stress one factor or another in generating their own corporate product categories, the factors should be as close as possible to those used in categorizing the NSF tables. Consistency in categorization tends to be more important than precision.

At this point in the process, the confidence the planner has in his estimates is likely to be low. The only answer is continued reevaluation of the sophistication and half-life factors. As the planner acquires additional relevant information and as he gains experience in the procedure, the accuracy of his estimates and the confidence he has in them will increase rapidly.

Using Comparative Data

Having gathered data on his organization and worked out a way of comparing it to national averages, what has the planner gained? Nothing less than an accurate insight into an R&D funding level that will help keep his organization ahead of competition. The point is, his organization's research expenditures must be in line with the spending of other organizations using either the same technologies or technologies of similar sophistication. The rationale was explained previously. Summarizing, it was noted that the rates of growth of technologies of equal sophistication were potentially equal. To this is added the recognition that in most cases technology tends to advance about as rapidly as the consumer is willing to accept the products of the advanced technology. Since this is a matter of buyer psychology rather than the nature of the technology, there is justification for believing that the accepted rate of growth for all technologies of common sophistication should be about the same. One can make a simple test of this assertion by noting how frequently his products of similar manufacturing half-life also have similar sophistication factors.

The arguments that were offered in justification for lumping products of similar sophistication and half-lives together in the first step of this procedure apply with equal validity here. The possible advantage of collation is that it permits the achieving of an averaged investment strategy indicator, a figure in which the planner can have greater confidence because it is based on a large sample size and is therefore, in the statistical sense, more likely to approach the "true" figure.

The next point to consider is that high and low figures describing industrial practices are shown in the National Science Foundation tables. Whether the planner should be guided by the high, low, or an averaged figure is a matter of corporate policy and strategy. Corporate policy must be considered and involves philosophic and strategy questions, including these: Shall I be the industry leader? Shall I keep abreast of the industry technically and see if a major market develops? In the over-all environment, competitors' actions must be followed closely, but there are other factors, such as interest rates, business expectation, economic forecasts, and so on, to be identified.

For the present it will be assumed that the planner has selected one figure for each product classification out of the possible ones and will proceed as though it were the only choice.

If the corporation has a single product line, or if all products have a common sophistication and half-life factor, the planner need only multiply the selected NSF percentage figure by the corporate net sales to determine an estimated total R&D budget. If two or more product classifications must be considered, each is treated separately, associating each product category with its own sales, and the estimated corporate R&D budget is the sum of the several calculations. This is the planner's first cut at a total corporate R&D budget.

Separating Research from Development

Between all U.S. industries that support R&D programs, the development efforts absorb about 80% of the total money allotted with the remainder going to research in science and technology. Thus, it is obvious that the total dollar investment is far more sensitive to a change in development needs than to an equivalent change in research.

During periods of financial austerity, far greater savings can be realized through the deferment of the development program than through a cut in the research budget. Austere periods do occur and cuts must be made despite an objective funding guide. Hopefully, when the economic fortunes of the corporation improve, an attempt will be made to accelerate the development of new products or to introduce an expensive new process that has been held back. As a result, the total research budget may be far in excess of that calculated with the procedures outlined.

It must also be noted that, except in large corporations, there is little or no need for a constant rate of introduction of really new products. The demands of the market and the practices of the competition may well require a large rise and ebb of new product introductions. Money for product or process development will similarly rise and fall over the years.

Thus, it is clear that a number of exogenous factors enter into the determination of the most acceptable development budget level for any given year. The total R&D budget calculated by the planner is, however, a useful guide for the long term.

In research the situation is usually different. The acquisition and training of new scientists and engineers is so costly that this factor alone dictates the avoidance of significant changes in the size of the research program from year to year. Since on the average the research portion of a budget is about 20% of the total, there is a strong argument for keeping it at a stable level even when the development part of the budget is gyrating.

While 20% is the general breakout figure for research, it can vary from one type of research to another. Here again, the National Science Foundation has tables describing average funding practices for the several product categories in terms of basic and applied research. These are given as percentages of total research and development. The result is the desired guidance figure for the corporate research budget. The further step of dividing this last figure into the basic and applied research categories, as suggested by the headings in the National Science Foundation tabulations, is not advised for the planner.

Activities within the Research Budget

The reasons for not pursuing the NSF subdivision into classes of research lie in the nature of the data-collection process. Those who fill in the annual NSF questionnaires are supposed to be guided by a set of careful definitions, but they tend to differ widely in their interpretations of these definitions. Too often the research expenditures reported to the NSF are those that were budgeted by the respondents under basic and applied labels but had many other objectives. They may have been doing something other than supporting the investigative programs required by the operating divisions, gaining the scientific and technical knowledge leading to new or improved products, or enhancing technological capability. In some industries, of which the pharmaceutical is a prime example, laboratory efforts involved in new product testing and evaluation equal or exceed those addressed to the actual discovery of the product. Obviously a planner in a pharmaceutical company must recognize that the industry-wide data include testing and evaluation in their reported research budget.

What about organizational support of several highly esteemed scientists involved in what the stockholders are told is "important, long-range, basic research"? Now, there is no real way to break out the amount or real value of this work. But the planner should recognize that he has built in some funds for this purpose, because this is a common practice and its existence is reflected in the over-all NSF data. Based on his own organization's practices, he must choose to retain this built-in amount, or adjust it up or down.

Learning to live with the NSF data takes time and experience. This discussion should have made it clear, however, that while they are useful in broader categories, some of the ways in which they are broken down are not to be taken at face value. One result is that at the corporate level no attempt should be made to differentiate between research activities for budgeting purposes. Once a research budget is established, the technical director of the laboratory can apportion this budget in accord with his own definitions and needs.

Special Requirements of Education

To this point research requirements and budgets have been tied directly to satisfying the immediate objectives of the government or the corporations; immediate in the sense of direct or obvious rather than in the sense of time. However, in case of the federal government or with very large corporations with their rather unique R&D requirements, there is an extra research cost. This is the investment in educating scientists and engineers to satisfy the future needs of laboratories. This task cannot assuredly be accomplished through general support of the colleges and universities. It appears to be best accomplished through contracts and grants directed at those professors whose work is of specific interest.

The validity of this statement is attested to by another of the Project HINDSIGHT findings. Although the Department of Defense has supported research in about 200 colleges and universities throughout the United States since 1945, the larger share of this support has gone to a relatively small group of them, primarily for specific studies. The top 23 universities, in terms of this support, awarded approximately 25% of the Ph.D. degrees in the physical sciences and engineering from 1945 to 1966; they also awarded about 11% of the M.Sc. degrees in the same fields. Project HINDSIGHT identified 1295 scientists and engineers who had made significant contributions to defense weaponry and, on a 50% sampling basis, determined their educational background. Fully 50% of the Ph.D. degrees in the high-performer group, and 46% of the M.Sc. degrees held by this group had come from the 23 universities mentioned.

It seems clear that the Department of Defense, by supporting selected professors to undertake research in areas of specific interest, had influenced the career choice of students. Wittingly or not, it had assured itself a supply of well-schooled, favorably oriented scientists and engineers. If, for the future, the major departments and research supporting agencies of the federal government, and the "General Motors" and "American Telephone and Telegraphs" of the nation wish to assure themselves a continuing supply of young professionals, they will have to undertake well-planned programs of support for relevant sections of the academic community.

This support should not be justified as acts of benevolence, as is typical to some corporations, but as a means of satisfying selfish interests of the research and development divisions. Wherever possible, programs should be developed and managed by the heads of these divisions and the costs of the programs regarded as training expenses. This requirement for taking an active interest in the schooling of future scientific and technical personnel can only become greater as the education trend continues to more and more specialization and as scientific and technical knowledge in each field increases to the point that even further specialization becomes necessary.

An Alternative Technique

The planning tool outlined above is most clearly designed for companies with well defined product lines and sales expectations. Where, as in the case of the Department of Defense, the objective of most of the research effort is a product-like equipment, the government planner may find application of the method—picturing his organization as a tremendous, multi-product conglomerate. In his case, the counterpart for net sales might well be the purchases by the Department for the equipping and support of the combat forces.

But, where the research efforts of the government agency never culminate in a manufactured product, the suggested procedures are totally inapplicable.

The entire concept of product sophistication or that of half-life becomes meaningless. There are no industrial data to which one can look for guidance. A completely different approach to budget estimation is necessary. In companies, too, there might well be situations where the NSF historical data cannot serve as guide.

Earlier in this chapter a plot entitled, "Relationship between Improvement, Complexity, and Requirement for New Technology" was presented (p. 148). In a very speculative manner, the relationships shown there can be a basis for estimating research budgets. However, since the data used to prepare this plot came from large, expensive systems, the degree to which it can be generalized is hard to estimate. And additional data may not be readily available or may be suspect.

In this budget-planning procedure the only objective of the research sponsor is the achieving of the research results needed to permit him to develop an advanced product with a specified product improvement. He must rely on quantitative planning techniques and must define his development objectives in terms of relative cost effectiveness—the product improvement needed.

Having defined his objectives in this way, he need only calculate the required number of scientific and technological advances needed to achieve that objective (these would be the "events" plotted in Fig. 8.1). Working back through the research program, he must then estimate the number of research starts necessary to achieve the objectives. To get the total research budget is then a matter of multiplying the number of starts by an average cost per research task.

This exercise is not quite as speculative as it might appear at first. The study from which Figure 8.1 was taken developed some general cost figures for research. It suggested that the median cost for a "scientific" event was $60,000; for a "technology" event, $45,000. It further noted that the ratio of required scientific advances to technical advances was about 1:10. Unfortunately the particular study did not investigate this obviously essential factor: "How many funded research tasks result in knowledge that is directly useful to a product as opposed to those that are not?" On this point, perhaps the experience of the corporate planner can supply the needed information. Discussions between the author and several research managers suggest that the success-to-failure ratio varies widely among different industries. In the pharmaceutical industry it is perhaps 1:30; 1:3 or 1:4 in the automotive industry; somewhere in between for the others.

Summing up, the following procedural approach to this latter concept of research budget estimation is suggested:

1. Use Figure 8.1 to calculate the number of events required for each equipment to be improved.

2. Correct the number of events computed to reflect your company's experience with a success to failure ratio.

3. Total the number of research efforts required for all projects.

4. Compute the science-to-technology distribution (approx. 1:10).

5. Calculate the research budget estimate on the basis of $60,000 per scientific effort and $45,000 per technological effort.

This speculative procedure has ignored two more salient factors. First, no attention has been paid to how soon the improved product is desired. Second, the treatment contains an implicit assumption that each scientific or technological advance offers only a unique use. Project HINDSIGHT, however, does offer some data on these matters.

Initially, of course, the time to be allowed for the needed research is a management decision. There is no obvious upper limit on the period, but there must be a lower limit. In the case of a complex weapon system, experience suggests that about 15 to 18 years may be required to gather all of the requisite knowledge. This figure might be reducible with better planning, but there is certainly a significant number of years required to carry a new scientific thought through to a practical device.

With regard to the matter of multiple use, the HINDSIGHT data suggests a probability of 0.8 that an advance will find three or more applications. There are important exceptions: for example, the advances that led to the transistor found an untold number of applications. Conversely, the data suggest that after an advance has been used about three times, a further advance is required to satisfy a new need. At any rate, the planner might be justified in reducing the budget estimate achieved in step 4 by a factor of three to account for the probability that he had overestimated the number of unique events required.

Again, the budget estimate generated through this latter procedure must be adjusted upward to account for such additional requirements as the training of future scientists.

Conclusion

The task of estimating a proper research budget for the organization, whether federal or in the private sector, is indeed difficult, but it is not impossible. Further, the stakes involved, whether they be in terms of resources involved or in terms of the risks and dangers of inordinately high or low budgets, are so great that despite the difficulty the task must be accomplished. The intent of this chapter was to demonstrate to the student of management or to the professional manager that there are real and logical paths to this objective.

It is clear that the budgeting process must account for phenomeno-
logical aspects of the growth of technology, the threat of competition
in the market place or on the international scene, and the psychology
of the consumer. To the extent that the interactions of these factors
are understood they can be dealt with. Examples of how this can be
done have been offered. Admittedly these attempts to come to grips
with a very difficult problem represent early steps into a new field for
the management scientist: a quantitative approach to research-budget
estimates. In this sense, much of what has been offered is properly
subject to question. Undoubtedly the suggested techniques will be
modified and improved upon. They are offered in the hope that they
will provide a base from which better techniques can evolve. They are
not a final answer to the problem of estimating a research budget.

9

Using Technical Forecasts

Marvin J. Cetron

"Some people see things and ask why. I dream of things and ask why not?" Robert F. Kennedy

The realization that technological forecasting methods could help answer these questions was catching hold slowly when many R&D planners were rudely shaken by a new reality: a leveling-off or even a cutback in most government-sponsored research efforts in 1967 and 1968. With NASA's post-Apollo projects whittled back, Department of Defense research budgets cut extensively, and other usually expanding budgets on a shorter rein, the need to make hard choices in funding became more critical than ever. Many planners are turning to technological forecasting to help them make these difficult selections.

In this chapter I will explain some of the approaches being examined in the Navy Department as well as some of the directions being actively explored in industry. The truth is, however, that this field is still in an evolutionary phase and most work now being done in one organization cannot be codified enough for adoption in others. At best, what is being done can provide many helpful hints for planners grappling with their own resource-allocation problems.

It is vital to remember that a technological forecast is not a picture of what the future *will* bring. Rather, it is a prediction, with a level of confidence and in a given time frame, of a technical achievement that could be expected for a given level of budgetary and manpower support.

The foundation underlying technological forecasting is the tenet that individual R&D events are susceptible to influence. The times at which they occur—if they can occur at all—can be modulated significantly by regulating the resources allocated to them. Another basic tenet of technological forecasting is the belief that many futures are possible and that the paths toward these futures can be mapped.

In use, a technological forecast can be looked at from two vantage points. One, in the present, gives the forecast user a view which shows the path that technological progress will probably take if not consciously influenced. In addition, the user will see critical branch points in the road—situations where alternative futures are possible. He will also gain a greater understanding of the price of admission to those branching paths.

The second vantage point is in the future. The user selects or postulates a technical situation he desires. Looking backward from that point, he can then discern the obstacles that must be overcome to achieve the result he wants. Once again, he is brought up against the hard realities of what he must do to achieve a desired result. As one user has said: "The process substitutes forecasting for forecrastination."

Making Basic Forecasts

At this point, it is worth reviewing some of the basics of making technological forecasts. The idea is not new. Leonardo da Vinci is probably the prime example of the scientific and technical forecaster whose knowledge and imagination enabled him to foresee many developments far in the future. Science-fiction writers from Jules Verne to Arthur Clarke have also peered into the future, often with great success. As long as one remains within the general bounds of known natural laws, he is safe in forecasting almost any technical achievement and will enjoy some success. But a highly developed imagination offers little help for the technological planner; the odds are not good enough.

To reduce the odds, most technological forecasts today fall into four categories: intuitive, trend extrapolating, trend correlating, and growth analogy. In *intuitive forecasting*, an individual may make an educated guess or he may call on polls or panels of experts for advice. A technique that promises to produce more objective intuitive forecasts is the Delphi method, developed by Olaf Helmer of the Rand Corporation.

In one version, a group of experts in a chosen field might be asked to name technical breakthroughs or inventions urgently needed and realizable within the next 50 years. They are polled by written questionnaires, eliminating the open debate generally found in panel decision-making. As a result, the influence of certain psychological factors is reduced: a persuasive speaker, unwillingness to abandon publicly expressed opinions, or the bandwagon effect of majority opinion. In a second round of questionnaires, participants are asked to give a time scale for achieving each of the items selected. They are also asked the reasons for their earlier opinions. These data are correlated and fed back to each with a request that he reconsider his earlier beliefs and submit new estimates. The result is usually some sort of a consensus.

The strength or weakness of the Delphi or other polling systems rests upon the knowledge or intuition of selected experts. It assumes that the consensus estimate is generally correct without an examination of basic data. Most other forecasting methods are tied directly to the basic technical data. The *trend extrapolation* technique, for example, is based on two fundamental assumptions: the forces that created the prior pattern of progress are more likely to continue than to change; the combined effect of these forces is more likely to extend the previous pattern of progress than it is to produce a different pattern.

One difficulty in using this technique, however, is that the longer the period of the forecast, the greater the probability that one or more of the assumptions made will become invalid. The yield strength of a material, for example, will go up as its density is increased, but there is a theoretical limit.

The *trend correlation* method, on the other hand, uses two or more identifiable trends in a technical field and tries to determine the probable relationship of one to the other. Plotting the speeds of military and transport aircraft indicates that the transports lag by a predictable amount. Therefore, looking at current or future military aircraft gives a good insight into the future of airliners.

Finally, forecasting by *growth analogies* recognizes that progress in a specific technical development has an exponential characteristic initially, changes its slope, and then tapers off toward a horizontal asymptote. This approach, however, is good only for a short term—ten years at the most. In many cases, a new development will take over the improvement rate as the old one is running out of steam. Mercury-vapor lamps, for example, started improving dramatically just as incandescent lighting had reached its limit.

The four techniques discussed have one common aspect: They depend on historical data and projection. There is no provision in them for the systematic introduction of management plans and actions. To take these into account, the forecaster must still rely on intuitive judgment. Newer and more sophisticated attempts at forecasting, however, include a systems analysis and a mathematical modeling approach. Basic to these methods is the interaction of human awareness of economic, social, and geopolitical needs with the technical state of the art. The technical inputs are formulated by methods like those mentioned, but they are then examined for nontechnical feasibility.

Putting Forecasts to Work

In most cases a manager does not have a total system to work with. Instead, he has the results of trend extrapolations or other regular technological forecasting projections. How does he use these data? While there are many approaches, the following case shows one which the Navy Department is examining to determine which techniques can best help decide which R&D projects to fund.

We begin with a technical planning flow chart that shows the "shredding out" of all the bits and pieces that comprise the makeup of a new vehicle. Assume that we have a technological forecast for each and every parameter of the shred-out. The forecasts, at each level of the breakdown, are the probable paths that various technologies will take. Armed with this type of data, a meaningful discourse can ensue between the user and producer. For a given set of operational requirements and performance characteristics called for by the user, the technical planners can respond with data that tell the user by what alternative means his needs can be satisfied and when he can expect these to be accomplished. Many of the tradeoffs—between steam, diesel, and nuclear energy, for example—become clear.

Operations officers, however, are not usually quite so acquiescent in accepting what a planner sees ahead. When faced with a military threat, or an anticipated threat, they want an effective answer to that threat by a specified date. The same holds true if they wish to create a new force of their own. In these situations, planners are taking a vantage point at some time in the future and try to discover whether they will have the technology they need by that time.

Quite likely an examination of the technology forecasts to that point in time will reveal that the users are not likely to get what they want. Now, this in itself is useful information and represents an approach that is not yet widely used in industry.

However, this view of the technological forecasting task is not the only one. There is the question of which path to take to achieve a desired result. By deciding on our needs in the future and looking at the forecasts, we can spot the principal obstacles standing in our way, and the magnitude of those obstacles. The inference is clear: If the given goal is to be achieved, the efforts must be applied in the areas containing the major obstacles. Or, we can settle for something less with a clear knowledge of what that something less will be. Often this analysis will show that two or more paths may be taken to achieve the needed or acceptable capabilities. The point here is that an environment of flexible choices is engendered, choices of which the user was not previously aware. A truly comprehensive technological forecast is backed up not only by the material and data used in generating the specific forecasts but also by supplementary analyses of various subfactors that could influence each technological forecast. Forecasts like these help indicate the future posture of an enemy or competitor. While you don't know what he *will* do you at least have a better idea of what he *could* do.

Mechanics of Decision-Making

Now let's return to our example and see how a specific decision can be analyzed, based on the forecasting techniques utilized at the Annapolis Division of the Naval Ships Research and Development Center. Forecasts for ship propulsion systems are given in terms of specific weight, reliability, noise, etc. The next level of consideration takes us into the area of subsystem segments: transmission, energy converter, thrust producer, etc. Each of these key into an associated set of parameters which in turn key into specific forecasts. In this fashion, we can work our way down the chart of Figure 9.1, eventually going into any degree of detail we wish.

This information is used for very practical decisions. Marine gas turbines, for example, have a tremendous potential for development. The possibilities for high-power, lightweight, compact power plants are unmatched in any other type of unit. These characteristics are particularly vital for powering new-concept vessels such as hydrofoils and air-cushion craft. In the last few years there has been a rapid growth in the horsepower capacity of gas-turbine units. Engines as large as 43,000 horsepower have been built, and units exceeding 50,000 horse-

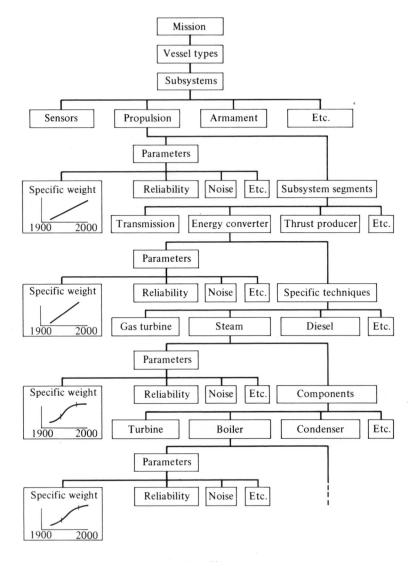

Figure 9.1   Technical Planning Flow Chart

power are projected. This growth trend will probably continue but at a decreased rate as limitations of mechanical, thermal, and ducting size are approached. However, much larger power outputs will be built by using multiple gas generators to drive a single turbine. Power outputs as high as 150,000 horsepower have already been attained by this method. The R&D manager's problem is to decide which aspects of turbine development are most critical.

The development trends for the specific weight, volume, and fuel consumption for a simple cycle gas turbine are shown in the first three graphs in Figure 9.2. In all of these the trend correlation (lead-follow relationship) was used in the study. Aircraft gas-turbine technology has been the leader because the marine environment led to problems of corrosion. Now that materials and other problems are being overcome, the curves are coming together; the aircraft experience gives some indication of what can be expected in future naval turbines.

As shown in the next graph, the compressor, combustion, and turbine efficiency have reached a plateau according to a growth analogy study. Any future improvement will be limited. Consequently, these component efficiencies will have an insignificant effect on future engine characteristics. The reason for recent improvements, moreover, is that the compressor-pressure ratio has gone up. But any further increase will be small. Because of improvements in blade loading, compressors are now designed to an optimum pressure ratio determined by turbine inlet temperature. And this blade loading, which has enabled engines to obtain higher pressures with fewer stages, appears to be approaching a limit.

This combination of forecasts shows that the addition of more heat energy within the same basic engine configuration—the major contributing factor to recent engine improvement—is likely to be the key factor in future improvement. Extrapolation of the curve to temperatures in excess of 2500° F is based on laboratory tests in which operating temperatures as high as 4000° F have been achieved— another trend correlation forecast.

As a result of this forecasting approach we now know where our R&D efforts should be concentrated. These are the *high* payoffs:

1. Cooling of turbine blades and other components in high-temperature ambients. This will allow higher turbine inlet temperatures.

2. New materials and protective coatings for these high-ambient components. This will increase high-temperature capabilities by increasing resistance to high-temperature oxidation and sulfidation. An increased resistance to thermal fatigue and creep is also required.

3. Improved materials, designs, and fabrication techniques for regenerative gas turbines to reduce their cost, weight, and bulk.

4. Further application and adaption of aircraft gas turbines and technologies to ships.

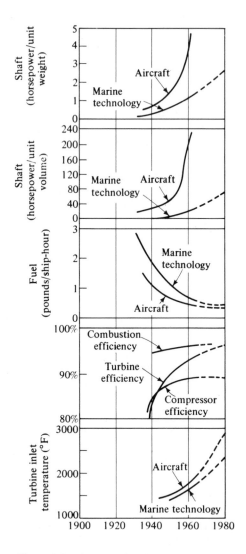

Figure 9.2   Gas-Turbine Characteristics

Technical areas where relatively *low* payoffs for the expended effort could be expected are attempts to improve efficiency of combustion, compressor, and turbine, and attempts to increase significantly the blade-loading or compressor-pressure ratio unless accompanied by major design changes.

The Over-All Picture

Up to this point we have been discussing the technological forecasting needed for one problem in a laboratory. But any organization has many such problems. Here the question becomes one of the allocation of resources of men, money, and materials. The evaluation scene therefore shifts from the technical specialist to the department manager, the head of research, and the over-all planners. The forecast data must be fitted into their approach if it is to be really useful.

Naturally, forecasting cannot be considered in a vacuum. General policy and the over-all environment must be integrated into the analysis. A company considering its strategy, for example, must consider many questions, including these: Shall I be the industry leader? Shall I keep in the ball game technically and see if a major market develops? In the general environment, competitors' actions must be followed closely, but there are other factors, such as interest rates, business expectation, and so on, to be taken into consideration. The road map of R&D planning (Figure 9.3) shows one organization of factors. A quick glance at the figure shows clearly how the forecasting element acts as a catalyst in setting and implementing corporate goals. At present only a handful of the largest corporations are really utilizing their technical potential, as shown in careful forecasting, in this kind of *total* planning process.

The next question is how you grind the technical forecasts into this total picture. A discussion of these methods would be a long story in itself. But I should mention that all systems used in the Department of Defense employ three major factors in the appraisal process: military utility, technical feasibility, and financial acceptability. Each of these factors is amenable to quantification and can be fitted into a model that compares the value of each component project or system. With about fifteen key items and thousands of calculations, it is necessary to program the job on a computer to get usable information quickly. However, these computer processes are simply a tool to aid the decision-maker; the machine merely arranges the material in accordance with his instructions so that he can focus his attention quickly on those areas that require his special knowledge and judgment.

One of the simpler techniques being investigated by the Navy utilizes Appraisal Sheet No. 1 which addresses itself to problems of military utility. Military utility with respect to development atmosphere is a measure of R&D work in terms of its usefulness in meeting the U.S. Navy's General Operational Requirements (GOR). To be useful,

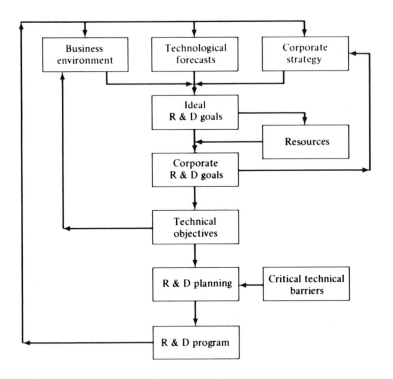

Figure 9.3   Road Map of R&D Planning

hardware or information must provide a new or improved capability in the shortest possible time after its need is recognized. Thus, military utility is made up of three interdependent criteria: value to naval warfare, responsiveness, and timeliness. In this condensed version, we will consider only value to naval warfare.

This criterion considers the extent of the contribution of a task area objective (TAO), a unit of work, in terms of its inherent as well as its military operational value. The importance of a task is measured by its relative impact on any individual naval warfare category as well as by the number of categories receiving a contribution from the task objective. This is done by multiplying the assigned value of the warfare category by the impact value of the contribution, to arrive at a value for each individual category. The sum of these values will determine the total value to naval warfare of the TAO.

Appraisal Sheet No. 1: Value to Naval Warfare

General Operational Requirements (GOR)	Impact of Task Contributions *										Value to Individual Category
	1.0	.9	.8	.7	.6	.5	.4	.3	.2	.1	
Merit Figures											
31 — Strike Warfare											
6 — Airborne attack											
3 — Surface attack											
5 — Submarine attack											
4 — Amphibious assault											
7 — Sea based strategic deterrence											
3 — Airborne anti-air warfare											
3 — Surface anti-air warfare											
31 — Antisubmarine Warfare											
5 — Airborne ASW				X							3.5
4 — Surface ASW						X					2.0
5 — Submarine ASW						X					2.5
10 — Undersea surveillance								X			3.0
2 — Mining											
3 — Mine countermeasures											
2 — ASW ancillary support									X		0.4
23 — Command Support											
3 — Command and control											
4 — Naval communications											
4 — Electronic warfare											
1 — Navigation											
4 — Ocean surveillance											
5 — Reconnaissance & intelligence											
1 — Environmental systems											
1 — Special warfare											
15 — Operational Support											
2 — Logistics											
4 — Personnel											
2 — Astronautics											
2 — Aviation support											
2 — Ship support											
2 — Ordnance support											
1 — NBC defense											

Total Value to Naval Warfare = 11.4

* Scale of Definitions

1.0 Creation of radically new mission concepts (meets overriding critical need)
.7 Revolutionary extension of capabilities
.4 Incremental or marginal improvement of capabilities
.2 Increase in economy

The figures of merit, or point values assigned to each naval warfare category are dummy figures; they were assigned for this example only. The actual number of points assigned to these 29 naval categories is equal to 100; the points are assigned for test purposes on the basis of the importance of each of these categories in the 1975 and 1980 time frame, since this is when most of our current exploratory development work will find its way into the fleet. The operational users provided the test figures based on the present world situation and their estimates of the most probable future situations.

When the warfare area specialist checks the boxes for the impact of the task area objective contributions, he considers the descriptors at the bottom of the page. In some cases the four descriptors do not adequately describe the contribution; in those cases he interpolates between these numbers. Naturally, the credibility of the ratings of technical feasibility and the probability of success increase if they are rated by personnel who have the necessary technical expertise and competence.

The top half of Appraisal Sheet No. 2 solicits the opinion of the technical specialist regarding the probability of achieving the total task area objective. It considers whether the task could be successfully accomplished from a scientific and technical point of view. Technical risk also takes into consideration the degree of confidence in the prediction that the remaining portion of the total objective can be attained. The degree of confidence usually assesses the factors of the present state of the art, either implicit or explicit. This technical appraisal is naturally based on technical forecasts and includes time factors and resource levels as well as the competence of the investigating team.

The technical specialist checks the box that best describes his opinion regarding the task area objective being evaluated, as well as the number of different concurrent approaches being taken which are also a measure of probability of success. The areas called "Sacred Cow?" and "Who Says?" were also considered in what we call the management environment. They solicit opinions on the acceptability of the effort. Here the evaluator is asked to give what he believes to be "the Washington environment" considerations concerning this effort.

Let us now analyze the bottom of Appraisal Sheet No. 2. The total program is calculated by value, expected value, and desirability index for three funding levels, by the computer. The inputs for military utility come from Appraisal Sheet No. 1. Suppose the proposed task area objective (TAO), or R&D effort, is to devise a system able to detect submerged submarines a given distance away from a sensor,

Appraisal Sheet No. 2

<hr>

Probability of Success

☐ 80-100% chance of meeting TAO.
☒ 30- 80% chance of meeting TAO.
☐ 0- 30% chance of meeting TAO.

Number of Concurrent Approaches

☐ 1	☐ 3	☐ 5	☐ 7	☐ 9
☐ 2	☒ 4	☐ 6	☐ 8	☐ 10 or more

Sacred Cow?		Who Says?	
S-1	☐ President	S-4	☐ ASN (R&D) (Asst. Secretary of
S-2	☐ Congress		Navy for R&D)
S-3	☐ DOD	S-5	☐ JCS (Joint Chiefs of Staff)
		S-6	☐ CNO (Chief of Naval Operations)
		S-7	☐ CND (Chief of Naval Development)
		S-8	☐ Other

Summary

No. of GORs 5
Value (V) 11.4
Probability of Success (P_s) 0.9375
Expected Value (EV) 11.4 × 0.9375 = 10.7
Optimum Funding 2 Million
Desirability Index (D) 5.35

say 20 miles. We shall consider the criterion "Value to Naval Warfare." Of the 29 naval General Operational Requirements shown in Appraisal Sheet No. 1, the TAO would be of value and contribute only to five GOR's: Airborne ASW, Surface ASW, Submarine ASW, Undersea ASW, and ASW Ancillary Support.

With respect to airborne ASW, the success of the R&D venture in this example is considered a "revolutionary extension of capabilities," and is accorded 0.7 point. At the same time, airborne ASW is said to contribute 5 out of the 100 units assigned to all the GOR's. Thus, the value of the TAO to naval warfare with respect to airborne ASW is 0.7 × 5 = 3.5. The other categories can be similarly evaluated for their contributions, and the total value of this TAO to naval warfare is summed at 11.4, as shown on the appraisal sheet.

For our calculation of the Probability of Success (P_s) in meeting the TAO, we use the probability chart shown in Table 9.1. In this chart, n is the number of concurrent approaches used to accomplish the TAO, and C a number arbitrarily assigned to the chances of succeeding in a given approach. We use: 80 to 100% chance of success— $C = 0.8$; 30 to 80% chance of success—$C = 0.5$; 0 to 30% chance of success—$C = 0.2$.

Table 9.1   Tabulation of Probability of Success (P_s)

n \ C	0.8	0.5	0.2
1	0.80000	0.50000	0.20000
2	0.96000	0.75000	0.36000
3	0.99200	0.87500	0.48800
4	0.99840	0.93750	0.59040
5	0.99968	0.96875	0.67230
6	0.99993	0.98438	0.73786
7	0.99997	0.99219	0.79029
8	0.99999	0.99609	0.83223
9	0.99999	0.99805	0.86578
10	0.99999	0.99902	0.89263

We assume that all approaches n have the same chance of success, and therefore the same value of C. If each n were to have a different C, a more involved calculation would have been necessary. The number assigned to the probability of one approach failing is then $(1 - C)$, and that assigned to the probability of n approaches failing is $(1 - C)^n$.

Further, if we assume that at least one of the approaches taken will succeed, the number assigned to the probability of success P_s is $1 - (1 - C)^n$. This figure for P_s is filled in on Appraisal Sheet No. 2 under the appropriate column.

Consider this example: On an Appraisal Sheet No. 2, we might have had 4 approaches ($n = 4$) with a 30-80% chance of meeting TAO ($C - 0.5$). Then the number corresponding to the probability of success is 0.93750 or 93.75%. From our previous example we calculated the total value of a given TAO to be 11.4. Therefore, the expected value is $11.4 \times 0.9375 = 10.7$.

The preceding has been a discussion of concurrent approaches. If the task area were made up of phased or sequential operations, these probabilities would be handled in a different manner.

Three funding levels are utilized in the concurrent approach: the actual optimum, maximum, and minimum. The actual optimum consists of the latest approved fiscal data. For each subsequent year, funds are entered based on what is estimated as necessary to achieve the completion date if the task area is supported at an optimum rate. An optimum rate is one that permits aggressive prosecution using orderly developmental procedures—not a crash program.

The maximum consists of what could effectively be expended in advancing task area completion data. Maximum funding is the upper limit in which unlimited resources are assigned in order to accelerate the accomplishment of a TAO.

The minimum consists of what could be utilized effectively to maintain continuity of effort and some progress toward fulfilling the TAO. Minimum funding is the threshold limit below which it would not be feasible to continue further efforts in the task area. The formula for obtaining the desirability index is

$$\text{Value } (V) \times \text{Probability of Success } (P_s) = \text{Expected Value } (EV)$$

$$\frac{\text{Expected Value } (EV)}{\text{Funding Level } (C)} = \text{Desirability Index } (D)$$

The final desirability index numbers now provide a way to compare a great multitude of current and proposed R&D projects. By carrying out similar evaluations on the basis of responsiveness to expected needs, the timeliness of the projects, and other criteria, it is possible to combine all the information about the project and come up with its total warfare value. The end results of an R&D planning effort like this are computer printouts that rank every project according to its value in the over-all program. In the Navy, this comes to more than 700 separate R&D projects.

Conclusion

It should be stressed again that these quantitative techniques are not intended to yield decisions but rather information that will facilitate decision-making. Indeed, these techniques are merely thinking structures to force methodical, meticulous consideration of all the factors involved in resource allocation. I am firmly convinced that if

I had to choose between any machine and the human brain, I would select the brain. The brain has a marvelous system that learns from experience and an uncanny way of pulling out the salient factors or rejecting useless information. It is wrong, however, to say that one must select intuitive experience over analysis or minds over machines. They are not alternatives, they complement each other.

The real concern should be directed toward using the collective judgment of technical staffs (technological forecasts) and decision-makers in such a manner that logically sound decisions are made and greater payoff is achieved for the resources committed, and that less, not more, valuable scientific and engineering time is expended. To make an incorrect decision is understandable, but to make a decision and not really know the basis for the judgment is unforgivable. The area of good resource allocation certainly must have advanced beyond this point; otherwise, a pair of dice could replace the decision-maker more effectively than a computer.

Even all the above disclaimers do not defuse critics of the whole idea—and there are some very vocal ones around in government and business. Some are simply reacting against what they say is an attempt to mechanize what must always remain a job for human evaluation. They feel that building up a logical system, computerizing the output, and putting numbers on what should remain gut decisions may give some managers a false sense of security. They may come to believe that the numbers represent the whole equation and they may then abdicate their role.

Appendix A
Survey of Quantitative Methods

Marvin J. Cetron

This appendix provides a summary of a number of known techniques for quantitative evaluation of R&D projects. The successful application of quantitative methods to problems such as inventories, queueing, transportation, and other problems requiring decisions on resource allocation or scheduling, has at least made it conceivable to raise the question of whether comparable quantitative evaluation methods could also be applied to research and development projects. The advent of the computer has made such applications appear feasible where the R&D efforts are large in number. The desired outputs from such quantitative methods would be an evaluation of a prescribed selection of projects or, better yet, a procedure for scheduling projects or allocating resources among competing projects.

Interest in such quantitative methods, especially within the Department of Defense, has become quite high within the past few years. As a result of this interest, the author has conducted a survey of methods, both completed and on-going, which have been devised in industry and government, and had evaluated those methods against a fixed set of factors. While the original purpose of this survey and evaluation was to form a basis for recommending a system for application within one of the military services, the results may well be of interest to others and are therefore presented here.

Features of the Methods

The various methods covered in our survey took into account various items of information about the R&D projects to be evaluated and provide various items of information as output from the evaluation. Fifteen different features were found that could describe the items of input and output of the various methods. No single method possessed all the features. The various features are described in some detail below.

1. *Utility measure:* Does the method take into account some measure of the utility or value of success of a particular R&D project? This measure may be share of a market, profitability, some measure of military worth, and so on.

2. *Probability of success:* Does the method explicitly take into account an estimate of the probability of success of each individual R&D project?

3. *Orthogonality of criteria:* Are the criteria used by the method mutually exclusive (orthogonal), rather than being highly correlated or having a great deal of overlap?

4. *Sensitivity:* Has the sensitivity of the output to small changes in the input been checked? A high degree of sensitivity to small variations in input is undesirable, since it causes the output to become unstable in the presence of minor perturbations in the input.

5. *Rejected alternatives retention:* When a project is rejected for funding, is it retained for later consideration in the event of a budget increase or other adjustment, rather than being discarded completely?

6. *Classification structure:* Does the method provide a structural relationship between the R&D project and a hierarchy of higher-level goals of the organization?

7. *Time:* Does the method take into account scheduling requirements or provide scheduling information as an output?

8. *Strategies:* Does the method permit the user to take into account several possible scenarios, world environments, market situations, and so on?

9. *System cross support:* Does the method give a system development credit for support which it provides to another system development?

10. *Technology cross support:* Does the method give a project for advancement of technology credit for support which it provides to the advancement of other technologies?

11. *Graphical display:* Is the output amenable to presentation in some graphical form which gives the user a condensed picture of the evaluation of various projects?

12. *Flagging:* Does the method flag problem areas, to bring them to the attention of the responsible management?

13. *Optimization criteria:* What criterion for optimization does the method use, and what constrains are considered? All methods used supplied a composite score from a number of factors, to obtain a ranking, or employed some form of maximum (discounted) net value.

14. *Constraints* considered by the methods were: budget, skills available, facilities available, competitor efforts, raw materials available, and time limitations.

15. *Computerization:* Is the method implemented in a computer program, and is it a linear program or a dynamic program? Those marked as computerized are known to the authors to have been programmed for some machine. Most of the techniques could be computerized if desired.

Ease of Use

Each method was evaluated according to several criteria bearing on ease of use, as described below.

1. *Data requirements:* While in general the more data a method uses as input, the more information it provides as output, the ease of use can be adversely affected by the amount of data. Two factors enter into the needs for data: the level of organization at which data are obtained, i.e., individual work unit, subsystem, system, etc.; and the quantity of data required on each effort.

2. *Manual:* Is manual operation of the method possible or reasonable to consider?

3. *Computer program:* If a computer is required, has the method been programmed for some computer?

4. *Running time:* If the method has been programmed, what is the running time for one cycle of evaluation or allocation?

5. *Updating:* What is the ease of updating the system to take into account new information, whether the new information is developed periodically or new items come in on an unscheduled basis?

6. *Proficiency level:* What level of proficiency is required of the operator (not the manager who is using the output)? Can it be handled by a clerk? Does it require a skilled technician? Does it require a professional?

7. *Outside help:* Is help or information required from persons outside the R&D organization in evaluating goals set by others, environments not under control of the R&D organization, and so on?

Area of applicability

Few of the systems appeared to be applicable throughout the entire R&D spectrum. Some were more applicable to one portion of the spectrum than to others. The methods are rated as being applicable to research, to exploratory development, to advanced development, or to engineering development.

Description of methods

Each method surveyed is briefly described below. It is identified by the name or names of the originators, unless some acronym or title has been used to designate it. Methods 1 through 10 and their descriptions are from the Baker-Pound article "R&D Project Selection: Where We Stand," printed in *IEEE Transactions on Engineering Management, EM-11*, No. 4, December 1964.

1. *Mottley-Newton, 1959:* A decision theory approach. Project proposals are rated with respect to a number of evaluation criteria. An over-all score is computed and used to rank the alternatives. Selection criteria are considered with respect to constraints including research budget, risk, and over-all program balance.
2. *Gargiulo et al., 1961:* A decision theory approach. Project proposals are rated with respect to a number of evaluation criteria. An over-all score is computed and used to rank the alternatives. Constraints such as research budget, skills available, facilities available, and competitor efforts in the area are considered.
3. *Pound, 1964:* A decision theory approach. Project proposals are rated with respect to a number of weighted selection objectives. An over-all score is computed and used to rank the alternatives. The budget constraint is considered.
4. *Sobelman, 1958:* An operations research approach. For each alternative project, estimates are made of average value per year, economic life, average development cost per year and development time. Selection is accomplished by maximizing discounted net value, perhaps subject to constraints.
5. *Freeman, 1960:* An operations research approach. For each alternative project, an estimate is made of the probability distribution of net value. Selection is accomplished by maximizing expected discounted net value, subject to constraints on the total budget, facilities, and personnel. A linear programming formulation is used.

6. *Asher, 1962:* An operations research approach. For each alternative project, estimates are made of the discounted net value of the project and probability of success. Selection is accomplished by maximizing expected discounted net value subject to constraints on the man hours available and on the raw materials available. The optimal manpower allocation is indicated by the result. A linear programming formulation is used.

7. *Hess, 1962:* An operations research approach. For each alternative project, estimates are made of the discounted gross value as of several points in time. Probabilities of success are also estimated. Selection is accomplished by maximizing expected discounted net value subject to a budget constraint for the first period. The optimal allocation to each project is indicated for each period. A dynamic programming formulation is used.

8. *Dean-Sengupto, 1962:* An economic analysis and operations research approach. The optimal research budget is first determined. Then for each alternative project, estimates are made of the discounted net value and the probability of technical and commercial success. Selection is accomplished by maximizing expected discounted net value subject to a budget constraint. A linear programming formulation is suggested.

9. *Disman, 1962:* An economic analysis approach. For each alternative project, an estimate is made of the discounted net value (not including R&D costs). This estimate, perhaps modified by a probability of technical and/or commercial success is considered to be the maximum expenditure justified. The ratio of the maximum expenditure justified to estimated project cost is an index of the desirability of the project.

10. *Cramer-Smith, 1964:* An economic analysis and operations research approach. An application of portfolio selection and utility theory to the problem of research project selection. For each alternative project, estimates are made of net values and probabilities of occurrence. Utility curves are also obtained. Projects may be ranked on the basis of expected value or expected utility. Lack of project independence is also mentioned.

11. *Esch, "PATTERN," 1963:* Combination decision theory approach and operations research approach. A continuing, large-scale, corporate effort to assign quantitative, relative values to the importance of conducting R&D on the various technology deficiencies which now stand in the way of the achievement of national security objectives for the decade 1968 to 1978. The model considers national survival, threat

force structure, capability, prestige, cost effectiveness, requirements, scientific implications, feasibility, effort, risk, capability improvement, and operational advantages. This technique is the first full-scale application of the heuristic "relevance tree" concept developed in 1958 by H. Wells in his Master's thesis at Ohio State University.

12. *Blum, 1963:* A mathematical treatment leading to a methodology of ranking R&D events in the project by their cost, risk, time, and value. The methodology puts into sequence the efforts by a version of the DOD and NASA PERT-cost technique.

13. *Bakanas, 1964:* A model to aid in the selection of applied research and development tasks for inclusion in a long-range R&D program. A structure relating the conceptional elements of the R&D program; formats for delineating the characteristics of the conceptional elements; mathematical relations between the expected program value and military priority, probability of task success, task cost, and program cost; and a rank-ordering procedure to select a program of maximum expected value. A computer program aids in formulating the R&D program.

14. *Dean, 1964:* An operations research approach. Mathematical models consider the relevant resource variables, noncontrollable variables, parameters, and constraints that are responsive to corporate goals and yield solutions for allocating technical resources to projects. The scoring model permits determination of important factors in a profitability model.

15. *Hill-Roepcke, 1964:* An operations research approach. A mathematical model considering the military value of the objective for technology, the technical probability of success, the expected value of the individual efforts, and a method to select the optimum program from many such efforts.

16. *Nutt, 1965:* An operations research approach. A deterministic model that quantifies the value or technical payoff of each research task. The model developed considers the world environment, the Air Force missions, future weapons systems configurations, laboratory-technical objectives, and the timeliness, complexity, and scope of each research effort. The result consists of recommended funding levels of efficient tasks along with suggested tasks for close scrutiny or possible elimination. A modified linear program.

17. *Cetron, "PROFILE," 1965:* Decision theory of approach designed to aid in exploring the total structure of project selection decision problems in the context of the R&D manager, and R&D processes relevant to the design and implementation of management systems for planning, appraising, and controlling resource allocation among

various projects. PROFILE's nine quantified criteria (value to war-fare, task responsiveness, timeliness, long-range plan, probability of success, technological transfer, manpower facilities, and funding) are used in developing a task "Profile" as well as in determining the military utility, the technical feasibility, and the application of resources for each project.

18. *Rosen and Saunder, 1965:* An operations research approach. A modification of Hess's dynamic programming approach by placement in the context of different optimization criteria for obtaining optimum expenditure patterns. Optimization criteria are used for obtaining optimum expenditure patterns. They are: expected profit; total expected output; life expected output; and a minimum fixed percent return on nondiscounted expenditure.

19. *Sacco, 1965:* An operations research approach. A refinement to the Hill-Roepcke model that permits dynamic programming to be used, thus achieving a more nearly optimum R&D program.

20. *Albertini, 1965:* An operations research approach. A methodology for the evaluation and selection of R&D tasks directed toward the determination of materiel development objectives. A mathematical choice model to assist management in the synthesis of pertinent information for the purpose of selection, within applicable constraints, of a maximum expected value program of research and development effort. Specifications in the form of flow charts are included for computerization.

21. *Berman, 1965:* An economic analysis and decision-tree approach. The approach considers the incremental cost of the project in R&D resources, the incremental production and operating and manning costs of introducing the new technology, and the incremental military value of the technology.

22. *Sobin-Gordon, 1965:* A comparative method that analyzes alternative applications of resource allocation techniques and attempts to establish the value of these techniques against various frames of reference. The analytical method thus developed (basically using ordinal values converted to relative value made up of interdependence of different proposals, definiteness of applications, capability values, probability of success, and military utility) will be used to optimize the selected principles of resource allocation in the dynamic multiple project environment. Linear programming will be used. Principal application to laboratory selection of efforts.

23. *Albertini, 1965:* An operations research approach to synthesize information pertinent to the planning process for the purpose of determining which long-range technical plan tasks to recommend for

funding. This technique begins with given major barrier problem areas (MBPA's), operations on these MBPA's using the following criteria: expected technical value, annual cost of a configuration, annual monetary quota cost of a configuration. A computer program helps formulate the recommended R&D program.

24. *Wells, 1966:* A decision theory approach to store, track, and properly relate judgments concerning systems; to show the impact of these judgments; to permit real-time iterations of planning problems to facilitate the assessment and selection of system candidates for development. Criteria are: threat, types of war, policy objectives, functions, systems contributions, force structure, technical feasibility, schedule and cost, and budget.

25. *Cetron, "QUEST," 1966:* An operations research approach. QUEST utilizes a double set of matrices, consisting of the sciences, technologies, and missions, developed with the technology parameter common to both. By having figures of utility assigned to each mission and by determining the value of the contribution of each technological area to each mission, a cumulative quantified value for each technological area is related to each scientific area and the relevant impact of each of the scientific disciplines is identified with each technological area.

26. *Dean-Hauser, 1966:* An economic analysis and operations research approach. An application of project selection under constrained resource conditions. By using mathematical models, computer programs, and available information concerning costs, uncertainties, and military values, it is possible to obtain optimum solutions. The Case Western Reserve study has developed a mathematical model for handling the large number of alternatives through the use of a series of simpler computerized methods, where the results of one stage are used in the succeeding stage. A dynamic programming formulation is used.

27. *Belt, 1966:* A decision theory approach based on quantified subjective judgments on the predicted value of a successful laboratory project outcome, the likelihood of success of the project in terms of its technological achievability, the specific plan of attack and the suitability of the proposed performers of the work, and the predicted cost. This technique stops short of producing a single numerical rating of project value but gives the decision-maker the opportunity to select from a group of alternative projects.

28. *De l'Estoile, 1966:* A decision theory approach. This refined rating scheme uses a formula including four factors: military utility, probability of technical success, possibility of realization in France,

and direct and indirect economic impact (including the cross support to the civilian sector of the economy). This total system, because of the large number of projects involved, has been computerized.

29. *Martino et al., 1967:* An operations research approach. Factors taken into account are importance of military missions, criticality of technological effort to mission, and level of technology required. Funds are allocated among technical projects on the basis of maximum marginal payoff per dollar, within a budget total.

30. *Caulfield-Freshman, 1967:* A decision theory approach. Development project proposals are rated with respect to six weighted selection categories, consisting of progress of program, military utility, technical risk, resources, management environment, and technological transfer; an over-all score is computed and used to rank the alternatives. This technique is used to develop a task "profile" that serves as an aid in the allocation of resources.

Comparison of Methods

The various methods are compared as to features, ease of use, and area of applicability in Tables A-1, A-2, and A-3 respectively. An entry of X in the matrix indicates that the method has the feature, satisfies the criterion, or is applicable to that area. For level of information or data required, the methods are coded L for little or none, M for a moderate amount, and C for a considerable amount. These evaluations are subjective, of course, but will provide some guidance as to the ease of use.

Summary

Several methods for appraisal of R&D programs have been evaluated against a set of criteria. The capabilities and limitations of each of the methods have been indicated. Each method, within its capabilities and limitations, can provide assistance to the management of an R&D enterprise in appraising the worth of its R&D effort. In particular, the use of quantitative methods tends to eliminate bias, provide a degree of consistency, and force managers to render their judgments more explicit in evaluating R&D programs. While some of the techniques described lack certain features, these usually can be added with some modification, if desired.

The value of any of the appraisal methods is further limited by two factors: the validity of input information supplied by the laboratory

Table A-1   Features of the Methods

	Utility Measure	Prob. of Success	Orthog. Criteria	Sensitivity	Retain Rej. Alt.	Class Struc.	Time	Strategies	Sys. Cross Support	Tech. Cross Support	Graph. Displ.	Flag.	Optimization Criteria *	Constraints †	Computerized
1. Mottley-Newton, 1959	X	X	X	X				X	X				1	1, 6, 7	X
2. Gargiulo et al., 1961	X	X	X					X		X	X		1	1, 2, 3, 4	
3. Pound, 1964	X	X					X						7	1	
4. Sobelman, 1958	X	X					X						7		
5. Freeman, 1960	X	X	X					X					7	1, 2, 3	X
6. Asher, 1962	X	X	X										7	2, 5	X
7. Hess, 1962	X	X					X						7	1	X
8. Dean-Sengupta, 1962	X	X							X	X			7	1	X
9. Disman, 1962	X	X	X										7		
10. Cramer-Smith, 1964	X	X						X	X				7	1	
11. Esch, "PATTERN," 1963	X	X	X	X				X	X	X	X		1, 2		X
12. Blum, 1963	X	X	X					X	X				6	6	
13. Bakanas, 1964	X	X	X	X				X					3	1, 6	X
14. Dean, 1964	X	X	X	X	X	X							4		
15. Hill-Roepcke, 1964	X	X	X					X					2	1, 6, 7	
16. Nutt, 1965	X	X	X	X	X	X	X	X		X	X		1, 2, 3	1, 2, 3	X
17. Cetron, "PROFILE," 1965	X	X	X	X	X	X	X	X		X	X	X	1, 2	1, 2	X
18. Rosen-Saunder, 1965	X	X											3, 3, 4, 7	1	X
19. Sacco, 1965	X	X	X					X		X			3		
20. Albertini, 1965	X	X						X		X	X		2	1, 6, 7	X
21. Berman, 1965	X	X						X	X	X			5		
22. Sobin-Gordon, 1965	X	X		X	X								1	1, 2, 3, 7	X
23. Albertini, 1965	X	X	X					X						1, 6, 7	
24. Wells, 1966	X	X	X	X	X	X		X		X			2	1, 7	X
25. Cetron, "QUEST," 1966	X	X						X	X	X	X	X	1, 2	1, 7	
26. Dean-Hauser, 1966	X	X	X	X	X	X		X				X	2, 3	1, 6	X
27. Belt, 1966	X	X					X				X	X			
28. De l'Estoile, 1966	X	X										X	3		X
29. Martino et al., 1967	X		X					X	X	X	X		3	1, 7	
30. Caulfield-Freshman, 1967	X	X			X	X	X	X	X	X	X	X	1, 2, 3	1, 7	

* Optimization criteria: 1. Ordinal ranking; 2. Expected value; 3. Cost benefit; 4. Profitability; 5. Incremental costs; 6. Composite score; 7. Discounted net value
† Constraints: 1. Budget; 2. Skills available; 3. Facilities available; 4. Competitor efforts; 5. Raw materials available; 6. Risk; 7. Program balance.

Table A-2   Ease of Use

	Data Req'ts.	Manual Oper'n Poss.	Comp. Prog. Avail.	Comp. Run Time	Diffic. of Updating	Operator Profic. Level	Need for Outside Help
1. Mottley-Newton, 1959	L	X	X		L	T	L
2. Gargiulo et al., 1961	M	X				T	L
3. Pound, 1964	C	X				T	L
4. Sobelman, 1958	M	X					
5. Freeman, 1960	C	X	X			T	
6. Asher, 1962	C		X			T	
7. Hess, 1962	C		X			T	
8. Dean-Sengupta, 1962	C					T	
9. Disman, 1962	C						M
10. Cramer-Smith, 1964	M	X					M
11. Esch, "PATTERN," 1963	C		X	C	C	P	C
12. Blum, 1963	M	X			L	T	
13. Bakanas, 1964	C		X	M	L	T	
14. Dean, 1964	M	X			L	P	L
15. Hill, Roepcke, 1964	C			M	L	T	L
16. Nutt, 1965	C		X	L	L	P	C
17. Cetron, "PROFILE," 1965	L	X			L	P	M
18. Rosen-Saunder, 1965	C		X			T	
19. Sacco, 1965	C			L	L	P	L
20. Albertini, 1965	C		X	M	L	T	
21. Berman, 1965	C			C	L	T	
23. Albertini, 1965	C		X	M	L	T	L
24. Wells, 1966	M		X	L	L	P	C
25. Cetron, "QUEST," 1966	C	X			M	P	C
26. Dean-Hauser, 1966	C		X	L	L	P	L
27. Belt, 1966	M	X			M	P	L
28. De l'Estoile, 1966	C		X	C	C	P	C
29. Martino et al., 1967	C	X			M	P	C
30. Caulfield-Freshman, 1967	C	X			M	P	C

Symbol keys
   Computer running time: L—little; M—moderate; C—considerable.
   Difficulty of updating: L—low; M—moderate; C—considerable.
   Need for outside help: L—little or none; M—moderate; C—considerable.
   Operator proficiency: C—clerk; T—technician; P—degreed professional.

Table A-3   R&D Areas of Applicability

	Research	Expl. Devel.	Adv. Devel.	Engr. Devel.
1. Mottley-Newton, 1959	X	X	X	X
2. Gargiulo et al., 1961		X	X	X
3. Pound, 1964		X	X	
4. Sobelman, 1958			X	
5. Freeman, 1960				X
6. Asher, 1962			X	X
7. Hess, 1962				X
8. Dean-Sengupta, 1962				X
9. Disman, 1962		X	X	X
10. Cramer-Smith, 1964	X			
11. Esch, "PATTERN," 1963		X	X	X
12. Blum, 1963		X	X	X
13. Bakanas, 1964		X	X	
14. Dean, 1964		X	X	X
15. Hill-Roepcke, 1964		X	X	
16. Nutt, 1965		X	X	
17. Cetron, "Profile," 1965		X	X	
18. Rosen-Saunder, 1965				X
19. Sacco, 1965		X	X	
20. Albertini, 1965		X	X	
21. Berman, 1965		X	X	X
22. Sobin-Gordon, 1965	X	X	X	
23. Albertini, 1965	X			
24. Wells, 1966			X	X
25. Cetron, "QUEST," 1966	X	X		
26. Dean-Hauser, 1966		X	X	X
27. Belt, 1966		X	X	
28. De l'Estoile, 1966		X	X	X
29. Martino et al., 1967	X	X		

workers and management staff; and the effective support and use of the system by higher management. If management supports a method and makes proper use of it, and furthermore insures that the input information is as valid as humanly possible, the methods can provide a very valuable tool for improving the management of an R&D organization.

Considering the limitations of the methods described, there is clearly much room for further refinement and improvement of quantitative methods for appraisal of R&D programs. However, even in the absence of these refined methods, the spectrum of existing methods can provide the R&D manager with valuable assistance in appraising his program.

Acknowledgment

The author of this appendix is indebted to Joseph Martino and L. Roepcke for their valuable assistance in its preparation.

Appendix B
"Braille," A Case Study on Quantitative Approaches to Aid in R&D Planning[1]

Marvin J. Cetron

In various industries, particularly those that are dynamic and very competitive, Technological Forecasting (TF) has already become an accepted tool of management. TFs have proved to be most useful in guiding a corporation's R&D effort, provided the forecasting outputs are properly integrated[2] into the companies' over-all planning structure and meaningfully related to corporate objectives. The most accurate forecast does not mean much, however, unless it is utilized and eventually influences action.

Forecasting as such should be the primary concern of various technical specialists (or marketing and production staffs where appropriate). But the weighing of probabilities, at which point in time and with which level of confidence a certain technological or scientific goal might be achieved, is a task solely for the experts in the R&D department who by virtue of their competence, experience, and over-all knowledge of a given field can alone provide the proper outputs.

It is frequently at this stage that the forecasting process stops and this for a number of reasons: An over-all plan within the company is not available or has not been made, company objectives are lacking, experienced transfer personnel capable of relating (coupling) scientific outputs to technological needs and marketing goals are missing, or middle management simply does not know how to utilize the forecast.

---

[1] This study was published as a section of Cetron, Marvin J., *Technological Forecasting: A Practical Approach*, New York: Gordon and Breach, 1969.
[2] Cetron, M. J., "Using Technical Forecasts," *Science and Technology*, July 1968.

196

In my contacts with many planning organizations, both in private industry and government, I have encountered an additional barrier to the utilization of technological forecasts which is perhaps the single most important reason why TFs are not used more broadly: Most planning models, incorporating project selection and resources allocation features, make use of R&D appraisal methods that are too complex, require too many data, and are too time-consuming and too costly to operate. Yet, simple practical models are often frowned upon and not used either. The literature is full of examples of appraisal techniques that got no further than the journals in which they were published, since for the reasons enumerated here they were never used. All of these "resistances against introduction" seem to fit into one of two categories: Either the forecast and planning procedures are too philosophical and complicated and cannot be utilized in the real world, or else they are too simple-minded, that is to say, not impressive enough to be considered seriously by the decision-makers. In this latter case, the technical management feels that all that they are doing is to manipulate quantitative subjective judgments as if they were technological data. This may well be so, but at least such approaches structure and clarify our thinking and in this way greatly aid in the planning, evaluation, and decision-making processes.[3]

We wish to present here a simple but practical model, proven and tested, which contains all the basic elements necessary to arrive at meaningful decisions, does not require a type 360 computer, and yet can easily be expanded in scope and sophistication should this be desired. This simple approach to corporate planning has been utilized not only by a number of small companies and by government agencies (who substitute "utility" for "profits") but also by large corporations and academic institutions.

For our exercise we have chosen the "Mighty Charge Corporation," a fictitious company producing various power sources.

The company, with sales of $3,000,000, makes a gross profit of 30% ($900,000; net after taxes $450,000) and has an annual R&D budget of $90,000. It employs about 500 people and produces primary (nonrechargeable) batteries: MnO_2/Zn, mercury dry cells, etc., and secondary (rechargeable) batteries: Ni/Cd, Ag/Zn, and lead-acid types.

---

[3] Cetron, M. J., Martino, J., and Roepcke, L., "The Selection of R&D Program Content —Survey of Quantitative Methods." *IEEE Transactions on Engineering Management*, EM-14, No. 1, March 1967.

Motivated by a desire to have both short- and long-term growth potential, the company now plans to manufacture fuel cells (H_2/O_2, CH_4/O_2, NH_3/O_2, or some such system), and seriously considers establishing a capability in direct thermal conversion: thermoelectric, thermionic, or MHD devices. Even though the company is small, management thinks modern, as evidenced by an integrated though inexpensive planning procedure.

We are assuming[4] that the board of directors has agreed on a number of company objectives and determined their merit, that is, their relative contribution to the over-all objectives, as listed in Table 3.1 (page 45).

Conveniently the total of the figures of merit is 100. Any other figure will do, but it should then be normalized[5] to 100 for ease of manipulation of the data.

With the necessary assumptions made and the objectives selected, we can proceed with the evaluation of our proposed R&D program as part of the company's systematic planning effort.

We begin with the value sheets (Table B-1), which assess the impact which each of the company's present or future products might make toward achieving the corporate objectives. The Figures of Merit (Column I) were already established by the board of directors and assigned on the basis of the relative importance of the various selected corporate objectives. Now a marketing or other nontechnical expert evaluates and fills in Column II. He should know the corporate situation thoroughly and when making his evaluation take into consideration the descriptors at the bottom of the sheet (Scale of Definitions). In cases where these three descriptors do not adequately fit the contributions, he interpolates between the numbers. For example, a new development with respect to product I (primary batteries in this hypothetical case) is considered slightly more than an "improvement of the current product" when related to contributing toward the "10% share of total market" and is accorded 0.4 point (Column II). The Figure of Merit of this corporate objective had been assigned 15 units out of the available 100. Thus, the value to this individual category is $0.4 \times 15 = 6.0$ (Column III). The other categories, similarly evaluated for

---

[4] The assumptions and corporate objectives presented in this case are used for illustrative purposes in order to demonstrate the methodology and feasibility of the procedures. Figures used here were specifically changed from those of a real working concern because we wanted to prevent any similarity or association to any existing company. Such information as for instance corporate objectives is normally proprietary, and the examples selected might even be contradictory in a real business environment.

[5] Cetron, M. J., "PROFILE," in Jantsch, E. (ed.), *Technological Forecasting in Perspective.* Paris: OECD, 1967, pp. 228–29.

Table B-1   Specimen Value Sheets for the Mighty Charge Corporation

Value Sheet 1

Product: Primary batteries

Figure of Merit	Column I — Corporate Objectives	1.0	.9	.8	.7	.6	.5	.4	.3	.2	.1	Column III — Value to Individual Category
12	1. Low volume, high margin									X		2.4
15	2. 10% share of total market							X				6.0
18	3. 12 to 15% annual growth rate								X			5.4
14	4. High versatility										X	1.4
10	5. Five years to reach maximum profits									X		2.0
12	6. Not more than 25% govt. business									X		2.4
19	7. Cash flow, 6% of investment							X				7.6

Column II: Impact of Product Contribution

Total Value (V) to Corporation   27.2

Value Sheet 2

Product: secondary batteries

Figure of Merit	Column I — Corporate Objectives	1.0	.9	.8	.7	.6	.5	.4	.3	.2	.1	Column III — Value to Individual Category
12	1. Low volume, high margin										X	1.2
15	2. 10% share of total market							X				6.0
18	3. 12 to 15% annual growth rate							X				7.2
14	4. High versatility									X		2.8
10	5. Five years to reach maximum profits							X				4.0
12	6. Not more than 25% govt. business									X		2.4
19	7. Cash flow, 6% of investment									X		3.8

Column II: Impact of Product Contribution

Total Value (V) to Corporation   27.4

Table B-1 (*cont'd.*)

Value Sheet 3

Product: Fuel cells

Figure of Merit	Corporate Objectives	1.0	.9	.8	.7	.6	.5	.4	.3	.2	.1	Value to Individual Category
		Column I				Column II — Impact of Product Contribution						Column III
12	1. Low volume, high margin	X										12.0
15	2. 10% share of total market						X					7.5
18	3. 12 to 15% annual growth rate						X					9.0
14	4. High versatility			X								11.2
10	5. Five years to reach maximum profits										X	1.0
12	6. Not more than 25% govt. business			X								9.6
19	7. Cash flow, 6% of investment									X		3.8

Total Value (V) to Corporation   54.1

Value Sheet 4

Product: Direct thermal conversion

Figure of Merit	Corporate Objectives	1.0	.9	.8	.7	.6	.5	.4	.3	.2	.1	Value to Individual Category
		Column I				Column II — Impact of Product Contribution						Column III
12	1. Low volume, high margin										X	1.2
15	2. 10% share of total market									X		3.0
18	3. 12 to 15% annual growth rate								X			5.4
14	4. High versatility		X									12.6
10	5. Five years to reach maximum profits										X	1.0
12	6. Not more than 25% govt. business									X		2.4
19	7. Cash flow, 6% of investment										X	1.9

Total Value (V) to Corporation   27.5

Scale of Definitions for "Impact of Product Contribution" (Column II):
    1.0 Critical line of service (defensive product)
    .7 Extension of existing product line(s)
    .3 Improvement of current product

their contributions and the total value of this product to the corporation (V) are summed at 27.2. The number of definitions can be expanded when adapting this model for other planning purposes. The expert then proceeds to do the same for the other products under consideration.

We now turn to the Appraisal Sheets Table B-2. The top half of these forms solicits the opinion of the technical specialist regarding the probability of achieving the technical objective. It considers whether the task could be successfully accomplished from a scientific and technical feasibility point of view. Technical risk also takes into consideration the degree of confidence or prediction that the remaining portion of the total objective can be attained. This latter usually assesses the factors of the present state of the art, either implicit or explicit. This appraisal is naturally based on technical forecasts and includes time factors and resource levels.

The credibility of the ratings of technical feasibility and the probability of success increase with the technical competence of the personnel qualified to judge these factors on the basis of the ability and experience of the individuals and/or organizations carrying on the development efforts. Therefore a technical specialist, preferably an R&D man still working at the bench, should check the box that best describes his opinion regarding the technical objective, as well as that giving the number of different concurrent approaches, these also being a measure of probability of success.

There is appended, for illustrative purposes, a fuel cell forecast. The forecaster assigned a 30-to-80% chance of meeting the technical objective, such as a new H_2/O_2 fuel cell (product 3) and he used three concurrent approaches to achieve this goal. The appropriate boxes on the Appraisal Sheet were checked.

The third area, Management Environment, solicits an opinion on the acceptability of the effort in the management structure. Here the evaluator is to give what he believes to be the management considerations concerning this effort, and he will check the applicable box.

Last, the appraisal summary is completed. For our calculation of the probability of success (P_s) of meeting the technical objectives (TO) we use the probability chart shown in Table B-3. Here, n is the number of concurrent approaches used to accomplish the TO, and C is a number arbitrarily assigned to the chances of succeeding in a given approach. We designate:

$$80 \text{ to } 100\% \text{ chance of success: } C = 0.8$$
$$30 \text{ to } 80\% \text{ chance of success: } C = 0.5$$
$$0 \text{ to } 3\% \text{ chance of success: } C = 0.2$$

Table B-2   Appraisal Sheet 1

Primary batteries

Chance of Meeting Technical Objectives with Level of Confidence (C)
( ) 80–100%
(X) 30–80%
( )   0–30%

Number of Different Concurrent Approaches (n)
(X) 1   ( ) 2   ( ) 3   ( ) 4   ( ) 5
( ) 6   ( ) 7   ( ) 8   ( ) 9   ( ) 10 or more

Management Environment
( ) Board of Directors   ( ) President   ( ) V.P. Marketing
( ) V.P. R&D   ( ) V.P. Production   ( ) Other

Appraisal Summary
Number of Corporate Objectives:
Value (V):   27.2
Probability of Success (P_s):   0.5
Expected Value (EV):   13.6
Funding (F):..20   (in thousands)
Desirability Index (D):   0.68

We assume that all approaches n have the same chance of success, and therefore the same value of C. The number assigned to the probability of one approach failing is then $(1 - C)$; that for the probability of all approaches failing is $(1 - C)^n$. Further, if we assume that at least one of the approaches taken will succeed, then the number assigned to P_s is $1 - (1 - C)^n$.

   Example (Product 3): We have three concurrent approaches ($n = 3$), with $C = 0.5$. Thus the number corresponding to P_s is 0.875.

   We had assumed that all approaches had equal chances of success. If the chance of success for each individual approach is different, then we use the formula:

$$P_s = 1 - [(C_1)(C_2)(C_3)] \ldots .$$

Example: We have four approaches, n_1 to n_4. The chances of success are:

Table B-2   Appraisal Sheet 2

Secondary batteries

Chance of Meeting Technical Objectives with Level of Confidence (C)
( ) 80–100%
(X) 30–80%
( )   0–30%

Number of Different Concurrent Approaches (n)
(X) 1   ( ) 2   ( ) 3   ( ) 4   ( ) 5
( ) 6   ( ) 7   ( ) 8   ( ) 9   ( ) 10 or more

Management Environment
( ) Board of Directors   ( ) President   ( ) V.P. Marketing
( ) V.P. R&D   ( ) V.P. Production   ( ) Other

Appraisal Summary
Number of Corporate Objectives:
Value (V):   27.4
Probability of Success (P_s):   0.5
Expected Value (EV):   13.7
Funding (F):   25   (in thousands)
Desirability Index (D):   0.55

$$
\begin{aligned}
C \text{ of } n_1 \qquad & C_1 = 0.5 \\
C \text{ of } n_2 \qquad & C_2 = 0.2 \\
C \text{ of } n_3 \qquad & C_3 = 0.5 \\
C \text{ of } n_4 \qquad & C_4 = 0.8 \\
P_s = 1 - [(0.5)(0.2)(0.5)(0.8)] &= 0.960
\end{aligned}
$$

For convenience, the P_s for several values of n have been calculated and are listed in Table 9.1 (p. 180).

Now back to our appraisal summary. The probability of success P_s is multiplied with the value V from the Value Sheet to get the expected value EV. Thus, for product 3 we obtain: $V \times P_s = EV$, or $54.1 \times 0.875 = 47.3$. Completion of this project is estimated to require a funding of \$80,000 ($F = 80$). The desirability index D is then calculated by dividing the expected value EV by F: $EV/F = D$, or $47.3/80 = 0.59$.

Table B-2   Appraisal Sheet 3

Fuel Cells

Chance of Meeting Technical Objectives with Level of Confidence (C)
( ) 80–100%
(X) 30–80%
( )   0–30%

Number of Different Concurrent Approaches (n)
( ) 1   ( ) 2   (X) 3   ( ) 4   ( ) 5
( ) 6   ( ) 7   ( ) 8   ( ) 9   ( ) 10 or more

Management Environment
( ) Board of Directors   ( ) President   ( ) V.P. Marketing
( ) V.P. R&D   ( ) V.P. Production   ( ) Other

Appraisal Summary
Number of Corporate Objectives:
Value (V):   54.1
Probability of Success (P_s):   0.875
Expected Value (EV):   47.3
Funding (F):   80   (in thousands)
Desirability Index (D):   0.59

Carrying out these same calculations for the other products, we can rank our projects according to their desirability index and can use the result as a basis for our decisions; else we can use the EV values or other factors for the same purpose.

These techniques are not intended to yield decisions but rather to furnish information that will facilitate decision making. Indeed, they are merely thinking structures to force methodical, meticulous analysis. The data plus the analysis only give us information. It takes this information plus judgment to render the decisions.

In our case, management decided to pursue R&D work for products 1, 2, and 3 only and to drop product 4. The research deficit was to be made up by seeking government support for the fuel cell venture.

Table B-2   Appraisal Sheet 4

Direct thermal conversion

Chance of Meeting Technical Objectives with Level of Confidence (C)
( ) 80–100%
( ) 30–80%
(X) 0–30%

Number of Different Concurrent Approaches (n)

(X) 1	( ) 2	( ) 3	( ) 4	( ) 5
( ) 6	( ) 7	( ) 8	( ) 9	( ) 10 or more

Management Environment

( ) Board of Directors	( ) President	( ) V.P. Marketing
( ) V.P. R&D	( ) V.P. Production	( ) Other

Appraisal Summary

Number of Corporate Objectives:
Value (V):   27.5
Probability of Success (P_s):   0.2
Expected Value (EV):   5.5
Funding (F):   30   (in thousands)
Desirability Index (D):   0.18

Certainly our result is not like the output of a linear programming model which one might want to utilize if there were more products and R&D programs to be considered, but the authors wish to stress the point that in their opinion management decisions should be made by managers and not by a system, not even a highly sophisticated computerized system. There are places where operation research techniques[6] are not only desirable but requisite, but in the case of R&D management a maximum amount of flexibility must be retained and freedom of decision is the manager's prerogative. This is absolutely essential if the decision-maker is not only to be given responsibility but also to be held accountable for the work under his control.

[6] Cetron, M. J., and Monahan, T. I., "An Evaluation and Appraisal of Various Approaches to Technological Forecasting," in Bright, J. R. (ed.), *Forecasting for Industry or Government*. Englewood Cliffs, N.J.: Prentice-Hall, 1968, pp. 144–79.

Fuel Cell Forecast

Background

A fuel cell is a direct energy converter that produces electrical energy by electrochemically combining a fuel and an oxidant. The basic components of a single fuel cell are two electrodes and an electrolyte. Fuel is oxidized at one electrode with the release of electrons to an external circuit to do useful work. Electrons are returned to the other electrode where the oxidant is reduced. The electrical circuit is completed with the transport of ions across the electrolyte. A practical fuel cell battery consists of a number of these individual cells in an appropriate electrical array together with the necessary structural supports, fuel, oxidant, electrolyte, coolant, and electrical current distribution components.

There are several characteristics of fuel cells which make them attractive for a variety of applications. Some of the unique features are:

High Efficiency: Fuel cells are not subject to Carnot-cycle limitations and thus are more efficient than other energy conversion systems. Over-all thermal efficiencies greater than 50% are presently obtainable.

Low Noise: Like conventional primary or secondary batteries, fuel cells are inherently quiet because of the lack of moving parts. This makes them attractive for submarine applications.

High-Overload Capability: Fuel cells can operate at power outputs several times the normal rated power for several hours without significantly reducing the lifetime of the system.

Current Status

The concept of a fuel cell and the first laboratory demonstration model date back to the early 19th century. Improvements through research and development over the past five years have advanced fuel cell technology to the stage where engineering development of power plant systems appears technically and economically feasible for many different applications. Some fuel cells that have reached this state of development use fuels such as hydrocarbons (including alcohols), hydrogen, ammonia, and hydrazine. Oxygen is the common oxidant, whether it is supplied from a cryogenic tank, by dissociation of hydrogen peroxide, or from atmospheric air. The reliability of such systems has been demonstrated again and again by perfect space flights in which spaceships used H_2/O_2 fuel cells as a power source.

Hydrocarbon Fuel Cell Systems. From the standpoint of fuel costs, fuel logistics, and ease of handling, fuel cells operating on liquid hydrocarbon fuels are the most attractive for a large number of applications. Systems under development include indirect systems in which the hydrocarbon fuel is reformed to produce hydrogen either in an external or an internal reformer using the excess heat to support the endothermic reforming reaction, and direct systems for the electrochemical oxidation of the hydrocarbon fuel at the fuel cell electrode. A hydrocarbon fuel-cell system is shown schematically in Figure B-1, in which the principal subsystems are the hydrogen reformer and fuel cell battery. The reformer generates hydrogen from a hydrocarbon fuel. After purification, the hydrogen reacts electrochemically with the oxidant in the fuel cells.

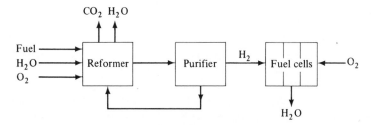

Figure B-1   Hydrocarbon Fuel-Cell System (Schematic)

The H_2/O_2 fuel cells for this system are more advanced in their development than any other type. The U.S. space program provided the major impetus for the engineering development of such cells. Naturally, the fuel cell concepts associated with this well-funded effort have other capabilities. A well-developed technological base has been established by the space programs which will be applicable to many other future developments.

The following paragraphs provide data on the three principal versions of H_2/O_2 fuel cells as distinguished by the type or condition of the electrolyte employed. These are ion-exchange membrane electrolytes, free electrolytes, and fixed electrolytes.

Ion-Exchange Membrane System: The fuel cells for the Gemini spacecraft were of the ion-exchange-membrane (IEM) type and consisted of an organic cation exchange membrane as the electrolyte, with electrodes made of teflon-bonded platinum deposited on a very thin, fine-mesh tantalum-palladium screen. The fuel cell electrode power density was about 28 watts per sq. ft. Power density for Gemini fuel cell modules was about 0.6 kw per cubic ft at normal rated load and about 1.6 kw per cubic ft at peak overload conditions.

Further improvements in the IEM cell are in the development stage. Reduced-catalyst-loading cells (5 to 10 g per sq ft) have operated for 3000 hours and reportedly have polarization characteristics similar to those of the higher-catalyst-loading cells. Present cell production facilities can produce cells as large as 17 by 72 in.; Gemini cells were 8 by 8 in. A 1-to-1 polarization characteristics ratio has been demonstrated in a scale-up to an 11-by-22-in. electrode.

Free Electrolyte Systems: There are two main types of free electrolyte fuel cell systems presently in engineering development; the moderate-temperature, low-pressure modified-Bacon system and the low-temperature, low-pressure thin-carbon-electrode system.

As the power source for the Apollo Command and Service Module, the modified-Bacon fuel cell system was the beneficiary of the largest effort that has yet been expended in fuel cell development. It has the highest efficiency of any known H_2/O_2 fuel cell at a given current density, because of the higher operating temperatures.

Unfortunately these high fuel-cell efficiencies do not come without penalty. To operate at temperatures in the range of 400° F at three or four atm pressure requires about 80% potassium hydroxide (KOH), which is solid at room temperature. Hence, one problem is the start-up and shut-down of modules. Also, the mechanical stresses due to the unavoidable phase changes during repeated start-up and shut-down may further reduce reliability. Another problem, resulting from operation at these higher temperatures, is cathode corrosion.

Two versions of low-temperature free-electrolyte systems have also been under development. The earliest of these employed catalyzed, $\frac{1}{4}$-in. thick, baked carbon electrodes and a 25% KOH electrolyte. Pilot systems up to 30 kw have been built. The electrodes currently used consist of a 0.030-in. nickel plaque to which is applied a carbon layer and 1 to 2 g of precious metal catalyst per sq ft. This system has operated at about 150° F with a circulating 12 N-KOH electrolyte. The guaranteed performance characteristics of these power plant modules are depicted in Figures B-2 and B-3.

The compactness of the design and the low electrode cost suggested by the low-catalyst loading are attractive features of the thin-carbon electrode. A circulating electrolyte also has many advantages, the principal ones being greater latitude in the dynamics of control of termal energy and by-product water removal, better temperature uniformity, thermal energy removal at its origin, and compact module construction.

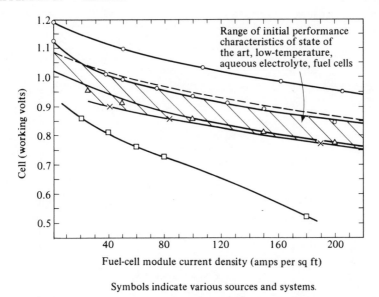

Figure B-2   Volt-Ampere Characteristics of H_2/O_2 Fuel-Cell Module

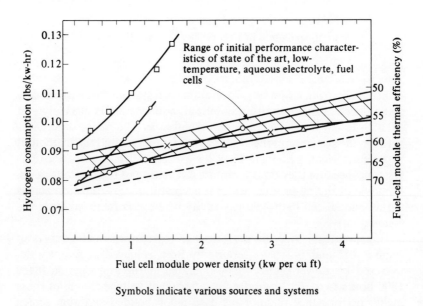

Figure B-3   Power Density versus Efficiency for H_2/O_2 Fuel-Cell Modules

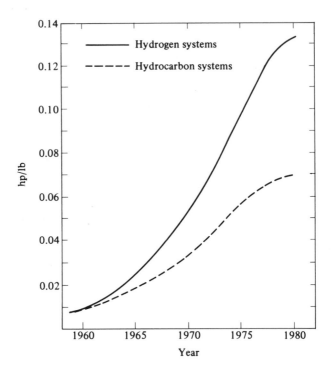

Figure B-4   Output of Fuel-Cell Systems in HP per Unit Weight

Fixed Electrolyte Systems. Several fuel cell systems presently under-going development use an immobilized, aqueous KOH electrolyte in a 0.020- to 0.030-in. thick asbestos membrane. The major differences between the systems are the types of electrodes used and the method of by-product water removal. They have been called "static-moisture-systems" because they do not require circulation of the reactant gases. Removal of the by-product water is accomplished by diffusion across the individual-cell hydrogen gas cavity where it is removed from the system.

Improvements over the performance represented in the curves of Figures B-2 and B-3 have reportedly been achieved in recently de-livered 2 kw power plants which operated at 100 amps per sq ft for 1800 hours to a 10% degradation in terminal voltage. Some of these higher performance plants have used teflon-bonded-platinum screen electrodes.

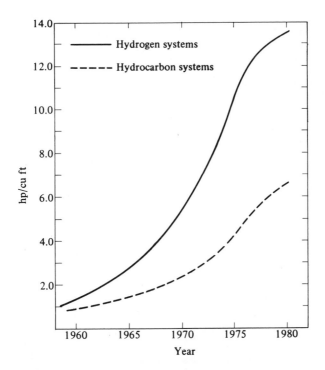

Figure B-5 Output of Fuel-Cell Systems in HP per Unit Volume

Another fuel cell which uses an immobilized KOH electrolyte in a thin asbestos membrane is being developed for the use of precious-metal, catalyzed screen electrodes. Catalyst loadings have been nominally 16.5 g per sq ft cell with platinum as the primary constituent. Product water removal is accomplished by condensation from recirculating reactant gases. Heat removal has been achieved with a circulating coolant or a circulating electrolyte.

Development of this fuel cell system is being pursued in several places. Single cell tests have shown power degradation rates of 2 to 3% per 1000 hours up to test durations of about 2000 hours. Power plants in the nominal 1-kw range have been built for industrial customer evaluation.

Performance characteristics of fuel cell modules based on estimates from developmental-model "compact cell" units are also plotted in Figures B-2 and B-3.

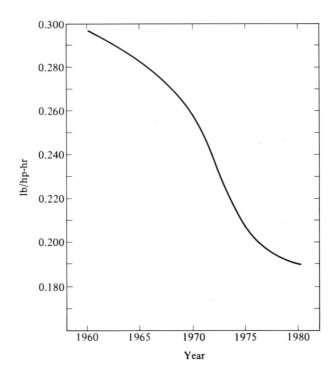

Figure B-6   Specific Fuel Consumption of Hydrocarbon Fuel Cells

Pilot-plant facilities have been developed for teflon-bonded-platinum screen electrodes which have a catalyst loading of 43 g per sq ft. These electrodes have been tested at $100°$ C, 50% KOH in 0.020-in. fuel cell asbestos, and atmospheric pressure reactant gases. Polarization data from these tests are plotted in Figure B-3. The volt-ampere characteristics of these high-performance electrodes were incorporated into an engineered module configuration which uses physically identical electrodes (in a fixed electrolyte design) to provide an optimistic estimate of fuel cell power density and efficiency that might be produced by present technology. The results of this analysis are shown as a dashed line in Figure B-3.

Performance Summary. The range of initial performance characteristics, in terms of power density and efficiency, for low-temperature, low-pressure, aqueous electrolyte fuel cells is indicated by a cross-

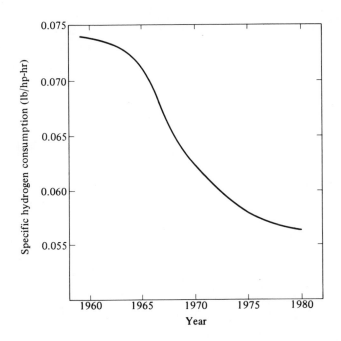

Figure B-7 Specific Fuel Consumption of Hydrogen Fuel Cells

hatched band in Figures B-2 and B-3. Rather than attempt to relate a single point of performance for a specific fuel cell to a given application, it is deemed more appropriate to consider this range of capabilities as representative of the technological base from which the development of other fuel cell power plants must emanate.

Reliability Summary. The performance spectrum of present low-temperature, H_2/O_2 fuel cells does not consider the reliability aspects of the various fuel cell systems operating at these power densities. A summary of the more pertinent reliability information available on the various fuel cells is given in the following paragraphs:

Thin-Carbon Electrode System—A lifetime of 10,000 hours mean time before failure (MTBF) is possible for cell modules of 0.375 sq ft thin carbon electrodes based on 50 amps per sq ft. This 8-cell stack

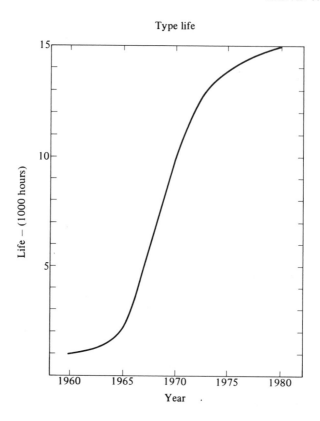

Figure B-8   Life Expectancy of Fuel-Cell Systems

lifetime is being structured into nominal 1-kw modules to provide a quoted module reliability of 0.989 for the 1000-hour guaranteed performance period.

Fixed Electrolyte Cell—Lifetimes of 2000 hours have been obtained on recently built breadboard systems operating at 100 amps per sq ft. Single cells using the latest 9-mg catalyst per sq cm electrodes show power degradation rates of 2 to 3% per 1000 hours up to 1800 hours on test. A 2.0-kw module using these electrodes and rated at 19 lbs per kw showed no statistically significant degradation in the 1000-hour acceptance test.

Apollo—Production-model 2-kw power plant systems are now quali-

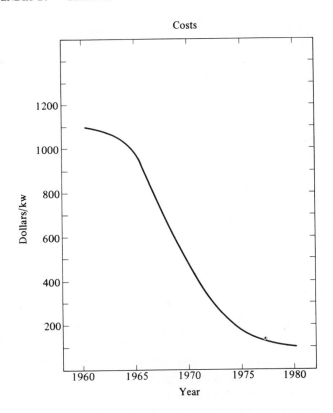

Figure B-9 Projected Costs of Fuel-Cell Systems

fied for the Apollo mission power profile of 1500 hours. NASA expects the lifetime to be improved to 2000 hours.

Ion-Exchange Membrane—Life data available on the Gemini production-model power plants show spacecraft power profile lifetimes ranging from 300 to more than 1000 hours.

This life-data summary is for the most part based on operation at the relatively high current densities (100 amps per sq ft and higher) that are dictated by a need for low-weight fuel cells in short mission space applications. Contrast this with missions to 60 days which may be considered for certain other fuel cell applications. If it is assumed that 100 watts per sq ft is the maximum electrode power density required at the high power operation, then the average power density over a typical 60-day mission is about 15 watts per sq ft. There is no incentive to make the average electrode power density higher by designing for higher power density at peak load because tradeoff studies indicate that the electrode power density should be in this range to achieve minimum total weight and volume. In reliability investigations it was determined that for a constant current density on the cells the voltage degradation per unit time is proportional to the square of the current density.

One source indicates that its fuel cell voltage degradation rate with time is probably more nearly proportional to current density. A more conservative estimate indicates that operation of fuel cells, in the range of 15 to 25 watts per sq ft, will probably improve the lifetime by a factor of 3 or 4 over the 50 to 100 watts per sq ft operation of current fuel cells.

Forecast of Future Developments

The projected capabilities of various fuel cell systems are portrayed graphically in Figures B-4 through B-9. They do not necessarily represent an evolutionary improvement along a time-proven-trend curve, such as the projections for conventional thermal power plant systems. Rather, they are based largely on engineering judgment and studies of the limited amount of engineering systems data available in present fuel cell technology. The projected capabilities indicated are believed to be technically feasible if the necessary resources are allocated. Available resources may permit the realization of selected capabilities within the time periods indicated. The chance of meeting the technical objectives outlined is estimated to be 30 to 80%.

The general pattern and time schedule of development, initial application and evolutionary improvement to provide the capabilities indicated are as follows:

1966-1970   Exploratory and advanced development of prototype systems using low temperature H_2/O_2 fuel cells supplied by hydrocarbon fuel reformers and cryogenic fuel and oxidant storage systems.

Exploratory development of moderate-temperature, low-pressure systems and low-temperature, high-pressure systems.

Research on high and low temperatures, direct hydrocarbon oxidation systems.

1970-1975   Engineering improvement of low-temperature indirect hydrocarbon and cryogenic fuel systems to improve power density, increase life and lower cost.

Initial engineering development and application of moderate temperature indirect hydrocarbon systems.

Initial application of low temperature, high pressure systems.

Exploratory development of direct hydrocarbon fuel oxidation systems.

1975-1980   Engineering improvement of moderate-temperature, low-pressure systems and low-temperature, high-pressure systems. Initial application of low- and high-temperature, direct hydrocarbon fuel oxidation systems.

Acknowledgment

The author is indebted to Dr. Bodo Bartocha for his valuable assistance in preparing this case study.

Bibliography

Ackoff, Russell L., *Scientific Method: Optimizing Applied Research Decisions.* New York: John Wiley and Sons, 1962.

———, (ed.) *Progress in Operations Research,* Vol. I. New York: John Wiley and Sons, 1961.

———, "Specialized Versus Generalized Models in Research Budgeting." Paper presented at the Second Conference on Research Program Effectiveness, Washington, D. C., July 27–29, 1965.

———, Arnoff, E. Leonard, and Churchman, C. West, *Introduction to Operations Research.* New York: John Wiley and Sons, 1957.

Adams, J. G., Nellums, Howard, R. E., "Engineering Evaluation—Tool for Research Management," *Industrial and Engineering Chemistry,* XLIX, May, 1957, 40A.

Albertini, J., *The QMDO Planning Process as it Relates to the U.S. Army Material Command.* Cornell Aeronautical Lab. Report No. VQ-2044-H-1 on USAMC Contract DA-49-185 AMC-237(X), Aug. 31, 1965.

———, *The LRTP Planning Process as it Relates to the U.S. Army Material Command,* Cornell Aeronautical Lab. Report No. VQ-2044-H-2 on USAMC Contract DA-49-186 AMC-237(X), Oct. 30, 1965.

———, *LRTP Mathematical Model Brochure.* Cornell Aeronautical Lab. Report No. VQ-2044-H-3 on USAMC Contract DA-49-186 AMC-237(X), Oct. 30, 1965.

Amey, L. R., "The Allocation and Utilization of Resources," *Operations Research Quarterly,* June, 1964.

Andersen, Sigurd L., "Venture Analysis, A Flexible Planning Tool," *Chemical Engineering Progress,* March, 1961, pp. 80–83.

———, "A 2x2 Risk Decision Problem," *Chemical Engineering Progress,* May 1961, pp. 70–72.

Anderson, Carl A. "Notes on the Evaluation of Research Planning." Paper presented at the Research Program Effectiveness Conference, Washington, D. C., July 21–23, 1964.

Andrew, G. H. L., Assessing priorities for technical effort, *Operational Research Quart.*, Vol. 5, September 1954, pp. 67–80.

Ansoff, H. I., Evaluation of Applied Research in a Business Firm, Technological Planning on the Corporate Level, Bright, J. R. (ed.), *Proc. Conf. at Harvard Business School,* Harvard University, Cambridge, Mass., 1962, pp. 209–24.

Anthony, Robert H., and Day, John S., *Management Controls in Industrial Research Organizations.* Cambridge, Mass.: Harvard University Press, 1952.

Asher, D. T., "A Linear Programming Model for the Allocation of R&D Efforts," *IRE Transactions on Engineering Management,* EM-9, No. 4, December 1962, pp. 154–57.

———, and Disman, S., "Operations research in R&D," *Chem. Engineering Progr.,* Vol. 59:1, January 1963, pp. 41–45.

Aumann, R. J., and Kruskal, J. B., "Assigning Quantitative Values to Qualitative Factors in the Naval Electronics Program," *Naval Research Logistics Quarterly*, March 1959, p. 15.

Bakanas, V., *An Analytical Method to Aid in the Choice of Long Range Study Tasks,* Cornell Aeronautical Lab. Report No. VQ-1887-H-1. USAMC contract DA 49-186 AMC-97(X), May 19, 1964.

Baker, N. R., and Pound, W. H., "Rand D Project Selection: Where we stand." *IEEE Transactions on Engineering Management.* Vol. EM-11, No. 4, Dec. 1964.

Barmby, John G., "The Applicability of PERT as a Management Tool," *IRE Transactions on Engineering Management*, Vol. EM-9, No. 3, Sept. 1962.

Battersby, A., *Network Analysis for Planning and Scheduling*, New York: St. Martins Press, 1964.

Baumgartner, John S., *Project Management.* Homewood, Illinois: Richard Irwin Press, 1963.

Beckwith, R. E., "A Cost Control Extension of the PERT System," *IRE Transactions on Engineering Management,* Vol. EM-9, No. 4, Dec. 1962.

Belt, John Robert, "Military Applied R&D Project Evaluation," U.S. Navy Marine Engineering Laboratory, Annapolis, Md., June 1966 (unpublished thesis).

Berman, E. R., "Research Allocation in a PERT Network Under Continuous Activity Time-Cost Functions," *Management Science,* Vol. 10, No. 4, 1964.

———, Draft: *Theoretical Structure of a Methodology for R&D Resource Allocation,* Research Analysis Corp., McLean, Va., May 26, 1965.

Bensley, Dean E., "Planning and Controlling a Research and Development Program: A Case Study." Master's Thesis, Massachusetts Institute of Technology, Cambridge, 1955.

Berstein, Alex, and de Sola Pool, Ithiel, "Development and Testing of an Evaluation Model for Research Organization Substructures." Paper presented at the Research Program Effectiveness Conference, Washington, D. C., July 21–23, 1964.

Blinoff, V., and Pacifico, C., *Chem. Processing,* Vol. 20, Nov. 1957, pp. 34–35.

Blood, Jerome W. (ed.), *The Management of Scientific Talent.* New York: The American Management Association, 1963.

Blum, Steven, *Time, Cost, and Risk Analysis in Project Planning*. U.S. Army Frankford Arsenal Report, Aug. 22, 1963.

Bock, R. H., and Holstein, W. K., *Production Planning and Control*. Columbus: Charles E. Merrill Books, 1963.

Bonini, Charles P., Jaedicke, Robert K., and Wagner, Harvey M., *Management Controls: New Directions in Basic Research*. New York: McGraw-Hill Book Company, 1964.

Boothe, Norton, et al., *From Concept to Commercialization, A Study of the R&D Budget Allocation Process*. Stanford University Sloan Program, The Graduate School of Business. Stanford, Calif.: Stanford University, 1962.

Brandenburg, R. G., *A Descriptive Analysis of Project Selection. A Summary Report*. Pittsburgh, Pa.: Carnegie Institute of Technology, July 1964.

————, *Toward a Multi-Space Information Conversion Model of the Research and Development Process*, Carnegie Inst. of Tech. Management Sciences Res. Report No. 48, Aug. 1965.

Bright, James R. (ed.), *Technological Planning on the Corporate Level*. Proceedings of the Conference at Harvard Business School, Harvard University, Boston, 1962.

Busacker, Robert G., and Saaty, Thomas L., *Finite Graphs and Networks: An Introduction With Applications*. New York: McGraw-Hill Book Company, 1965.

Bush, George P., *Bibliography on Research Administration, Annotated*. Washington, D. C.: The University Press, 1964.

Carroll, Phil., *Profit Control—How to Plug Profit Leaks*. New York: McGraw-Hill Book Company, 1962.

Caulfield, Patrick, and Freshman, Robert, "Technology Evaluation Workbook," HQ Research and Technology Division, AFSC, Bolling AFB, D.C. January 1967.

Cetron, Marvin J., "Programmed Functional Indices for Laboratory Evaluation, 'PROFILE,'" Paper presented at the 16th Military Operations Research Symposium (MORS), Seattle, Wash., Oct. 10–14, 1965.

————, and Freshman, Robert., Some Results of "PROFILE." Paper presented at the 17th Military Operations Research Symposium, Monterey, Calif., May 21–25, 1966.

————, "Quantitative Utility Estimates for Science & Technology 'Quest'" paper presented at the 18th MORS, Fort Bragg, N. C., Oct. 19–21, 1966.

————, and Davidson, Harold F., "Methodology for Allocating Corporate Resources to Objectives for Research and Development (MACRO R&D)" *Industrial Management Review*, Cambridge, Mass.: Massachusetts Institute of Technology, Winter 1969.

————, Martino, J., and Roepcke, L., "The Selection of R&D Program Content —Survey of Quantitative Methods," *IEEE Transaction on Engineering Management*, Vol. EM-14, No. 1, March 1967, pp. 4–12.

——, "Using Technological Forecasts," *Science and Technology*, July 1968, No. 79, pp. 57–63.

——, and Monahan, T. I., "An Evaluation and Appraisal of Various Approaches to Technological Forecasting," *Technological Forecasting for Industry and Government*, ed. Bright, J. F.; Englewood Cliffs, N. J.: Prentice-Hall, 1968.

——, and Weiser, L., "Technological Change, Technological Forecasting and Planning R&D—A View from the R&D Manager's Desk," *The George Washington Law Review—Technology Assessment and the Law*, Vol. 36, No. 5, Washington, D. C., p. 1091.

——, *Technological Forecasting: A Practical Approach*. New York, N. Y.: Gordon and Breach, Science Publishers, Inc., 1969.

——, and Hauser, L. E., *Advanced Material Systems Planning*. Case Institute of Technology, Operations Research Group Tech. Memo. No. 65. ONR-AMC Project Nonr-1141(19), Sept. 15, 1966.

Charnos, A., "Conditional Chance-Constrained Approaches to Organizational Control." Paper presented at the Research Program Effectiveness Conference, Washington, D. C., July 21–23, 1964.

——, and Stedry, A. C., "Optimal Real-Time Control of Research Funding." Paper presented at the Second Conference on Research Program Effectiveness, Washington, D. C., July 27–29, 1965.

Churchman, C. West, *Prediction and Optimal Decision*. Englewood Cliffs, N. J.: Prentice-Hall, 1961.

——, Kruytbosch, C., and Ratoosh, Philburn, "The Role of the Research Administrator," Paper presented at the Second Conference on Research Program Effectiveness, Washington, D. C., July 27–29, 1965.

Clark, Wallace, *The Gantt Chart*. London: Isaac Pitman and Sons, 1938.

Clarke, Roderick W., "Activity Costing—Key to Progress in Critical Path Analysis," *IRE Transactions on Engineering Management*, Vol. EM-9, No. 3, Sept. 1962, p. 132.

Combs, Cecil E., "Decision Theory and Engineering Management," *IRE Transactions on Engineering Management*, Vol. EM-9, No. 4, Dec. 1962.

Cook, Earle, F., "A Better Yardstick for Project Evaluation," *Armed Forces Management*, April 1958, pp. 20–23.

Cramer, Robert H., and Smith, Barnard E., "Decision Models for the Selection of Research Projects," *The Engineering Economist*, Vol. IX, No. 2, Jan.-Feb. 1964, pp. 1–20.

Crisp, R. D., "Product Planning for Future Projects," *Duns's Review and Modern Industry*, March 1958.

Dantzig, George B., *Linear Programming and Extensions*. Princeton: Princeton University Press, 1963.

Daubin, Scott C., "The Allocation of Development Funds: An Analytic Approach," *Naval Research Logistics Quarterly*, III, Sept. 1958, pp. 263–76.

Davidson, Harold F., "Surveys as Tools for Acquisition of Research Management Information." Paper presented at the Research Program Effectiveness Conference, Washington, D. C., July 21–23, 1964.

Davis, Keith, "The Role of Project Management in Scientific Manufacturing," *IRE Transactions on Engineering Management,* Vol. EM-9, No. 3, Sept. 1962, p. 109.

——, "Allocation of Technical Resources in a Firm." Paper presented at the Research Program Effectiveness Conference, Washington, D. C., July 21–23, 1964.

——, "Stochastic Networks in Research Planning." Paper presented at the Second Conference on Research Program Effectiveness, Washington, D. C., July 27–29, 1965.

——, and Sengupta, S., "On a Method for Determining Corporate Research Development Budgets," *Management Sciences, Models, and Techniques,* Vol. II, Churchman, C. W., and Verhulst, M. (eds.), New York: Pergamon Press, 1960.

——, and Glogowski., *On the Planning of Research.* ONR-AMC Project NOOR1141(19), July 1965.

Dean, Burton V. (ed.), *Operations Research in Research and Development.* Proceedings of a conference at Case Institute of Technology, New York: John Wiley and Sons, 1963.

——, *Scoring and Profitability Models for Evaluating and Selecting Engineering Projects,* Case Institute of Technology, Clrveland, Operations Research Group, 1964.

Dean, Joel, *Managerial Economics.* Englewood Cliffs: Prentice-Hall, 1951.

——, "Measuring the Productivity of Capital," *Harvard Business Review,* Jan.–Feb. 1954.

De l'Estoile, "Resource Allocation Model," Ministère des Armées, Paris, France.

DeVries, Marvin G., *A Dynamic Model for Product Strategy Selection.* Industrial Development Research Program Institute of Science and Technology. Ann Arbor: The University of Michigan, 1963.

——, "The Dynamic Effects of Planning Horizons on the Selection of Optimal Product Strategies," *Management Science,* Vol. X, No. 3, April 1964, pp. 524–44.

Disman, S., "Selecting R&D Projects for Profit," *Chem. Engineering,* Vol. 69, Dec. 1962, pp. 87–90.

Dooley, Arch R., "Interpretations of PERT," *Harvard Business Review,* March-April, 1964, pp. 160–71.

Drucker, Peter F., "Twelve Fables of Research Management," *Harvard Business Review,* Jan.-Feb. 1963.

——, *Managing for Results.* New York: Harper & Row, 1964, pp. 25–50.

Easton, David, *A Systems Analysis of Political Life.* New York: John Wiley and Sons, 1965.

Eisner, Hoard, "Generalized Network Approach to the Planning and Scheduling of a Research Program," *Operations Research,* Vol. X, 1962, pp. 115–25.

————, "The Application of Information Theory to the Planning of Research." Paper presented at The Institute for Management Science, American International Meeting, Washington, D. C., September 12–13, 1963.

Elmaghraby, Salah E., "An Algebra for the Analysis of Generalized Activity Networks," *Management Sciences,* Vol. X, No. 3, April 1964, pp. 494–514.

Emlet, H. E., "Methodological Approach to Planning and Programming Air Force Operational Requirements, Research and Development (MAPORD). Analytic Services Report 64-4, Analytical Services Inc., Falls Church, Va., Oct. 1965.

Esch, Maurice E., "Planning Assistance Through Technical Evaluation Pattern." Paper presented at the 17th National Aerospace Electronics Conference, Dayton, Ohio. May 11–12, 1965.

Ewing, David W. (ed.), *Long-Range Planning of Management.* New York: Harper & Brother, 1958.

Flood, Merrill W., "Research Project Evaluation," *Coordination, Control, and Financing of Industrial Research*, Albert R. Rubenstein (ed.). New York: Columbia University, King's Crown Press, 1955.

Fong, L. B. C., "A Visual Method of Program Balance and Evaluation," *IRE Transactions on Engineering Management*, Vol. EM-8, Sept. 1961, pp. 160–63.

Ford, L. R., Jr., and Fulkerson, D. R., *Flows in Networks.* Princeton: Princeton University Press, 1962.

Freeman, Raoul J., "An Operational Analysis of Industrial Research." PhD. dissertation, Department of Economics, Massachusetts Institute of Technology, Cambridge, Massachusetts, 1957.

————, "A Stochastic Model for Determining the Size and Allocation of the Research Budget," *IRE Transactions on Engineering Management*, Vol. EM-7, No. 1, March 1960, pp. 2–7.

————, "Quantitative Methods in R&D Management," *California Management Review*, Vol. XI, No. 4, Summer 1960, pp. 36–44.

————, "A Generalized Network Approach to Project Activity Sequencing," *IRE Transactions on Engineering Management*, Vol. EM-7, No. 3, Sept. 1960, pp. 103–07.

————, "A Survey of the Current Status of Accounting in the Control of R&D," *IRE Transactions on Engineering Management*, Vol., EM-9, No. 4, Dec. 1962, pp. 179–81.

Fry, B. L., "SCANS—System Description and Comparison with PERT," *IRE Transactions on Engineering Management*, Vol. EM-9, No. 3, Sept. 1962, 122.

Galbraith, John Kenneth, *The Affluent Society.* New York: Mentor Books, 1958.

Gargiulo, G. R., and others. "Developing Systematic Procedures for Directing Research Programs," *IRE Transactions on Engineering Management,* Vol. EM-8, No. 1, March 1961, pp. 24–29.

————, "Research on a Research Department: An Analysis of Economic Decisions on Projects," *IRE Transactions on Engineering Management,* Vol. EM-7, No. 4, Dec. 1960, pp. 166–72.

Goldberg, L. C., "Dimensions in the Evaluation of Technical Ideas in an Industrial Research Laboratory," M.S. thesis, Northwestern University, Evanston, Ill., 1963.

Guy, K., *Laboratory Organizations and Administration*. London: Macmillan & Company; also New York: St. Martin's Press, 1962.

Hackney, J. W., "How to Appraise Capital Investments," *Chemical Engineering,* May 15, 1961, pp. 146–67.

Hahn, W. A., and Pickering, H. D., "Program Planning in a Science-Based Service Organization." Paper presented at the Second Conference on Research Program Effectiveness, Washington, D. C., July 27–29, 1965.

Hansen, B. J., *Practical PERT Including Critical Path Method,* Washington: America House, 1964.

Harrel, C. G., "Selecting Projects for Research," in *Research in Industry: Its Organization and Management,* C. C. Furnas (ed.), New York: Van Nostrand, 1948, pp. 104–44.

Heckert, J. E., and Willson, J. B., *Business Budgeting and Control*. New York: The Ronald Press, 1955.

Henke, Russ, *Effective Research & Development for the Smaller Company*. Houston: Gulf Publishing Company, 1963.

Hertz, David B., *The Theory and Practice of Industrial Research*. New York: McGraw-Hill Book Company, 1950.

———, and Rubenstein, A. H., *Costs, Budgeting and Economics of Industrial Research*. Proceedings of the First Annual Conference of Industrial Research. New York: Columbia University Press, 1951.

———, and Rubenstein, A. H. (eds.), *Proceedings of the Third Annual Conference on Industrial Research: Research Operations in Industry*. New York: Columbia University Press, 1953. See especially Stewart, J. A., p. 55, and Hartstone, E., p. 153.

———, and Carlson, Phillip G., "Selection, Evaluation, and Control of Research and Development Projects," in *Operations Research in Research and Development,* Dean, B. V. (ed.). New York: John Wiley & Sons, 1963, pp. 170–88.

Hess, Sidney W., "On Research and Development Budgeting and Project Selection." Ph.D. dissertation, Case Institute of Technology, Cleveland, 1960.

———, "A Dynamic Programming Approach to R&D Budgeting and Project Selection," *IRE Transactions on Engineering Management*, Vol. EM-9, No. 4, December 1962, pp. 170–78.

Heyel, Carl (ed.), *Handbook of Industrial Research Management*. New York: Reinhold Publishing Corporation, 1959.

Hickey, Albert E., Jr., "The Systems Approach: Can Engineers Use the Scientific Method?" *IRE Transactions on Engineering Management,* Vol. EM-7, No. 2, June 1960, p. 72.

Hildenbrand, W., "Application of Graph Theory to Stochastic Scheduling." Paper presented at the Second Conference on Research Program Effectiveness, Washington, D. C., July 27–29, 1965.

Hill, F. I., and Roepcke, L. A., "An Analytical Method to Aid in the Choice of Long Range Study Tasks." Paper presented at the 1964 U.S. Army Operations Research Symposium at Rock Island, May 25–27, 1964.

Hill, Lawrence S., "Toward An Improved Basis of Estimating and Controlling R&D Tasks." Paper presented at the Tenth National Meeting of the American Association of Cost Engineers, Philadelphia, Pa., June 1966.

Hitchcock, L. B., "Selection and Evaluation of R&D Projects," *Research Management*, Vol. 6, May 1963, pp. 231–44.

Hodge, M. H., Jr., et al., *Basic Research as a Corporate Function*. The Graduate School of Business, Stanford University Sloan Program, Stanford University, California, 1961.

Honig, John G., "An Evaluation of Research and Development Problems." Paper presented at the Research Program Effectiveness Conference, Washington, D. C., July 21–23, 1964.

Horowitz, Ira., "The Economics of Industrial Research." Ph.D. dissertation, Massachusetts Institute of Technology, Cambridge, 1959.

Hugues, "La Programmatation de la Recherche Appliquée," Centre de Prospective et d'Evaluations, Le Progrès Scientifique, No. 18, April 1968.

Janofsky, L., and Sobleman, S., "Balancing Equations to Project Feasibility Studies." Paper presented to Operations Research Society of America, Detroit, October 10, 1960.

———, and Milton, Helen S., "A Proposed Cost-of-Research Index," *IRE Transactions on Engineering Management*, Vol. EM-8, No. 4, Dec. 1961, pp. 172–76.

Johnson, E. A., and Milton, H. S., "A Proposed Cost-of-Research Index," *IRE Transactions on Engineering Management*, Vol. EM-8, Dec. 1961, pp. 172–76.

Johnson, Richard A., Kast, Fremont E., and Rosenzweig, James E., *The Theory and Management of Systems*. New York: McGraw-Hill Book Company, 1963.

Joint Commanders, Army Materiel Command, Navy Material Command, and Air Force Systems Command, Report on Technological Forecasting. Washington, D. C.: Joint Secretariat, June 1967.

Karger, D. C., and Murkick, R. G., *Managing Engineering and Research*. New York: The Industrial Press, 1963, pp. 193–253.

Kelley, James E., Jr., and Walker, Morgan R., "Critical-Path Planning and Scheduling." *Proceedings of the Eastern Joint Computer Conference*, 1959.

———, and Walker, Morgan R., "Critical Path Planning and Scheduling. Mathematical Basis." *Operations Research*, Vol. IX, 1961, pp. 296–320.

Kiefer, D. M., "Winds of Change in Industrial Chemical Research," *Chemical Engineering News*, Vol. 42, March 1964, pp. 88–109.

Klein, B., and Meckling, W., "Applications of Operations Research to Development Decisions," *Operations Research*, May-June 1958, pp. 352–63.

———, "The Decision-Making Problem in Development," in *The Tate and Direction of Inventive Activity*. Princeton: Princeton University Press, 1962, pp. 477–508.

Kliever, W. R., and Bancroft, R. Z., "Choosing and Evaluating Research Projects, *Prod. Engrg.*, June 1953.

Koontz, Harold, *Toward A Unified Theory of Management*. New York: McGraw-Hill Book Company, 1963.

Landi, D. M., *A Model of Investment Planning for Research and Development*. Evanston: Northwestern University, 1964.

Leermakers, J. A., "The Selection and Screening of Projects," in *Getting the Most from Product Research and Development*. New York: American Mgmt. Assn., 1955, pp. 81–94.

Levy, F. K., Thompson, G. L., and Wiest, J. E., "Multiship, Multishop, Work-load-Smoothing Program," *Naval Research Logistics Quarterly*, Vol. XI, March 1962.

Lipetz, Ben-Ami, *Measurement of Effectiveness of Science Research*. Carlisle, Massachusetts: Intermedia, Inc., 1965.

Lytle, A. A., "The Yardsticks for Research Success," *Prod. Engrg.*, Vol. 30, Oct. 1958, pp. 34–37.

Magee, John F., "How to Use Decision Trees in Capital Investment," *Harvard Business Review*, Sept.-Oct. 1964, pp. 79–96.

Manning, P. D., "Long-Range Planning of Product Research," *R&D Development Series 4*. New York: American Mgmt. Assn., 1957.

Marples, D. L., "The Decisions of Engineering Design," *IRE Transactions on Engineering Management*, Vol. EM-8, June 1961, pp. 55–71.

Marschak, T. A., "Strategy and Organization in a System Development Project," in *The Rate and Direction of Inventive Activity*. Princeton: Princeton University Press, 1962, pp. 509–48.

———, "Models, Rules of Thumb, and Development Decisions," in *Operations Research in Research and Development*, Dean, B. V. (ed.). New York: John Wiley & Sons, 1963, pp. 247–63.

Marquis, Donald G., "Organization and Management of R&D." Paper presented at the Research Program Effectiveness Conference, Washington, D. C., July 21–23, 1964.

Marshall, A. W., and Meckling, W. H., "Predictability of the Costs, Time and Success of Development," in *The Rate and Direction of Inventive Activity*. Princeton: Princeton University Press, 1962, pp. 461–75.

Martino, J., Caulfield, P., Cetron, M., Davidson, H., Liebowitz, H., and Roepcke, L., "A Method for Balanced Allocation of Resources Among R&E Projects." AF Office of Scientific Research Technical Report, Washington, D. C., Feb. 1967.

Massey, Robert J., "A New Publication: Department of the Navy RDT&E Management Guide." Paper presented at the Research Program Effectiveness Conference, Washington, D. C., July 21–23, 1964.

McMaster, Samuel B., "Study of Project Selection Techniques in an R&D Organization." Unpublished Master's Thesis, Northwestern University, Evanston, 1964.

McMillan, Claude, and Gonzalez, Richard F., *Systems Analysis: A Computer Approach to Decision Models*. Homewood, Illinois: Richard Irwin Press, 1965.

Mees, C. E. K., and Leermakers, J. A., *The Organization of Industrial Scientific Research*, 2nd ed. New York: McGraw-Hill Book Co., 1950; especially Chapter 11.

Mellon, W. Giles, *An Approach to a General Theory of Priorities: An Outline of Problems and Methods,* Princeton University Econometric Research Program, Memorandum No. 42. Princeton: Princeton University Press, 1962.

Miller, D. W., and Starr, M. K., *Executive Decisions and Operations Research.* Englewood Cliffs, N. J.: Prentice-Hall, 1960.

Miller, Robert W., *Schedule, Cost and Profit Control with PERT.* New York: McGraw-Hill Book Company, 1963.

Miller, T. T., "Projecting the Profitability of New Products, Special Report No. 20." New York: American Management Association, 1957, pp. 20–33.

Morgenstern, O., Shephard, R. W., and Grabowski, H. G., "Adaption of Graph Theory and an Input-Output Model to Research Description and Evaluation." Paper presented at the Second Conference on Research Program Effectiveness, Washington, D. C., July 27–29, 1965.

Moshman, Jack, Johnson, Jacob, and Larson, Madalyn, "RAMPS—A Technique for Resource Allocation and Multi-Project Scheduling." *Proceedings of the Spring Joint Computer Conference,* 1963. Baltimore: Spartan Books, 1963, pp. 17–27.

Mottley, C. M., and Newton, R. D., "The Selection of Projects for Industrial Research," *Operations Research,* Vol. 7, Nov.-Dec. 1959, pp. 740–51.

National Science Foundation, *Science and Engineering in American Industry,* Final Report on 1953–1954 Survey, Washington, D. C., October 1956.

Norden, P. V., "Curve Fitting for a Model of Applied Research and Development Scheduling," *IBM Journal of Research and Development,* Vol. II, No. 3, July 1958, pp. 232–48.

———, "The Study Committee for Research, Development and Engineering (SCARDE)," *IRE Transactions on Engineering Management,* Vol. EM-8, March 1961, pp. 3–10.

———, "Some Properties of R&D Project Recovery Limits." Paper presented at the Second Conference on Research Program Effectiveness, Washington, D. C., July 27–29, 1965.

Norton, J. H., "The Role of Subjective Probability in Evaluating New Product Ventures," *Chemical Engineering Progr. Symp.* Ser. 42, Vol. 59, 1963, pp. 49–54.

Nutt, Ambrose B., "An Approach to Research and Development Effectiveness," *IEEE Transactions on Engineering Management,* Sept. 1965, pp. 103–112.

———, "An Approach to Research and Development Effectiveness," *IEEE Transactions,* Vol. EM-12, No. 3, September 1965.

———, "Ancillary Benefits of an Automated R&D Resources Allocation System." Presented to the American Society for Mechanical Engineers, Winter Annual Meeting, New York City; November, 1966, (ASME Report 66-WA/MGT-18).

———, "Considerations in Exploratory Development Planning in a DOD Laboratory," Presented to R&D Management Working Group, 19th Military Operations Research Society, Fort Bliss, Texas, April 25–27, 1967.

———, "A Compilation of Computer Programs in Flight Vehicle Technology 1964–1967," AFFDL-TF-68-66, April 1968.

————, "Implementing a Computerized Resources Allocation System in an Air Force Laboratory," Presented at IBM Aerospace Operations Research Seminar, Newport Beach, Calif., April 30, 1968.

————, "An Application of Goal-Oriented Forecasting in a Laboratory Environment," Presented to NATO Defense Research Group, Glazebrook Hall, National Physical Laboratory, Teddington, Middlesex, England, November 12, 1968.

————, "Technological Forecasting in an R&D Laboratory," Presented to the Third Forecasting and Planning Symposium; Alamogordo, New Mexico, April 1969.

————, "Testing TORQUE, A Quantitative R&D Resources Allocation System," Submitted for publication in the *IEEE Transactions on Engineering Management* in July 1969.

Nyland, H. V., and Towle, G. R., "How We Evaluate Return from Research," *National Association of Cost Accountants Bull.*, May 1956.

Olsen, F., "The Control of Research Funds," in *Coordination, Control and Financing of Industrial Research*, A. H. Rubenstein (ed.). New York: King Crown Press, Columbia University, 1955, pp. 99–108.

Pacifico, C., "Is It Worth the Risk?" *Chemical Engineering Progr.*, Vol. 60, May 1964, pp. 19–21.

Pappas, G. F., and MacLaren, D. D., "An Approach to Research Planning," *Chemical Engineering Progr.*, Vol. 57, May 1961, pp. 65–69.

Pound, William H., "Research Project Selection: Testing a Model in the Field," *IEEE Transactions on Engineering Management*, Vol. EM-11, No. 1, March 1964, pp. 16–22.

Quinn, James Bryan, *Yardsticks for Industrial Research: The Evaluation of Research and Development Output*. New York: The Ronald Press, 1959.

————, and Mueller, James A., "Transferring Research Results to Operations," *Harvard Business Review*, Vol. XLI, Jan.-Feb. 1963.

Rac, Robert H., and Synnott, Thomas, "Project RDE, A Framework for the Comprehension and Analysis of Research and Development Effectiveness," TM 63-22 Air Force Flight Dynamics Laboratory, Dayton, Ohio, October 1961.

————, "A Systems Development Planning Structure," ABT Associates, Inc., Cambridge, Mass., Nov. 18, 1965. Report to the Air Force Systems Command, May 1966.

————, An Automated Scenario Generator—ABT Associates, Inc., Cambridge, Mass., January 1966.

Raiffa, Howard, and Schlaifer, Robert, *Applied Statistical Decision Theory*. Boston: Division of Research, Harvard Business School, 1957.

Roberts, E. B., *The Dynamics of Research and Development*. New York: Harper & Row, 1964.

Roberts, C. S., "Product Selection—Witchcraft or Wisdom?" *IRE Transactions on Engineering Management*, Vol. EM-6, Sept. 1959, pp. 68–71.

Roman, Daniel D., "The PERT System: An Appraisal of Program Evaluation

Review Technique," *Journal of the Academy of Management*, Vol. V, No. 1, April 1962.

———, "Organization for Control," *Journal of the Academy of Management*, Vol. VI (Proceedings of the Annual Meeting, Pittsburgh, December 27–28, 1962).

———, "Project Management Recognizes R&D Performance," *Journal of the Academy of Management*, Vol. VII, March 1964, pp. 7–20.

———, and Johnson, Jacob N., "On the Allocation of Common Physical Resources to Multiple Development Tasks." Paper presented at the 18th Military Operations Research Society, Fort Bragg, N. C., Oct. 19–21, 1966.

Roseboom, J. H., Clark, C. E., and Fazer, W., "Application of a Technique for Research and Development Program Evaluation," *Operations Research*, Vol. VII, Sept.-Oct. 1959, pp. 651–53.

Rosen, E. M., and Saunder, W. E., "A Method for Allocating R&D Expenditures," *IEEE Transactions on Engineering Management*, Vol. EM-12, No. 3, Sept. 1965, pp. 87–92.

Rubenstein, Albert H. (ed.), *Coordination, Control, and Financing of Industrial Research*. New York: King's Crown Press, Columbia University, 1955.

———, "Evaluation of the Possibilities of Research Effort in a New Field of Technology," Sweden, Vol. 6, 1955, pp. 239–251.

———, "Setting Criteria for R&D," *Harvard Business Review*, Jan.-Feb. 1957, pp. 95–104.

———, and Horowitz, I., "Project Selection in New Technical Fields," *Proc. Natl. Electronics Conf.*, Vol. 15, 1959, pp. 24–47.

———, "Studies of Project Selection Behavior in Industry," in *Operations Research in Research and Development*, Dean, B. V. (ed.), New York: John Wiley & Sons, 1963, pp. 189–205.

———, and Haverstroh, C. J. (eds.), *Some Theories of Organization*. Homewood, Illinois: Richard Irwin Press, 1960.

———, "Some Common Concepts and Tentative Findings from a Ten-Project Program of Research on R&D Management." Paper presented at the Second Conference on Research Program Effectiveness, Washington, D. C., July 27–29, 1965.

Saaty, Thomas L., *Mathematical Methods of Operations Research*. New York: McGraw-Hill Book Company, 1959.

Sacco, W. J., *On the Choice of Long Range Study Tasks*. Ballistic Research Laboratories, Aberdeen, Md., Memo Report No. 1693, Aug. 1965.

Savage, J. J., *The Foundations of Statistics*. New York: John Wiley and Sons, 1954.

Scherer, F. M., "Time-Cost Tradeoffs in Uncertain Empirical Research Projects," *Naval Research Logistics Quarterly*, ONR, Vol. 13, No. 1, March 1966.

———, "Quantitative Utility Estimates for Science & Technology 'Quest'." Paper presented at the 18th MORS, Fort Bragg, N. C., Oct. 19–21, 1966.

Schweyer, Herbert E., "Graphs Can Reveal Project Feasibility," *Chemical Engineering*, Sept. 18, 1961, pp. 175–78.

Seiler, Robert E., *Improving the Effectiveness of Research and Development*. New York: McGraw-Hill Book Co., 1963.

Shank, R. J., "Planning to Meet Goals," *Optimum Use of Engineering Talent, AMA Report No. 68*. Cambridge: Riverside Press, 1961.

Shaller, H. I., "An Exploratory Study in Research Planning Methodology," ONR Tech. Report ACR/NAR-27, Department of the Navy, Washington, D. C., September 1963.

Sher, I. H., and Garfield, E., "New Tools for Improving and Evaluating the Effectiveness of Research." Paper presented at the Second Conference on Research Program Effectiveness, Washington, D. C., July 27–29, 1965.

Silk, Leonard S., *The Research Revolution*. New York: McGraw-Hill Book Company, Inc., 1960.

———, *The New Science of Management Decisions*. New York: Harper & Row, 1960.

———, "An Optimal Method for Selection of Product Development Projects." Paper presented at the 15th National Meeting, Operations Research Society of America, May 1959.

Sobelman, S. A., Modern Dynamic Approach to Product Development. Dover, N. J.: Picatinny Arsenal, Dec. 1958.

———, "An Optimal Method for Selection of Product Development Projects." Paper presented at the 15th National Meeting of the Operations Research Society of America, Washington, D. C., May 1959.

Sobin, Bernard, and Proschan, Arthur, "Search and Evaluation Methods in Research and Exploratory Development." Paper presented at the Second Conference on Research Program Effectiveness, Washington, D. C., July 27–29, 1965.

———, *Proposal Generation and Evaluation Methods in Research and Exploratory Development*. Research Analysis Corp., McLean, Va., Paper RAC-P-11, Nov. 1965.

Special Projects Office, *PERT Summary Report I*. Washington, D. C.: Bureau of Naval Weapons, Department of the Navy, 1959.

Spencer, M. H., and Siegelman, L., *Managerial Economics*. Homewood, Illinois: Richard Irwin Press, 1964, pp. 461–567.

Stanley, A. O., and White, K. K., *Organizing the R&D Function*. AMA Research Study No. 72. New York: American Management Association, 1965.

Steiner, George A., *Managerial Long-Range Planning*. New York: McGraw-Hill Book Company, 1963.

Stilian, C. N., et al., *PERT—A New Management Planning and Control Technique*. New York: American Management Association, 1962.

Stoessl, L., "Linear Programming Techniques Applied to Research Planning," Master's Thesis, U.S. Naval Postgraduate School, Monterey, Cal., 1964.

Stoodley, F. H., *A Study of Methods Which Could Improve the Relevance of Naval Applied Research and Exploratory Development*. Office of Naval Research Report, June 1, 1966.

Sullivan, C. I., "CPI Management Looks at R&D Project Evaluation," *Ind. and Eng. Chem.,* Vol. 53, Sept. 1961, pp. 42A–46A.

Taylor, Frederick W., *Scientific Management.* New York: Harper & Brothers, 1947.

Theil, H., "On the Optimal Management of Research; A Mathematical Approach." Paper presented at the conference of the International Federation of Operations Research Societies, Oslo, Norway, July 1963.

Thompson, R. E., "PERT—Tool•for R&D Project Decision-Making." *IRE Transactions on Engineering Management,* Sept. 1962, pp. 116–21.

University of California, *A System Engineering Approach to Corporate Long-Range Planning.* Department of Engineering Report EEP-62-1. Berkeley: University of California, June 1962.

Wachold, G. R., "An Investigation of the Technical Effectiveness of a Government Research and Development Test and Evaluation Organization." Navy Missile Center, Pt. Mugu, Cal., July 1965 (unpublished thesis).

Walters, J. E., *Research Management: Principles and Practice.* Washington, D. C.: Spartan Books, 1965.

Wasson, Chester R., *The Economics of Managerial Decision.* New York: Appleton-Century-Crofts, Inc., 1965, pp. 147–218.

Wells, H., "The Allocation of Research and Development Resources." Wright-Patterson Air Development Center, August 1958. Columbus, Ohio: Master's thesis, Ohio State University.

———, "Efficient Use of Groups in the Planning Process." Columbus, Ohio: Doctoral dissertation, Ohio State University.

———, Cannon, John R., and Oakes, Carl L., *The Wright Air Development Division Effort Allocation Guide.* Wright-Patterson Air Force Base, Ohio: Plans Division, WADD, June 1959.

———, "*Systems Planners Guide.*" Paper presented at the 18th Military Operations Research Society meeting, Fort Bragg, N. C., Oct. 19–21, 1966.

Wilson, E. Bright, *An Introduction to Scientific Research.* New York: McGraw-Hill Book Co., 1952.

Wright Air Development Center Plans Division, *Resource Allocation Trends for Technical Program Planning.* WCOP Technical Memorandum 58-2, Wright-Patterson Air Force Base, Ohio; Wright Air Development Center, 1958.

Index